# RAW

# RAW

## MY JOURNEY INTO THE
# WU-TANG

### LAMONT 'U-GOD' HAWKINS

FABER & FABER

First published in the UK in 2018
by Faber & Faber Limited
Bloomsbury House
74–77 Great Russell Street
London WC1B 3DA

First published in the USA in 2018
by Picador
175 Fifth Avenue
New York
N.Y. 10010

Printed and bound by CPI Group (UK) Ltd, Croydon CR0 4YY

A CIP record for this book
is available from the British Library

ISBN 978–0–571–34241–9

FSC
www.fsc.org
MIX
Paper from
responsible sources
FSC® C020471

2 4 6 8 10 9 7 5 3 1

# CONTENTS

# RAW

Time is a motherfucker. Time reveals shit. It wears things down. Breaks things. Crushes things. Kills things. Reveals truth. There's nothing greater than Father Time.

If you have patience, time will be on your side. And if you recognize how valuable time is, and if you know the right time to make your move, you'll be a bad motherfucker.

That's how I feel right now writing this book. The time is now for me to write all this shit down. It's time to write down not only my legacy, but the story of nine dirt-bomb street thugs who took our everyday life—scrappin' and hustlin' and tryin' to survive in the urban jungle of New York City—and turned that into something bigger than we could possibly imagine, something that took us out of the projects for good, which was the only thing we all wanted in the first place.

But first, we had to come from hell all the way up. New York City was a crazy place to grow up, especially in the 1970s, '80s, and '90s. There was so much energy on the streets and the clubs back then. That shit got into my system early and stays there to this day. Not just the club scene, but that whole era, the Mayor Koch, punch-you-in-the-face, snatch-your-pocketbook era. The whole Clan is from that era, and we convey it in our music, because that era molded us, it's still in us. We're constantly evolving and changing, but that core is where I draw my inspiration from. And not just what we saw, but everything we went through at that time.

When they built the projects, it was just an urban jungle; dangerous, but if you knew the rules, you could get by all right, maybe even have some fun occasionally. There'd be fights, usually with fists, maybe brass knuckles, maybe a knife. Drugs were around, sure, but not like they were later on.

But when crack hit my Park Hill neighborhood on Staten Island, that jungle became a goddamn war zone. Fists and knives turned to pistols and submachine guns. Bulletproof vests were hidden under sports jerseys. Bullets and bodies littered the streets, and often you didn't know who you could trust from day to day. People you thought were your friends, lured in by addiction or easy money, often became sneak thieves or stickup kids.

That fear, anger, and terror in the streets made the friends you could trust all the more precious. And in the early nineties, nine friends, each a master of his own craft, each with his own part to play, came together to form the legendary group you know as the Wu-Tang Clan.

RZA, the Mastermind: From creating the very idea of the Wu-Tang to gathering the members who would execute his plan to shaping the hooks, concepts, and themes of our early albums, RZA was the general whose orders we all followed. He had a great mind; he was very, very intelligent for his age. He wasn't no real hustling-ass dude, but to feed his family, he'd put that great mind of his to it and came up with things to put food on his plate. Wu-Tang was just one of those things that took us all higher.

GZA, the Genius: Often right beside his cousin RZA, GZA elevated his verses from the grimy, crime-ridden streets to higher planes of thought, consciousness, and expression. When he dropped his debut album, *Words from the Genius,* on Warner Bros., suddenly we could see the reality of music taking us out of the projects. I still remember me and Method Man listening to that tape and just vibing off it.

Method Man and Ol' Dirty Bastard, the Performers: We were all performers, but Meth and ODB were the two who always took shows to a higher level. Meth had his infectious enthusiasm and natural charm, and brought it from way back when he was kickin' New Edition dance moves at the P.S. 49 after-school center. ODB was just unpredictably wild, with insane stage charisma. Out of all of us, he was already a natural entertainer right out of the box—he was just early with it. Sometimes I used to look at him like he was fucking crazy, but he always knew what he was doing, every time.

Inspectah Deck, the Artist: As a kid, Deck was always looking out his apartment window at 160, down at everything going on in the street below. He absorbed all that shit and turned it into these vivid rhymes. His visual details, plus using words you hear news reporters use, just made it seem like he was reporting street news in his verses.

Ghostface Killah, the Storyteller: A troublemaker all his life who hit the streets early, Ghost made his stories come alive because when he rapped them, it felt like you were living them right along-side him.

Masta Killa, the Natural: A disciple of GZA, Masta's the only one of us whose first performance was with the fully formed Wu, but his ability to hold his own from the start was undeniable. I know everyone's roots in Wu-Tang—everybody except Masta Killa's. He's always just held himself real close to the vest. And that's just the way it is.

Raekwon, the Hustler: Creator of the "mafioso rap" subgenre, he was in the streets at an early age, pushing crack out of the gate down the block from Meth and me. One of my very first drug stories is of Rae and me trying to move this shitty weed we'd gotten from his cousin Rico. Drug dealing may not have been the best vocation, but it sure gave him a lot to rhyme about.

And me, U-God, the Ambassador: I was just a straight hard-core thug with the brain capacity to do a lot of shit, make things happen on my own, and hustle those bombs to get my bread. I was there from the very beginning, beatboxin' in the hallways of 160 with Rae and ODB, hustlin' on the streets with Meth, layin' down the first tracks at RZA's crib—I was there for all of it. Walking my own path, which had a detour or two, to be sure, but that path led inexorably to the Wu-Tang Clan, as I'd somehow known it would from the very beginning.

This is my story.

This is our story.

## STARTED OFF ON THE ISLAND

Growing up as hard, as rough, as wild, as crazy as we in Wu-Tang did, death was always a part of my life.

I remember the first time I saw somebody die. I was only about four or five years old. It was just me and my mother in the apartment. "Lovin' You" by Minnie Riperton was playing on a radio in the street. It seemed like whenever shit was going down, there was always music playing along with it.

Something was always happening in the Park Hill projects. I remember a commotion outside my window—I could barely reach the windowsill to look out to the street. A crowd was forming, making the uproar that drew my mother and me outside to see what was going on. By the time we arrived, the gathering had gotten bigger, so she put me up on her shoulders. I looked around the courtyard and up the street. All my neighbors, as well as half of 260 Park Hill Terrace, were outside.

Soon, the cops, firemen, and an ambulance showed up. A woman was standing on the roof of the project next door—280 Park Hill—threatening to jump. She was pretty young, talking to herself and yelling down at everyone as the cops tried to talk her down off the ledge.

I remember staring up at her till my neck was stiff. I didn't understand what was going on or what was about to happen.

At first, it seemed like she was going to be okay. She looked like she didn't really want to kill herself, but something still kept her from coming down off the ledge. I can still see her face—tormented, twisted in despair, her wide eyes staring down at the crowd seven stories below.

Then, without a word or warning that she'd had enough of making a spectacle, she jumped—or slipped and fell, I never knew which.

She flailed her arms for a second, then fell so fast I almost couldn't see her. She hit the fence first, then landed on the steps at the side entrance. Blood flew, people screamed, and the cops and paramedics ran up to the bleeding soon-to-be corpse. Everybody there, my mother and me included, just stood and stared at the body in shock and disbelief while they got her ready to be carted off.

I was a toddler, and already I'd seen death up close. The sound of her hitting the concrete steps would resonate with me forever. At the time, I couldn't understand what could make someone end their own life. As a five-year-old, you don't always recognize what you see, but I always felt like that was the moment that made me self-aware. It made me think of life and death for the first time. I was young as hell, but it made an impact on me.

I come from a long line of project babies. It seems like poor people always start from the bottom. Either you make it out of the projects or you stay there, sometimes for generations. I still know people that have been there for their entire lives. Never advanced, never went nowhere else, never explored the rest of the world outside their neighborhood. I guess they're content with that sort of life, but I knew early on it wasn't for me.

Only the pure of heart make it out of the ghetto. What that means to me is that when you really believe in what or who you are, you stay focused on yourself, and you don't hurt anyone while trying to get out. You don't connive, you don't do any ratchetness to get ahead, and you don't backstab someone else to get out.

You get out with determination, willpower, and persistence in pursuing what you believe in. If you really believe you can become a doctor, and you study to become a doctor, that's pure of heart.

Now, I became a songwriter, even though I had drugs and all that stuff in my world, and people was dyin', and I might have sold poison and all that, but underneath all that drama, I was still pure of heart. I never sold to a pregnant woman. I helped old ladies down the stairs. I still managed to keep my personal morals in an unrighteous setting. Even though I was doing wrong to get by, there were still lines I would not cross.

I know people that went through some hard shit, they were thieves or murderers, and then they changed their life around, got a job, had a family, and they got their shit together. Now, just because you killed someone, you might think you're done, man, you're gonna be fucked for the rest of your life. Not necessarily. Even if a person accidentally hurts somebody or they did a wrong deed, they can always correct their deeds by choosing to act on their pureness of heart. In other words, you choose a right path. You choose righteousness over negativity.

That's what I did.

My mother's from Brownsville, Brooklyn. She was raised in the same project building as Raekwon's mother, at 1543 East New York Avenue, in Howard Houses.

The Brownsville projects were the wildest, period. Ask anybody from New York City what part of Brooklyn is the roughest, they're gonna say Brownsville.

Some projects you could walk through. Some you couldn't. At its worst, you couldn't walk through Brownsville. You couldn't walk through Fort Greene or Pink Houses either. The tension and violence was always in the air in those places. Guaranteed there was gonna be fights topped off with a few people getting cut or stabbed, and even back then there might have been a shooting or two. Someone would probably end up dead by the end of the ruckus. That's why I don't like going back to my old projects nowadays; I feel like the spirits of my old comrades are calling to me. They're still haunting the projects they hustled at and got killed in.

When I was a kid, there was always someone looking to rob your sneakers, your coat, anything they could get their hands on. They would steal your fucking sneakers right off your feet. Back then, if you wore gold chains and shit, you better know how to shoot or how to fight. And the cops wouldn't really do shit to prevent a crime or deal with it after the fact. They just didn't care.

And when they actually did get involved, a lotta time it turned out worse for us. During the early seventies, law enforcement had no regard for life. My grandmother told me on more than one occasion that the cops in the Seventy-third Precinct in Brownsville were killing people in the neighborhood. She and a lot of her friends and family claimed that people would get escorted in, handcuffed and bleeding, and they would never be seen again. Guess the cops put them under the jail—literally. That's how treacherous it was in Brownsville.

Just getting in and out of the neighborhood was an adventure. My mother got her pocketbook snatched four or five times right in front of me. She had to call the police to escort us from the train station to my grandmother's building on several occasions because a group of kids were waiting on the corner to snatch the few dollars she had.

Each project or street had at least one gang or crew. You couldn't walk from one block to the next if you didn't know the right people. Thugs would come right off the stoop and get in your face. "Who you coming here to see? Why you think it's okay for you to walk through my block if I don't know you?"

The local gang, dressed in Kangols, Pumas, and Adidas tracksuits, hung around the bus stop near the Chinese restaurant on Pitkin Avenue. At the time, Pitkin Avenue was the shopping area in Brownsville. It was full of clothing stores, had OTB (Off-Track Betting), and dudes would be retailing stuff on the corner. There was also a slaughterhouse where they used to slaughter chickens. My grandmother would take me over there, and there would be chickens in a cage, and she'd get fresh chicken cut from the butcher.

We were always leery of these dudes, just like we were any time we went anywhere in the projects. I remember seeing them chillin' one time as some guy came riding toward them on a ten-speed. One of the gangsters came out of nowhere and whacked him over the head with a pipe, then took the bike and went and sat down on the bench. We just kept walking like we didn't see anything. No one else did anything or reacted, even though the dude who got hit was lying there twitching and bleeding.

My craziest Brownsville memory, though, involves Mike Tyson, who came from Brownsville. This was back in the seventies, before he was the world champion or had even started boxing. I was about eight years old, holding my mother's hand, walking down Pitkin Avenue by the OTB, when this dude came by and snatched my mother's earrings right off her earlobes. Left her with bloody ears and everything and just took off.

I was too young to remember exactly what he looked like at the time, but years later, when Tyson started getting famous, my mother saw him on TV and swore, "That's the guy who snatched my earrings!" It sounds crazy, and of course I don't have any proof, but that didn't stop me from fantasizing as a kid that a slew of Brooklynites and even some Manhattanites could say the same thing about the World Champ.

---

I don't know who my father is or where he comes from; I wish I could find out more about him. A big part of why I don't know much about him is because of how I was conceived.

My mother probably wouldn't want me to bring this up, because she hates me talking about it, but I was a product of rape. I was a rape baby. She told me my father had tricked her into believing he was a photographer and wanted her to model for him. He told her she was a natural beauty and all this other fly shit. He lured her to a spot and took advantage of her. She never pressed charges and never even reported it.

The only person who could have told me more about him was my mother's friend Carol. Carol used to be pretty good-looking back in her Brooklyn days. She liked to party and used to hang around with my father and the dudes he ran with. She was on drugs and eventually contracted HIV. She had a brain aneurysm and is currently in a mental ward in Brooklyn. She doesn't remember a goddamn thing now. Needless to say, she's not much help to me as far as learning about my dad.

When I was around ten years old, I remember asking about my father a lot, but Moms wouldn't tell me anything. She didn't tell me about him until I was a grown man. I'd been asking off and on for years, though. My dad was the missing piece of my whole life.

"Who's my dad though, Ma? Who is my dad?"

"God is your father!" she would always reply.

Finally, when I was twenty-one, she got into some of the details. She also explained why she kept me. She told me that one night, God came to her in a dream and told her not to abort this child, that I was gonna be a great man someday, so she kept me. That dream solidified her spirituality, her connection with God. My moms is real spiritual, I mean like super spiritual, so she always points out how it's funny that my name turned out to be U-God. "And now look at you," she told me once, as if confirming that the dream had been right.

She always emphasized that she never regretted having me, even during the tough times we went through. The way I see it, you've got to be a compassionate individual to love a child conceived the way I was.

When she told me, I was shocked. The average person, even if born accidentally, is still often born out of love, and to know I'd been brought into the world like that really rocked me. The whole situation seemed like a fluke accident—after all, my mother wasn't looking to get pregnant at the time, and certainly not by no fly-by-night photographer/rapist. But I had to accept that that was how I'd been born and that it wasn't going to stop me from being great.

Yet make no mistake, I'm the product of both my parents. I have the side that comes from my mother, like her good heart, but I also got my father's hustle. My father's side—I know my mother doesn't have it—must be where I get my internal drive from. Nobody else in my family has it, so it had to come from my father.

To this day, I have no idea where my pops is at. Even if I wanted to find him, I have no idea where to start looking. Those little bits Moms told me when I was older are all I really know about him. I want to know who he is, what else we have in common. Even though he tricked my mother, I was still his son. What features did I get from him? What habits? What disorders? Just a whole lot of questions I'll never know the answers to.

For the first twelve years of my life, it was just me and my mom. We were always close. She raised me from a boy into the respectable man I am now, and did it on her own during the Ed Koch era, some of the wildest times New York City has ever seen.

The 1970s, '80s, and '90s were probably the city's most violent times. Even before crack hit, NYC was teetering on bankruptcy. A lot of social programs got slashed, if not cut from the city's budget altogether.

All five boroughs had violent neighborhoods. Muggings, robberies, rape, assaults, and murders were all too common. You couldn't ride the train too late. Before crack, heroin was flowing, coke was flowing. Pimps, prostitutes, corrupt cops; all the New York City clichés were present and thriving.

Growing up, you always had to be aware of your surroundings. In the ghetto, in the projects, in those types of high-risk, high-violence parts of town, you always have to be aware, 'cause things could jump off at any moment. Like when I'm in the hood, I'm around these crazy motherfuckers. That doesn't necessarily mean I'm down with these motherfuckers, but it means I have to be aware what they're doin', 'cause if they're fuckin' around and I'm standing nearby, next thing you know my motherfucking head might get blown off by some motherfucker trying to get someone he got beef with.

So you grew up watching shit. You always had to be aware. You had the bullies to watch out for. You always had to be on point. And to this day it's like that for a black man living in a poverty-stricken area. It ain't the fact that you're involved in shit—'cause often you ain't doin' anything—it's that you're so confined and so closed off in an urban box, that you have to be aware of everyone and everything around you at all times.

What a lot of people really don't understand is how growing up like that changes a person for the rest of their life. I'm changed right now. It fucked me up, and I'm never going to be the same. I don't have any close friends. I can't have friends from Park Hill no more. I can't deal with those dudes. I can't deal with certain shit on the streets. I can't be around certain people. Why? Because now I'm slashed. I'm always mentally aware of certain situations that I wasn't aware of before. So I had to cut a lot of that stuff out of my life.

Eventually we left Brooklyn for Staten Island, and ended up in Park Hill.

In the late 1970s, welfare housing on the Island was going for a good rate. It was a chance for my mother and Raekwon's mother to move out of Brownsville, and at first Park Hill was nice. When we got there, it was a working-class neighborhood and still a community. There were buzzers on the lobby doors. There was grass behind the buildings. The school was right down the block.

I mean, I still grew up in the notorious Park Hill projects. But back when we first arrived, Park Hill and most of Clifton and even nearby Stapleton had all just undergone urban renewal. It was a predominantly black population, and the neighborhood still looked newish, so things didn't seem so rough.

Park Hill is privately owned, but federally subsidized. That's a bad combination, because the federal government guarantees the owners that the residents' rent will be paid. That sounds good, but not if the rent still gets paid whether repairs are made and upkeep maintained or not.

Still, at first, it wasn't too bad. It was still a housing complex and rugged, but you had a fifty-fifty chance of walking through or near it and not getting fucked with by the locals. But then things started getting broken, and they wouldn't get fixed for months, and sometimes not at all. As a result of the owners' neglect, Park Hill began getting worse and worse.

But I didn't see all that at the time. In a lot of ways, I had experiences like a lot of regular American kids. And there was a lot that was different, too.

I was a latchkey kid from the age of six or seven, which meant I was home alone, with no parental supervision, every day. Mom gave me the apartment key so I could let myself in after school, and *"YOU DON'T ANSWER THE DOOR OR THE PHONE FOR ANYBODY!"*

I'd have a babysitter when my mother could afford it. But there were slim pickings for good babysitters, and I went through a lot of them.

I remember one of my babysitters. She was a good person who kept a clean house and cared for me. She would give me my lunch and make sure I did my homework. She had two daughters, and all three of them would babysit me at her apartment. But she was also a straight-up heroin addict.

One day I walked into the living room at their place, and saw her shooting heroin right on the couch. Her hands were all swollen with needle holes, but at the time I didn't know what they were from. I can still see them now. Her boyfriend and a couple other folks I'd never seen before were there, too, all shooting that shit up.

You have to understand that my mother had no idea this was going on. She was busy working hard and going to school, trying to better our situation. So I just kept shit like that to myself.

And although that babysitter was a functioning drug addict, she was good to me. When I grew up, I never looked down on her. Plus, I didn't even know what they were sticking in their arms at the time anyway. Years later, I realized they were just hard-core heroin addicts. And when I say "hard-core," I mean *hard-core.*

I had another babysitter who was a little freaky. While she was babysitting me, she'd be playing with my penis. I never spoke up about it to anyone. I was too young to really know what was going on, but instinctually I knew she shouldn't be doing it. Regardless, I liked it—it was the first awakening of my sexuality. And I liked her, so I'll never reveal her name.

Growing up how we did, you'd think it was all hard times. We were too young to know we were "disadvantaged." You sort of have a feeling something's not right, but you're a kid, so you adapt and learn how to have your fun anyway. And there were a lot of good times and funny memories to balance out the hard-core ones.

Like Big Titty Rose. Big Titty Rose had the first pair of titties I ever saw.

We'd gone up to my friend's house to get some Kool-Aid, and there she was lying on the couch, butt-ass naked. She musta weighed about three hundred pounds. It was summertime and hot, so I guess she wasn't trying to put any clothes on. I was so intimidated by these big-ass titties. She didn't try to cover up or anything. She just lay there, changing the channel, with them big things hangin' out. I was young, maybe around six or seven, so they looked even more huge. I was just in awe, I remember. They didn't call her Big Titty Rose for no reason.

I might've been young, but there were still some girls that got me going. I watched a lot of TV as a kid, and I had a huge crush on Kim Fields's character, Tootie, from *The Facts of Life*. I noticed that the credits listed Tandem Production Company. So one day, I called Information to get the number of the company so I could speak to her directly. Even though I didn't speak to Tootie, I got an autographed picture of Kim on roller skates. She had braces on. I was in love with that girl right there. I showed my little friends and they were like, "Get outta here! How'd you get that?"

Clearly, I was very determined from a very young age. When I wanted something, I was gonna do whatever I had to do to get it.

When we weren't watching TV or running up and down the streets, my friends and I mostly hung out in the back of the projects.

Behind our building were a few acres of undeveloped land with grass and trees and two ponds. One pond was medium-sized and the other was real big.

On one side of the big pond were the whites, and on the other side were the blacks. If you tried to go to the other side, you'd get run out. This mob of white boys had motorbikes, and they tried to chase us back to the black side. They used to spray-paint KKK and all types of shit on the rocks to try and scare us off.

We mostly just stayed on our side of the pond. We'd be back there playing Huckleberry Finn and all types of shit. We used to catch catfish there. We'd make bike trails, dig for worms and salamanders. We'd hang rope from a tree and swing on it. We had our imagination and improvised back then. There was no PlayStation or Internet. Some of my friends didn't even have a TV or a phone in their apartment. No air-conditioning in the summer, so you might as well be outside.

We used to make rafts out of tires and old mattresses, and go out in the middle of the pond with the fucking things. We used to play in this huge Dumpster in the back of the building. It was grimy, but it was ours. There were lots of things in it—Dumpster diving was a gold mine for kids back then. You had your sticks. You had your chalk. You had your bike ramps. All types of shit.

We'd build bikes from the scraps we'd find: you'd find a wheel over here, a pedal over there, handlebars somewhere else. Once you got all the pieces together, you had to get a chain. We used to pop the chain and take the little links off with a wrench so it fit whatever bike we were working on. Sometimes we'd pull the back tire back as far as it could go and still stay on, and make the chain fit that way. The seat wouldn't match, the handlebars wouldn't match, but you were out!

We had so much fun. I remember Jack the wino in the staircase, smelling like Night Train, and Sassy, the gospel lady who lived downstairs and used to yell at us out the window, calling us little devils and shit.

Even the pack of wild dogs roaming the neighborhoods couldn't stop us from playing outside. Dudes would shoot dogs and leave their carcasses behind our building all the time. This was the late 1970s, and there was no real ASPCA, at least not in my hood. Sometimes the dogs would come after us while we were riding our bikes. But the weirdest shit was when two dogs got stuck together fucking on the street. Stuck together from butt cheek to butt cheek, and you'd have to throw a rock to separate them. Once they separated, one dog running one way and the second dog running the other way, the dog that had been doing the fucking, his dick would be bloodred. Strangest shit I ever saw in my life.

I didn't stay on the Island every summer, either. Back then, we all had the Fresh Air Fund. It was part of growing up in New York City back in the day. Even Mike Tyson has mentioned the Fresh Air Fund.

There were two types of programs in the Fresh Air Fund. One was where you stayed with a family up in the mountains, and another was where you stayed in a bunch of bungalows, more like a summer camp. I went to the camp, up north in the mountains, for about two weeks. I didn't want to go at first, crying and all, didn't want to leave my peoples. But it was good to get off the streets, and when it came time to leave the camp, I didn't even want to go home, I didn't want to leave the peoples I knew there.

I was an overly aggressive kid and already fighting, so it kind of felt like being sent away to jail, even though it wasn't anything like jail. I mean, you had four meals a day, you had a counselor watching over you, you had to make your bed every day, and there were inspections where you could win a prize for having the cleanest bunk. A lot of things that helped make us ready for the world, instilling some order into us.

But the craziest thing about camp is that's where I first found out about fame. There I was, hanging with every type of kid from all five boroughs, about three hundred of us in this one camp area, and I was one of the most famous kids up there. The whole camp knew me. I started young with that fame shit. I wanted to be the man. At camp they called me Yoda, because I had big ears back then, and everybody didn't call you by your name, they nicknamed you based on what you looked like.

I was one of the kids who my counselor looked on to keep the rest of the kids in check. He had a right-hand man—me—who was supposed to make sure that the kids wouldn't act up, and if they did act up, they'd get punched in the face. Every time I went to camp, I was regulating. I knew I had to set my claim when I arrived, so boom, that was it.

Me and another kid named Monster, who grew up in Brooklyn, we hung out a lot. The counselors liked both of us because we kept the other kids in check. I was the right-hand man, and Monster was the left-hand man.

One time Monster and I were taking a shower, and you only have a certain amount of time before the next bunk comes in. But we were taking our time, just sitting there talking and shit, and we ended up taking a little bit too long, and the older kids came in. We still had soap on us. We were still sudsy.

Those older kids said, "Yo, you shorties gotta bounce so we can get in the showers."

Now, Monster and me were already oily together; each of us had fought enough other kids to immediately overcome any hesitation to strike first and strike hard. I would punch your face in at the drop of a dime.

What I mean by *oily* is like, when you're about to be aggressive on someone, that first punch is like an icebreaker. If you haven't been in a fight for a long time, you might be hesitant to punch somebody in the face simply because you haven't done it in a while. After you hit three people in the face, it starts to become second nature. By the time you hit the fifth or sixth person in the face, it becomes a reflex.

So by this time, we were already geared up for violence—we had absolutely no problem punching any kids who got out of line in the face.

We just looked at these older kids like, "You know who the fuck you talkin' to?" Me and him end up going toe-to-toe with these motherfuckers in the showers, with our slippers on, covered in soap, just fucking these older kids up. By the time the counselors came in, all of us were all just covered in soap, and they're like, "Yo, what's goin' on in here?" And the other kids were like, "Hey, we're just trying to use the showers, just tryin' to get cleaned up in here."

Looking back on it now, I have to wonder what I was thinking back then. I was such a little, little man, I was insane. I was crazy.

So we got into a little rumble with those older kids, but after that, they respected us, no doubt. Whenever the whole camp would come together, they'd point to us and say, "There's those two little dudes. Don't fuck with those two, they'll fuck you up."

That was when I first found out that I liked that notoriety shit, I liked being known like that. We had heart. I had little to no parental guidance at the time, but I was still holding it down. It was around this time that I also realized I was able to stand up on my own, even as a little kid.

And that hasn't changed.

## GROWING UP ON THE CRIME SIDE

Staten Island was an interesting place to grow up, because a lot of it was still rural in the 1970s, when we first moved there. It was a bit removed from the electricity of the city. There were some aspects of life that were a little different than your typical city experiences. And it was a step up from Brownsville, at least before the crack era.

People think Staten Island is a joke. Staten Island is *no joke.* One thing about the Island is that it's a small town. Boroughs like Manhattan and Brooklyn are so big, I could pop someone and disappear like a fart in the wind. You couldn't do that on the Island, it was just too small. If you got into a beef with somebody, sooner or later you were gonna see them again. You couldn't run away from your problems. So you were gonna have to knuckle up, shoot, cut, stab, whatever—you had to make your claim. Either you were gonna get punked, or you were gonna do the punking. And that's just how the Island is.

Around this time, everything was gang-related. Now, when I say *gang* I don't mean that we all wore colors and went around shooting people and all that. At that time, people would just come together in a community and stick together. They all had something in common, same neighborhood, same school, whatever, and they would just come together. And that's how we grew up.

In my neighborhood, there was a gang called the Avenue Crew, older kids who used to bully us all the time. They were about fifteen or sixteen years old, and we were only about eight or nine years old. They'd come up behind us and say, "Look at you, you lil' punk motherfucker," and then run off. We became recreation for these motherfuckers. It was just like the Little Rascals. We were the little kids that got on their fucking nerves, and they got on our nerves. They would just fuck with us. I never sat up in the house and played by the window just looking outside, even though going outside meant risking getting beat up by the Avenue Crew.

Getting beat up was different from getting beat down. Beat down meant you got stomped out and obliterated. You were probably going to the hospital. Beat up just meant getting wedgies and your chest punched in, getting slapped around or karate-chopped in the neck. Aside from the wedgies and jumping us and giving us hard pops on the arm, and catching us with that classic "open chest," holding both arms down while whaling on your chest, they used to really try to hurt us. Man, they used to fuck us up. Like, they enjoyed it so much they used to stalk us every day. They'd run down on us and lump our legs up and take our little money. They'd hold us down and punch our legs until we couldn't walk.

After a run-in with them, we'd go up on the roof and throw gravel and rocks at them. Every roof in the Clifton and Park Hill projects was covered with a mess of loose gravel and small rocks, which made perfect throwing ammunition. Or we'd wait for them to get fresh wearing their best clothes or be shooting dice and we'd hit them with water balloons. But they'd always catch us later. We didn't care, though. It was like guerrilla warfare. Strike and run, and take the beating like a man when you get caught.

I was taking that punishment, and it made me tougher. I was

an only child, so I had no older siblings to fight for me, so I just took the beatings as best I could. I never lay down or ran away, though; I always tried to dish out as much as I was taking. At least after they beat me up, they knew who I was and would have a little more respect for me. Sometimes you can fight and lose, but still gain respect from that because you stood up for yourself.

And I carry that confidence with me everywhere I go. That's why I'm not scared to go anywhere. After getting beat up so much, you have no choice but to get better with your hands, too. I could dodge punches and weave my way out of the circle and dip if need be. I used to call that the Scooby-Doo. But it wasn't easy to get good at fighting; the only way was simply to fight. That came with a lot of beatings.

I'd be the one in the park punching other kids in the face over the swings or some shit because I was growing up in the projects. If you know anything about how most ghettos are, you know the projects are like the slum within the slum. Living in that environment kind of gave me a sixth sense. It showed me what to look for before it even popped off. It taught me how to hone that instinct and protect myself at all times.

Sometimes, we ran and got away, sometimes we couldn't. My man Looney, though, he could shake the Avenue Crew like Herschel Walker. I couldn't shake dudes like he could. He had the moves. He made the big kids chasing him fall on their face. He was that swift and agile. He was the illest shake artist. He would have the Avenue Crew slipping and sliding and falling in their British Walkers and Playboy shoes. He'd run up the ramp to the building and juke his way down the stairs and then run down the hill and hide behind a wall, and when the Avenue Crew would run past he'd run back up the hill and shake a few of them at the top of the hill, too, just for good measure. They couldn't ever catch him.

I remember once they burned down our clubhouse in retaliation for us having hit them with water balloons while they were all fresh in their new clothes and shooting dice. One winter they caught us out on the pond when it had frozen over. The mother-fuckers started jumping on the ice to crack it so we'd fall into the water. We probably would've died if the ice had cracked.

It was like a cycle. We'd try to fight back, but we were just little kids. We had to form our own crew. Since we were so young, we became the BCC—the Baby Crash Crew. It was made up of little kids in the neighborhood. We all started sticking together. It was Kane, GC, Vinny, Raekwon, Killa Kane, Zabo, Love God, Chaz, Miser, Hersch, Looney, Sea Bass, Cab . . . it was a lot of us.

We ended up forming the Baby Crash Crew on our own, which did calm things down in our project. It was made up entirely of the younger kids coming up in the neighborhood. From the BCC, which lasted from grade school to junior high, we became DMD, which stood for Dick 'Em Down, in junior high school. That eventually morphed into Wreck Posse in high school, which I'll get to later on.

We moved out to the Island, but we always kept our Brooklyn ties. I'm a mixture of Staten Island and Brooklyn, because I spent a lot of time in Brooklyn. When my mother was off work for a few weeks and wanted some alone time, she'd send me to my grand-parents, who lived in Brownsville, Crown Heights, and Clinton Hill. I saw so much shit going on there, it was crazy. All parts, too. I would be with my grandmother in Brownsville, or with my cous-ins in Tompkins Projects. My grandfather lived between St. James Place and Cambridge Place, right down the block from where Big-gie was from.

Brooklyn was a different kind of rough. It was just grimy. You had twenty or thirty projects over there: Brownsville, Fort Greene, Marcy, Tompkins, Red Hook, Gowanus, Bushwick. All these fucking neighborhoods, it was like concentration camps for poor black people. Same with the Bronx.

The really crazy shit was that I used to have to go from Staten Island all the way to Brooklyn by myself. My mother would give me the money to go there. I was so young, only eight or nine years old. I actually had to go on the train. I had to go take the ferry to the other side. Jump on the 4 train at Bowling Green, go to Eastern Parkway, get on the bus there, go to Brownsville, get off at the OTB on Pitkin Avenue and go see my grandmother. That amazes me. These kids nowadays, they wouldn't understand how independent we were at such a young age back then. Today, a parent would get locked up for child abuse for letting shit like that happen.

It was different back then; no adults fucked around with kids all that much. I'm sure there were probably abductions and all that weird shit, but for the most part, you stood on your own. My mother used to send me to get fucking cigarettes from the corner store at eight or nine years old. You can't do that now. They gonna be like, "Shorty, get the fuck out of here."

My grandfather was a war veteran. My grandmother was an accountant for the government. My grandfather didn't teach me anything. Most of my whole family didn't teach me anything. I got love from them, but I didn't really get any guidance on how to live my life, on right and wrong, about what to do and what not to do.

I got my guidance from the streets. I didn't have no father. My mother was my guidance a little bit, but she was more or less worried about food and clothing, stuff like that. When I had problems or drama in the street, I couldn't go to my mother and ask her how to handle that shit. I had to figure that shit out myself. Sometimes I made the right choice, and sometimes I made the wrong choice. You just learn as you go. That's how it is with a lot of black kids growing up.

———

Every so often when I visited my grandfather, I'd also see my favorite uncles—Uncle Matt and Uncle Jason—who used to take me all over Brooklyn.

Jason, my quiet younger uncle, has a humble spirit. But the humble ones are the ones you gotta watch. I'm a real humble dude as well, real nice, but don't push my buttons until I get angry, 'cause I just go berserk. It takes a lot to piss me off, but when I get pissed the fuck off, watch out. Jason was the same way—calm and quiet until it was time to let off, and then he would bring the thunder.

Jason was younger than me. He was my uncle because my grandfather got married twice and had children from both wives. Me and Jason used to run around in the streets all day long.

Uncle Matthew, on the other hand, had a friend named Q., who was like his twin. They weren't blood, but they looked exactly alike. Uncle Matt was notorious in that area—he and Q. and their friends showed me the definition of maniac. Back then, you had to have a reputation so other motherfuckers wouldn't fuck with you.

I recall Q. as a fucking maniac, too. I was maybe eight or nine at the time. I'd say he probably killed a couple motherfuckers at least. He'd rob you for your shoes, rob you for your chain. Punch you in the face, stab you, cut you, shoot you, whatever. He was just that type of man. He loved me, though. He used to put me on his shoulders all the time.

We'd be out at night, running all around Brooklyn with these crazy motherfuckers. They'd do robberies right in front of me. Once they hit some guy in the head with a brick and took his boom box. Bashed the shit out of him and kept moving. I just looked at the dude twitching on the ground, then ran to catch up with Uncle Matt and his friend Q. That thug shit kind of influenced me a little bit, too—as a kid, I looked up to both of these guys, and to them, this was normal behavior. It was just another part of my upbringing.

I didn't really let that stuff get to me too much. The sad thing about ghetto life is that crazy shit like the shootouts, the stabbings, the piss-filled staircases, and the junkies become the norm. You grow a thick skin and get desensitized to the environment around you.

It shouldn't be that way, though. There were some deaths that should've been reflected on more, that people should have honored more. Like this little girl, only about seven or eight years old, who got killed. She was in my class in public school. She was raped and thrown off the roof at the back of the building by this mentally disabled kid we knew as Big A., who walked around the neighborhood looking goofy all the time.

This fucked everybody up. When we heard what had happened, everybody cringed. We were all in disbelief that this shit had gone down. When we found out a rapist was walking around the hood, that affected everybody. Even though they caught him pretty quickly, the presence of the crime lingered for months. At school, they emptied out her desk during class. The thought of her being there one day and dead the next was surreal.

Years later, you walk right by that same place where they found her body, and it's as if nothing had ever happened there.


A lotta shit went down on the roofs of the projects; they were like our clubhouse. When I was nine or ten years old, we'd just run across the roof because we weren't supposed to be up there. Then we moved to throwing rocks off; then, when I got older, we were smoking weed, slap-boxing, rhyming, moving product, watching for cops.

Of course, other things happened up there, too. One guy tried to kill himself by jumping off 141, a seven-story building—not once, but twice. He survived both attempts, landing on the fence near the day-care area, and only broke his arm. Eventually, he ended up in the asylum.

Maybe despite all this, my mother did what she could to try and maintain my innocence and ensure I was a good kid. We had dinners together on Christmas, and she'd let me say grace and try her best to keep me mindful of God and the good things in life. It worked a lot of the time. I stayed in school and made good grades for the most part and didn't get myself into too much trouble.

At least, not yet.

# 3

## RUUUUMBLEEE!!

Fighting—the art of hand-to-hand combat—was a big thing growing up. You had to know how to use your hands. Guns weren't the weapon of choice until later—you used your fists or a knife. That's one thing about Island dudes; they know how to throw their joints.

I didn't have older brothers to hold me down, so I had to fight my own battles against kids my age and pretty much anybody else who tried me. To this day, fists aren't my last resort, they're my first.

That's why I sometimes have trouble relating to people who have never fought or who have never been punched in the face. How much can you know about yourself until you're in a physical altercation? There are people today who have never been punched in the face. That's why they'll knock right into you as they walk by in the street and not even excuse themselves. They have no basic respect for any-one around them. Not enough people living in New York today have been punched in the face. They could use that lesson, though. I feel that confrontation brings respect. People who keep doing sneaky shit keep getting away with it, often because no one's willing to call them on it.

Whether in humility or self-confidence, they need that lesson. Getting tested lets you find out who you are deep down. And I found out that deep down I'm a scrapper. I'm also respectful, though. If I bump into someone, I excuse myself. I'm a humble warrior. You can't go around looking for trouble, but you have to be ready when it comes. You can't walk around trying to be the toughest, because there's always someone tougher.

Just to join little crews and be cool with certain people, you had to fight. You had to shoot the joints. Can you imagine? Even the Avenue Crew, who used to beat us up, had to fight to be able to chill on the avenue. They had to deal with older dudes trying to push them off the block.

To be down with any crew, you had to slap-box: whoever got the most slaps off with an open hand won. Just because you lost the fight didn't mean you didn't get in, though. Win or lose, if you had heart to fight, you got in. Some kids didn't want to fight, so they couldn't be down. You couldn't be scared to fight.

I've gotten the shit slapped out of my face for five minutes straight when my hands weren't good yet. All that fighting and getting jumped and sometimes taking a beating is why I'm not afraid to scuffle to this day. And I will hold it down and do my just due with my hands. I prefer my hands to a gun any day. Guns and hands are two different games. A dude knows that you're good with your hands, he's not gonna fight you, he's gonna shoot you.

The problem with a gun is that it's a coward's weapon, because anyone can use it. I could put a gun in the hands of a two-year-old, blindfold him, and tell him to squeeze the trigger, and he'd kill somebody.

Now, for someone to come up on me, actually say something, and we get it on, we rumblin', and I catch him with an uppercut, a cross, kick him in his fuckin' abdomen, break his fuckin' leg and break his jaw with my right hand, knock him on his ass, do you

know the satisfaction in that? It's huge, and not just for the winner. That feels better than shooting someone, because he'll get
up and say, "Damn . . . that was some shit I just went through.
I'm not fuckin' with that dude no more." Or he might be the kind
of dude who thinks: *You know what? I like how he did this or that, I'm
gonna go learn and practice, and we gonna fight again.* He might be
one of those guys. But at the end of it all, we both get to walk away
and go see our families, and fight another day.

With a fight, there's a clear winner and a clear loser, and (usually) no one gets seriously hurt. Guns and drugs changed everything; but growing up, fighting brought out the real men on the
streets.

There is a science to fighting. Balance, technique, speed. Speed
kills. Fuck what you heard. Fuck all that slow, I'll knock you out,
big dude shit. No. Speed kills. I've seen David and Goliath stories
my whole life. I've seen little small dudes knock out dudes ten
times their fucking size and weight based on speed and speed
alone.

When you tap someone's jaw properly, their brain rocks. The
human brain is encased in fluid, and it has no shock absorbers,
so when it moves, it's going to hit the side of the skull. When someone gets hit, the fluid shifts and the brain shakes, and they get
knocked out. If you get hit and it wobbles your brain, no matter
how big you are, you're going to be fucking discombobulated, and
you're gonna fuckin' fall.

And your size doesn't matter. That was one of the things that
fighting in the streets (and later in jail) etched into my psyche.
Size does not matter one bit. I've seen big dudes get scooped by
small dudes and slammed on their heads. And I've seen small
dudes jump to punch a big man in the face and still knock him
right out.

Back in the day, you used to run out of your apartment when
you heard two motherfuckers fighting. It was like *Clash of the*

*Titans.* It was like a Mike Tyson main event. People would run out of their apartments and come out of the building to see certain people fight. Instead of being on TV, the shit was right in front of your face. These were our heroes growing up.

We'd sit there and they'd go at it and shoot the five until one dude was knocked out. It wasn't just entertainment for me like it was for most spectators. I wanted to watch so that I could learn. I studied dudes like Tameek. Billy Johnson used to knock guys out. Buddha knocked some people out. Arkim and Dupreme and Ubar all knocked people out, too. And they all used the 52 Hand Blocks.

They were superstars with the knuckle check. These dudes could rock a gold chain, and nobody would fuck with them. Back then, you couldn't rock any type of jewelry just like that, because someone was going to test you or rob you. If you were wearing a chain, you had to be someone who was known for shooting or cutting or knocking dudes the fuck out. And someone who didn't know you may still try and test, so you couldn't really rely on your rep to save you every time. You had to be ready to show and prove.

Now anybody can wear a chain in the goddamn hood. Nobody's doing shit to them. You can wear your Jordans and leathers and jewelry in good faith. Rarely are you gonna get tested. At least in comparison to when I was coming up. Fighting was just a way of life then. It was pretty much a given that you were going to have to fight or at least stand up for yourself if you hoped to keep whatever little fly shit you had.

Everybody wanted to be Bruce Lee back in the day. He was the main dude on TV, and played a major part in the 52 Hand Blocks. The 52 is like "the Continuing Fist" in tae kwon do. No matter what kind or how many punches you threw, if your opponent had mastered it, it was hard as hell to hit them. The 52 Blocks is both an offensive and defensive style that was developed on the street. It's elbows, arms, and a combination of hand movements that combines techniques from a half-dozen martial arts, including tae kwon do, monkey-style kung fu, jeet kune do, and who knows what else. That's why 52 Blocks was such a major advantage if you could master it. Size or ability didn't matter if you could block everything your opponent threw at you, then retaliate.

For whatever reason, the OGs didn't pass 52 down to the younger generation. Maybe it was because guns became more of a factor in settling disputes. Whatever the reason, 52 Hand Blocks is nearly a lost art today, with only a scarce few remaining who claim to know it. So few that people think it's a myth. It's not, though. If you tangle with one of these old heads that knows the 52, you're gonna get hit with a tornado. He'll hit you from your kneecaps to both sides of your dome.

Sha-Bon, or Shabby, who was down with the Avenue Crew, had a brother named Tameek who was a master at 52 Hand Blocks. You could not get your shit off with Tameek. He was a knockout artist in every sense of the word, and there is an art to the knock-out. He had big ol' mitten hands, and he could knock you out with either one. His defense skills were impenetrable. You could not land a single punch on this guy, and he would land all his. Believe it or not, this dude used to catch your punch and kiss your fist, then bust your shit.

I wanted to do a documentary with Tameek about the 52, but he got killed before I could. He was in the life, and tried to take over a drug building, and got shot in the back of the head. I wanted to interview him because he knew the blocks. He knew defense, but he also knew offense, how to come back from the block. Once he had neutralized his opponent's attack, he knew the best way to strike and drop them with one punch. That's lost knowledge. That died with him. That's a damn shame.

One of my best friends was named June June, aka Infinite, who I first met in high school. He was a six-foot-two-inch, wavy-haired, jet-black motherfucker, and a born fighter. I wish he were still alive; he could have become a heavyweight fighter.

He showed me about what having heart really meant and to not be afraid of anybody. Even if he was, he'd hide it real good and take them on anyway. I was smaller than a lot of other dudes, but I was already a fighter with heart, and had been for years. So he kept my little yellow ass around.

I learned so much from him. I learned that if I got into a fight and I got lumped up, I'd just take my beating. That's heart. And that's something I learned from him, because he lost fights, too.

He and I would be walking down the street or hanging out, and we'd see someone who had a rep for fighting.

"Yo, God, you think he could get me?" In other words, do you think he can beat me?

"I don't know, Infinite."

That's all he needed to hear. He'd go over and start a fight with the dude. Either he'd win or he'd lose. Usually he'd win, but if he lost, he'd take the loss. He wouldn't cry and go get his gun. He would say, "I'ma see that dude in three months."

That's all he'd say to whoever beat him. He'd go work out crazy hard for three months, then come back and challenge him to another fight. And he'd knock him the fuck out. Every. Time.

Infinite also taught me that you can take a loss and you can come back strong. That's the true heart of a champion. He was a notorious knockout artist on Staten Island. To this day, if I said his name there, people would know who he was.

I remember before he died, he got locked up at Rikers Island and came home with twenty-two cuts on his back and face. He showed me the scars on his back—it was gruesome. I asked him what happened.

"I was goin' to war in Rikers!" he said. "As soon as I arrived in the Four Building [the prison dorm], my name's ringin' bells. 'June June's in the house!'"

See, the moment you get in jail, you gotta act a certain way, or other dudes are gonna try to take advantage of you any way they can. That's your reputation, and if it's solid, it can protect you from a lotta shit. Of course, the bigger rep you have, the bigger target you can be, too. June June knew this, and since he had a rep for knockin' dudes out, he knew guys were gonna come at him, hoping to improve their rep by taking him down.

"Them lil' dudes all had to gang up on me, there musta been about twenty of 'em," June June said. "They climbed up on me, and I was knocking 'em out one by one. But after that, I came out of the infirmary, and the whole jail was dialed down."

That's just how he was. He was one of those dudes that everywhere he went, you always knew he was in the house. Everyone knew not to mess with him, or if they didn't know, they learned damn quick. Matter of fact, during that stretch was when he changed his name to Infinite. He went in June June, he came out Infinite.

I loved that man. He had a lot of people that didn't like him, but then he also had mad peoples who loved him. And he didn't like that many people, but I was lucky to be one of them. He even got along with my moms.

Unfortunately, like a lot of the good brothers I grew up with, he got killed. He ran up on some little shorty who was scared of him, and he shot June June in the chest with a .45. Just murdered him. The guy who shot him was a little sucka punk, but he feared June June, so he shot him. I always told June June he couldn't keep just running up on people like that. But he wasn't trying to hear that, and it got him killed.

# 4

# THE 5 PERCENTERS

I wasn't awakened and truly empowered as a black man in America until I started hanging out with the 5 Percent. That knowledge and experience provided the foundation for both the Wu-Tang Clan and my own manhood.

I would always see those brothers on the corner, talking positive and addressing issues in the community. The way they spoke and the terminology they used, I didn't really understand it at first, but when I was around thirteen or fourteen, it drew me in:

"Peace, Allah. Come build with the brothers in the cipher."

"The black man is God, don't believe in no mystery God in the sky!"

"Peace, God. What's today's Mathematics?"

My name, U-God, came from my enlightener Dakim, the person who gave me knowledge of self. The *U* in my name is short for *Universal*. The word *universal* means multidimensional, infinite, comprehensive. Basically, anything I put my mind to, I will figure out how to get it done. I was given the Universal name because I carry the Ambassador torch every day. I can go anywhere, I can talk to anyone, it's just who I am.

My full name is U-God Allah. The name U-God is a

statement saying that inside of you, the all, the making of you is
God. In our terminology, when we say God, it means being a supreme being. A supreme being's seed/sperm is dominant. He
can change the face of the earth physically.

Much of this comes from Islam and Muslim culture. Allah is
the All Eye Seeing. Christians and Catholics believe that God is
some mysterious force in the sky. We believe the black man is God,
and Allah is the All Eye Seeing (Jehovah, God, etc.). The black
man is the original man, the maker of civilization. How can you
tell the originator what is what?

Knowledge of self is the terminology of 5 Percenters—5 Percent
lessons taught blacks in America our true history and made us
understand the reality of how we got in our current situation in
America. Public schools and textbooks told us we were from
Africa, were slaves for four hundred years, freed eventually by
Abraham Lincoln, and further freed by Martin Luther King Jr.
This is not our true history.

Our true black American history is contained within 120 Lessons, which were given to us by Clarence 13X, who was a con-
temporary of Malcolm X. The 120 Lessons teach us that we were
stripped of our identity, broken down, and made to fear—and
that fear was implanted in our babies, everything done to control
us like cattle and property.

With this bit of knowledge that was given to us by Elijah Muhammad (who received it from Baby G, a half-black, half-white
man who disappeared without a trace soon afterward) and Wal-
lace Fard Muhammad before him, and a lot of very powerful Muslim guys who were awakened by some strange force, they passed
that on to us as kids. The Muslim degrees that we received as kids
are called the 120.

Clarence 13X brought these Lessons to the streets, gave them
to us to wake us up. He was different because he brought Islam
to the hustlers, pimps, drug dealers, and thieves on the street

corners who needed it most. The 120 was for gangsters, pimps, all the street dwellers in the black community. You received these Lessons and became enlightened depending on the type of person you were.

The majority of the world is the 85 percent. They are the deaf, dumb, and blind masses, basically Savages in pursuit of happiness, who are often poison-animal eaters (certain foods, like pork, make a person docile, and added antibiotics and artificial ingredients just make it worse), who have no knowledge of self, and therefore are slaves to the 10 percent who are in power.

The 10 percent are the slave owners and bloodsuckers of the poor masses, like priests and politicians. They control the system; they know the truth, but keep it to themselves, so they hide the facts proving who the true and living God is.

Then you have the 5 Percent, who are the Poor Righteous Teachers. They're trying to educate the 85 percent and awaken them out of their sleep state. Basically, the 5 Percent has to civilize the uncivilized. That makes up the entire 100 percent of the population on earth.

The 5 Percent Lessons taught you that everything in existence came from the black man, the Original Man, the father of civilization, God of the Universe. It's a great source of pride and takes a lot of reflection because as a kid, you get bombarded by so much white America that you don't know that blacks have contributed massive amounts of things to this world.

The 120 Lessons aren't prejudiced against white people; the Lessons are for us. The 120 taught us to unlearn the lies that shackled us and replace that with genuine attempts to fill in history that was purposefully left out of history books. From birth, we're bombarded with a single idea: that we were and are slaves. Our history is basically four hundred years of free labor. According to that version of history, we didn't invent anything, we didn't create anything, we were good for nothing else. So they took advantage of the place they put us in. They separated us. They fed us the wrong foods. And they keep us this way, with the trickery they use to do things. The 120 broke down everything.

Even at a young age, these degrees, the 120 Lessons, gave me and my crew our first real knowledge of self. You couldn't trick us with stupid shit anymore. Why? Because the degrees told us about the tricknology, how we were taught lies and deceit. They allowed us to see the truth of our situation.

The degrees also gave us high self-esteem, allowing us to carry ourselves differently, with the idea that we mattered in this world. I think that's a big problem with much of today's youth, especially black youth; they feel like they don't matter in today's society. Granted, much of today's society isn't helping—it's very clear to me that the deck is still stacked against young black men—but they have to rise above what society thinks of them in general and be true to themselves, hold their heads up high and keep doing what they're doing every day, regardless of what anyone else thinks.

But mainstream society keeps trying to throw that shit in our face like we give a fuck anymore. I mean like, "Know your place, boy." Naw, we don't know anything about that. We black people don't give a fuck about no place—what place you talkin' about? All I know is that as long as I got some money in my pocket, I can do whatever the fuck I wanna do. And anyone trying to tell us otherwise just makes us go harder.

We need to realize that we're standing on the shoulders of everyone who came before us. We're the seed of the seed of the seed of those ancestors that made our history. All of us, we're the best of the best right now. Those that made it, we survived everything that was thrown at us—diseases, plagues, violence, slaughter—to actually get to this level of humanity where we can actually read and write and chill on the couch and watch TV, do all the things we take for granted today.

We made it, we all survived to reach this point. But what comes next? What are you going to do with this life that your ancestors suffered and fought and bled and died for? How are you going to carry their legacy forward and leave your own mark—whether it be big or small—on the world? No matter what you choose to focus on, you should aspire to be the very best you can be, whether that's being a drug dealer or a fireman or a teacher. If you want to be a poet, if you want to be a rapper, if you want to be an athlete, whatever you want to do, just always be striving for more—more skill, more knowledge, more experience—to be the best at it.

When I was thirteen, my enlighteners were Dakim and Love God, who both dropped Supreme Mathematics into my lap. At the time, being 5 Percent was a big fucking deal. You had to know at least the basic Mathematics, or you were catching a beating. They never beat me because we were younger, and they were just happy the young Gods were picking up the lessons.

I got my degrees at fifteen. First came knowledge, which was just knowing the degrees. Then came wisdom, which was to be able to speak about the degrees. Finally came understanding, when the lightbulb came on and my world was forever changed—I was awake now.

Though Supreme Mathematics guided me through my teenage years, it really took hold of me when I got to about twenty-one years old. What really pulled me into it, the teachings of this offshoot of Islam, was that my last name is Hawkins. In case you don't know, the first English slave trader was named John Hardy Hawkins. He was the first Englishman to bring slaves to America. He was sanctioned by the pope. The Roman Catholic Church gave him the okay to enslave us and bring us to North America. When I found that out, it blew my mind. That pulled me in. I wanted to know what this shit was about and why I shared that devil's last name. Both my grandmother and I have tried to have our DNA analyzed, but the results have either been inconclusive or never came back.

The Mathematics encouraged me to learn how our families were split up and our history was stolen. How we were renamed after our masters. How we're still doing the same shit to each other years and years down the line. How we need unity and structure to better our situation, but fall victim to the manipulative ways of the powers that be until we can't stick together. We're still attempting to bring down anybody who is doing better than us in our community, like crabs in a barrel. Still doing stupid shit the powers that be want us to do. My own kind will throw each other into slavery for profit and power. Still fighting and killing each other over stupid, petty shit. And this isn't just a black thing, it's a human condition. But black people are more direct about trying to fuck up your shit.

Worse yet, our lack of knowledge has us trying to drink from this one little well of drugs, entertainment, and sports. There's so many ways to make money legitimately, but all we see is drugs, entertainment, and sports. See, that's the thing about knowledge. When you get knowledge, you don't even know you have it until you apply it. In essence, you don't even have it until it gets used.

What it really all comes down to is knowledge of self: what you know—knowing your history and where you truly come from—how you know it, who you know. Listen to the people around you, observe the world around you. The average person in the hood isn't seeing that; they're just going by what they know and their limited worldview. But there's more things under the sun than they can possibly imagine.

The illest aspect of the degrees that I internalized was to not look in the sky for salvation. Religion is only a moral ceiling; you still have to live life as though there are repercussions for the shit you do, but I realized as a kid that I couldn't rely on a mystery God.

People pray for things, then they think things are gonna come to them. Actually, that's not the way it works. God helps those that help themselves, that's basically what it means. You can't wait for a mystery God to bring you food, clothes, and shelter. You'd be out there on the streets homeless. The act of doing, that's where the blessing takes place.

And during the crack era of Park Hill, we needed to be reminded that we were the only ones who could save ourselves.

# 5

# HIP-HOP WAS OUR WAY OF LIFE

Eventually, my mother got kicked out of our old building at 260 Park Hill. The dude upstairs from us used to make so much fucking noise that she got into an argument with him. She and her boyfriend went up there and they all got into an even bigger argument, which ended up in a fight, so they kicked us out, and we moved across the street to 339 Vanderbilt Avenue.

While we were living there, I became best friends with the landlord's son, an older kid named Tom who lived below us. He was like a mentor to me, the big brother I never had.

Tom used to DJ at parties, and I'd help him with his records and gear. Crazy shit about Tom was that he used to make his own speakers. He'd go to a hardware store and get wood and cut out a box. Then we'd get amps, woofers, and tweeters from a used-electronics store and build the box around it and put insulation in it for soundproofing, and he'd have the best speakers in the hood for practically no money.

Tom had a friendly rivalry with Thurman, another DJ on the block, and they were always trying to one-up the other with speaker builds, whose was louder, all that. We were a little more innovative with the shit back then. And every

time there was a little party popping off, I'd be over there helping Tom, carrying records, whatever.

I was always listening to music while growing up. When I was
punished, my mother would send me to my room. All I had was
my box and my radio. We used to make our own tapes. We would
put the tape in the recorder, press the record button, and record
songs off the radio. We were listening to Mr. Magic's show and all
those old-school rappers, that's how you did it back in the day. I
started listening to rap in '84, but it has always influenced me. It
was *our* music. It wasn't popular like it is now.

Tom was my first real mentor for hip-hop, him and my uncle Matt.
Now, we'd heard hip-hop before this, but it wasn't super rhymes
and classic beats and all that. It was groups like the Treacherous
Three, Grand Wizard Theodore and the Fantastic Five, and the
Cold Crush Brothers. The movie *Wild Style* came out, which really
moved hip-hop culture forward.

My man Tom was already collecting records and DJing. He had
a mixer and two turntables, and we'd just be in the basement
listening to music all day long. It was here where I first started
listening to the roots of what would become the rap and hip-hop
the next generation would kick out. Sampling was just starting at
this time, and we would sample this song or sample that beat. We
would come up with ideas or concepts or put routines together,
things we still do to this day.

On top of this, Uncle Matt would come out to Staten Island
whenever he'd get in trouble, that was his little hiding spot. He'd
come and stay with us, and he'd bring tapes of live performances
from Harlem World, a popular club that hosted everyone who was
anyone in hip-hop, like Grandmaster Flash and the Furious Five,
Lady Smiley, Busy Bee Starski, Doug E. Fresh, and Kool Moe Dee.

Old rappers and all that stuff, and we'd listen to those on the stoop of the house all day long. That was where I started honing the craft of hip-hop. Hip-hop started getting into me at that time.

I still remember the first time I hung out with RZA. It was at a block party in Stapleton Park. Tom and I went down there together. Back then he'd give little house parties with the blue light or the red light, and Tom would get his big speakers out and the rest of his equipment and start DJing.

This time we were going to Stapleton to DJ in the park. RZA was also DJing there that day. I knew him from the projects when he lived across the street from my house on Vanderbilt. I also knew his brother Divine from P.S. 57. They had a big family that was always moving around. Actually, RZA ended up in Park Hill for a while, on the top floor of Building 350. Then he moved down the hill by our junior high school, P.S. 49, and was there for another good while. His house was near a path that ran from P.S. 49 through the neighborhood. Everyone used it to go from school back to Park Hill.

So RZA got on the turntables and started doing his cutting thing. To me, nobody could fuck with Tom, because he was my mentor. I was still impressed by RZA, though. It was a nice summer day, and I just happened to talk to him for a minute, and he was into the same things I was into. Little did I know that a few years later he'd be coming to the Hill to chill, and we'd recognize each other and become close friends.

In those years, RZA kept kind of popping up in my life; our paths just seemed to keep crossing every so often. It was him, a dude named Dondi, and this guy whose street name was To the Beat, who later died of cancer. He looked like Michael Jackson, with a big old Afro and a big old nose. But those three were like the stars of the hood back then. They'd go around in matching zodiac-sign sweatshirts and all that fly shit. They were always doing something hip-hoppy, and I was always attracted to that scene, and so was RZA.

He was always a smart motherfucker. What initially drew me to him was his mind. I could care less about what you got, what you doin', but if you can stimulate my mental, talk about some real shit, if you're a smart man, that's what drew me to him. Because I hate ignorance. Even as a kid, I hated ignorant motherfuckers.

At the time, he called himself Prince Rakeem Allah, and he was in tune with the Mathematics and knowledge of self—like I said, the man is a genius.

For example, RZA is a master of the 120. He, Genius, and Masta Killa mastered the Lessons back and forth, forth and back. They have that shit down pat. "RZA, what's the wisdom knowledge degree in the 1-40, the second and third paragraphs?" And he would know it and kick that shit verbatim at you.

When we first met, he asked me "What's today's Mathematics, God?" because my name was U-God Allah. Now, it happened to be the eighth day of the month, so we discussed the eighth degree: "to build, destroy, divine." We would first take it to the Supreme Mathematics: to build is to add on; *build* is another word for elevation: when you build, you elevate from the lowest to the highest forms of life. *Destroy* is to destroy all negativity within your circumference. *Divine* is another word for greatness—my mind is divine because it cannot be diluted. In other words, a person with knowledge of self cannot be diluted; he cannot be tampered with in any shape, form, or fashion because he knows the truth about himself and his surroundings. When you build with someone, it's like having a meeting of the minds, and that's why I was drawn to RZA.

This was during my cool nerd phase. I wasn't hanging around hooligans as much anymore. I was hanging out with Pachy, Eric,

Foe, Kenny, Tom, Mike, Abdul, Keith, Mark, Howie . . . a bunch of dudes, and a lot of them grew up to be somebody. One of them grew up to be a correctional officer, another one became a nurse. Abdul, who was a tall dude, at least six foot six or six foot seven, tried to get into the NBA, but couldn't make it and wound up playing in Italy. They weren't into street shit. I'm not saying they were exactly nerds, but to me nerds are cool. Nerds are non-threatening.

That's how I viewed RZA at first. He was a nerd, but he wanted to be down with the gangsters. I remember when I gave RZA half a man (a half kilo) of crack to sell one time, I got my money back, but he messed up his cut. I shoulda known he wasn't built for that kind of hustlin', but sometimes you gotta let some cats find that out for themselves.

The truth was that both of us weren't really into the streets. I mean, we hung out on the streets, but I wasn't really *out there* out there, if you know what I mean. But we wanted to chill outside, so we'd hang out on the stoop of the corner bodega. That was our hangout spot. And if we weren't there, we were hangin' at Tom's house. We'd be sittin' there all day and all night, just laughing, talking about stupid shit, records, just doing what kids did every day back then.

One thing that corner store had that I still remember was some fuckin' great heroes. They made great big sandwiches for five bucks. You could get turkey or roast beef and a quart of grape drink. That was the shit back in the day.


I also started running into Method Man around this time. I first met him at the P.S. 49 Center, the youth center. It was located between Stapleton and Park Hill, and we used to all go down to the center at about five o'clock at night, when it would open. We would be down there playing basketball, hanging out, and you get to mingle with all the kids from the projects.

That was when we were break-dancing, doing windmills and all that shit. So you had your Pumas on, and we had these suits called windbreakers, real slippery jackets and pants that you'd break-dance in, 'cause they gave you extra spin on the cardboard. Some days they would play music, songs like "Planet Rock" by Afrika Bambaataa & the Soulsonic Force, and "Candy Girl" and other New Edition songs that were really hot at the time.

Meth had one of them shag cuts in the back of his head back then, and he could dance motherfuckin' New Edition routines like it was nothing. He was doing them dance steps like he'd re-hearsed it. That was the first time I met him, when we were both around eleven years old at the 49 Center. This was even before he became known as Shaquan. He was fresh from Long Island, trying to find his way over here, trying to fit in. I saw him bustin' his New Edition moves and went over and started talking to him.

Meth's always been an upbeat character; his whole personality was always positive. Even when things were the roughest for us on the streets, he never was down on himself or life—unless he's high as a motherfucker, but other than that, that dude's energy is always goin'. To this day, he's still an upbeat dude.

Meth was in the same projects as me. He used to live upstairs on the floor with Sargee, another neighborhood DJ. So it was inevitable that we'd run into each other and laugh it up. You know, what's up, what's up, yadda, yadda, yadda.

Later on, after the Center, Meth threw out a couple of hood jams. Like, "My House, My House" and "Panty Raider" and all that fly shit. We were all like, "Wow, dude got talent."

And, you know, I ran into him again and we started talking. But it wasn't until we got our jobs at the Statue of Liberty later on, when we were like fifteen, that we really got close.

That's also about the time when his name became Shaquan; he became 5 Percent because everybody else was 5 Percent. He got his 5 Percent name from his mentor Rashawn. Rashawn was down with the Avenue Crew back in the day, same old shit, just another bully chasing us little kids when we were young. But he took Meth under his wing first.

So Meth started coming out of the house a little bit more by then. And I don't wanna throw dirt on him, but he was just a dirt bomb back then. The fuckin' dude never washed his clothes, he was just always raggedy. I mean, he was going through some shit. He was going through whatever he was going through, just like we all were at the time. We were all raggedy at some point. One time I had one pair of shoes, I was leanin' because my shoes were worn out on one side, I was trying to get my shit together, and my girl left me. It's the same shit. We all went through the same shit at the same time.

About this time, my mom took up with a man named Charles for several years, who was the father of my half brother, Issa.

Charles would babysit us. He raised me, too; between Uncle Matt and him, those two really put the "have no fear" type of shit in me. I can't even front on Charles, God bless the dead. He was no joke. He also made me into a fighter. He made me into a tough little boy, more aggressive, because I was the only child with my mother at the time—this was before my brother was born.

He was a Quran-reading man who jogged ten miles a day and played tennis. A real athletic dude, but he and my mother fought a lot, and sometimes he would put his hands on her. I remember trying to stand up for her one time. "Motherfucker! Don't hit my mother!" I tried to defend her, but I was only ten or eleven years old. I was a little frail thing back then, I probably weighed about seventy or eighty pounds.

One day, he met me after school. He dragged me behind the school building and put a knife to my neck. He did that because I was starting to become a little man. I think back on it now, he was trying to put fear in me. He wanted me to fear him. It worked for the first few seconds, but as soon as he let me go, I ran off and yelled back, "Fuck you, motherfucker! When I get older I'm gonna kill you!"

That was about the time when I started losing my fear of a lot of things. When you lose your fear of something or somebody, they have no authority over you. When he beat on my mother, he saw it in my eyes without me having to say, "Motherfucker, I'm gonna kill you." I still was a little guy. But I was still trying to find my little way in the world.

As I got older, I realized you don't have to worry about the old guys doing you harm. Adults put more thought and reason into their plans and actions. It's the youth, the kids, that you've got to worry about doing you harm. Not all of them, of course, but the ones that have lost their fear of everything, including death. The ones living on the street day to day, hand to mouth, falling into crime just to survive. Those little motherfuckers have heart, and they're fearless. When the kids start not caring and losing their fear, given the right situation, they would blow your fucking head off your shoulders.

After the knife incident, I ran back to my mother's house, and she put a restraining order on him. Even with that, he was still in and out of our lives. As I got older, I'd see him time and time again when he would come see my brother Issa.

Time moved on and things changed, and I grew into that little man, and then grew some more. It's funny—when you're young, you think you're grown, but really I was still a little snot-nose.

When I was sixteen or seventeen, I ran into Charles again. By this time I was making grown-man moves on the street, with plenty of people selling drugs for me. Charles saw how strong I had become, and I saw straight panic on his face. He knew I'd never forgotten what he'd done to my mother and me. So he moved out of the Stapleton projects on the Island to Marcy Projects in Brooklyn. Even though I could have done him dirty, I didn't—he was still my brother's father.

I also realized there was an upside to Charles being in my life at that time. He had family in the Stapleton projects, and we used to hang there all the time. Stapleton always reminded me of a maximum-security prison; the buildings all have balconies that look like jail tiers. In Stapleton, I ran into RZA more, and Ghostface Killah, too—if it wasn't for Charles, I probably never would have gotten to know those two.

I was going to school at P.S. 49 when I was fourteen or fifteen years old. It was right in the middle of Park Hill and Stapleton, and I became an ambassador between the projects. I was cool with everybody. That was a major thing, because at that time Park Hill peoples couldn't go to Stapleton, and vice versa. I overcame all that by being in Stapleton when I was a little kid, and I played with those kids. I had passes, and never had any beef with dudes from that project.

I was in and out of Stapleton all day. I'd go to Ghost's crib. I'd go see Den at his crib. I'd stop by Juice's crib and say what up to Dorian on the way. I'd even be up in Guy's house, and he's the one that shot my son by accident years later.

Eventually, this extended into New Brighton and West Brighton, the other projects on the Island, too. Because I went to high school with kids from both places, I was always interwoven into all the neighborhoods. Later on, that gave me the pass to sell big drugs in all those 'jects.

That played a huge part when I started hustling. People don't even know how much hustling I was doing, because I knew dudes in every project in Staten Island. I was the first one to conquer all those projects, put work in each one simultaneously, and have 'em all cooking at the same time.

Around this time, I was also starting to get with some of the girls in my neighborhoods. Like my first girlfriend. Well, she wasn't my first girlfriend, but she was the first bad one that I got with. She lived in a house close to Stapleton. She was smoking hot. She broke my virginity and turned me into a fucking animal.

I had met her while out one night, and I just went up to her. I just banged her. I wasn't her first, though. She was fucking already. By the time she got to me, I was probably the third or fourth on the list. She got around, and just by her putting me on the list, that was kind of cool, because that was a confidence booster for me.

But then she started fucking a drug dealer who had more money than me. I didn't have any money at the time; I was just a regular, good-looking young guy. And she liked me for who I was at first, but then drugs started coming into the hood, and the lure of that lifestyle pulled her in, going for the dudes with the gold chains and the cars, all that shit. She left me and started fucking around with this other dude. That was my first taste of C.R.E.A.M.—that cash rules everything around me.

I remember one night I was with one of my peoples, my best friend, Choice. It was raining, and I was thinking about everything I was going through, with this drug dealer taking my girl, and how I was flat broke. I was a real downer, on some damn "I don't have any bread, my money is wack" kick. I said right then and there that I was never gonna be broke ever again. Years later, Choice said, "After U-God said that shit, the man transformed himself. Sure enough, he's never been broke again in his whole fucking life. From that day on."

On Saturdays, we would have rec room parties. The rec room was at the bottom of the building, where everybody would just come on in and get down. These particular parties attracted the hardest motherfuckers from every project on Staten Island. It'd be at capacity, about a hundred people, but everyone would be trying to cram in there. They were like our own private little parties, packed with nothing but hood dudes smoking weed and hood broads, and we'd be in there doing our thing.

Funky G Grandville would DJ, and Scotty Watty—one of the illest street rhymers ever—would be on the mic as the Discotyzers. Or Schoolly D would be playing "PSK." You might see that cute girl from West Brighton or Stapleton that you saw on the bus earlier that week. You might see one of your crushes from school. You might see some of your partners from school or from another project. There might be a fight outside, there'd be sightings of people you might have beef with, but overall it'd just be a bangin' party.

I'd be in there with my man Jahmel, we'd be hanging with Bones, Love God, Kane, Hersch, Chaz, Marcus, the whole Wreck Posse crew, the whole Hill. Of course, you couldn't show up at a rec room party without looking your best. Park Hill was known for fly dudes who were always on some fly shit: Gucci down, Polo down, you name it. If it was high end, we were sporting it: gold teeth, ropes, cars.

The fashion of the day was Double Goose V leather bombers mostly, or sheepskin coats, all worn with Pumas and Kangols. You always took a kind of a risk wearing sheepskins, 'cause some dude might be trying to take your shit, even though that would have been suicide doing it on our turf. Besides, at the time I was carrying a sawed-off deer shotgun under my sheepskin, and usually just flashing that would shut any trouble down before it ever got started.

I guess it's like the young boys in their new Jordans and Kobes

now. Except back then we sweated Ballys. Shit don't change, just
new material to lust for, that's all.

Of course, since we had everyone from all over the Island coming over, every rec room party was a mix of all the neighborhoods.

Staten Island had five or six neighborhoods, and each one was
close-knit. And out of all of them, Stapleton and the Harbor
were both full of troublemakers—like Ghost. Stapleton dudes
like the Gladiator Posse weren't about gear or money, they always
came around to make trouble. Instead of getting money, they
wanted to shoot shit up or snatch a chain. That's why Stapleton
always had beef with everybody on the Island. That hood was
also the capital of angel dust (PCP), and in my opinion, that's
probably why they were so crazy. When I was hustlin' in Stapleton, I had three good workers over there. That's because I kept
my shit organized, unlike everyone else there.

Guys from the New Brighton projects were getting money, but
they were more about fighting and being known as good fighters. New Brighton was a gold mine for me when I started hustling,
because the typical New Brighton dudes wasn't getting money like
that.

Then we had notorious troublemakers throughout Staten Island that were just wild for nothing. Dudes like Corky, Cash, and
others would just come through and shoot the Hill up just for
reputation.

Mariner's Harbor dudes were also known as troublemakers.
They didn't play over there. Mal Gibbs from the Harbor was the
worst. He was known for all kinds of wild shit. If he was coming
at you, you better keep your heat on you, not stashed off somewhere. He was known for shooting, robbing, and kidnapping drug
dealers. He'd find out where you lived, run up in your house, tie
you up, and rob you.

Mal pulled shit all over the Island—except Park Hill. He never came to the Hill. I think he was kinda scared of us because dudes on the Hill were always ready. Motherfuckers would have their gats stashed in the bushes, in the motherfucking grass. They'd be ready for these dudes to come along and try something.

Mal got locked up, but he's home now. He might still be fucking around, he might get his life together, who knows? It's not the same on the streets anymore. He was a straight maniac. Certain dudes reached that maniac level in the street. And when they got locked up, sometimes it just made them even worse.

Some dudes would do their time and get out and end up going right back in again. Some of my mans did fifteen years and came home and got a job at Home Depot. They'd be like, "Fuck that life, man. I'm good, I got my girl, my little family, I'm cool, I'm good. I'm fucking decent, I'm gonna make my way from here."

And I was always like, "Yeah, yeah, you got the right idea, dog. You got the right idea."

Even the various neighborhood gangs would chill out at the rec room. We'd have dudes from the Avenue Crew, or the Paris Crew, or FMF or VO5 hanging with the Wreck Posse. Sometimes the Gladiator Posse would show up from Stapleton. Ghost hung out with the GD back then. The Cash Money Brothers (CHB) from the Harbor would drop by.

It was our part of town, so out-of-towners couldn't come through too fly or too tough or they'd get hurt, just like with most other housing projects. If you were an out-of-towner you're a UFO, so you had to be careful. You'd get hurt like that. Dudes would flip and strip you of everything if they got the chance. Even Brooklyn guys had to mind their P's and Q's. Can't just come through in Cazals and sheepskins, someone's gonna test you for that. Same rules applied when we went to Brooklyn or the Bronx or any other borough. It was just a part of the intricacies of growing up in New York City.

From 1983 to about 1986, it was all about the rec room. That shit was live enough to keep us enthralled for years. I was hanging out with Cappadonna a lot around then, and we were both in the DND (Dick 'Em Down Posse) together. We used to hang at the rec room parties and take mescaline and dance all night long. We had to go down to Stapleton for that, 'cause it had two things Park Hill didn't have: angel dust and mescaline. You pop two of them shits, and you'd be sweatin', dancin', and laughin' all fuckin' night long. And then you were done, you couldn't go to sleep either. And sometimes you'd get the wiggles, like your arms and legs would just shake for no reason.

In between those parties, there would also be some jams and house parties. Rachel and Robin were these two sexy little shorties that would throw parties in their basement, and their mom would let us set up the music. They would hook their place up with red lights or purple lights, and everyone would bring a little bit of liquor or whatever and have a good time.

They had a brother who used to dress like Prince, no lie. He used to dress just like the guy. He used to look like Prince, too, light-skinned, hair, the clothes, all of it, all the time. I bet he was feeling it when Prince died.

Summertime there would also be block parties; those were fun and pretty chill. Of course there'd be a few fights and maybe a little violence, but overall it was much more peaceful compared to the rec room parties, 'cause girls like Rachel and Robin, along with others, Dayna, Leslie, they were the good girls of the neighborhood, so shit never got too out of hand there. I wouldn't necessarily call them upper-class girls, but they definitely had more class.

These parties were the predecessor to the big, historic clubs we would hit later on. Before we would go to Union Square or the Latin Quarter with like a hundred Staten Island dudes. Before we'd see Salt-N-Pepa and fly-ass Spinderella. Before we'd see Scoob and Scrap, Big Daddy Kane's dancers, and the Fort Greene Posse. Before Red Parrot was popping off. Before any of that went down, we were in the rec room, and hip-hop was our way of life.

With all that stunting in our fly gear, you still had to be careful. There were a lot of crews and gangs in one place, so if one troublemaker fucked with someone in a gang, the gang is gonna find him. You ain't jumping one of my crew without a hundred dudes coming at you. This gang mentality started becoming very real at these rec parties and soon became the foundation of the Wu-Tang Clan—especially in our early days, you couldn't fuck with one of us if you didn't want to fuck with all of us.

Ghostface was friends with C Allah, a notorious gangster motherfucker from West Brighton. C Allah was invited to the Hill, and at one of the rec parties, decided to cut my man Sam Bones's face for no reason. He was too big for any of us to handle solo. And he must've thought we were too scared of him for cutting Bones, who was a hundred pounds soaking wet and just a kid.

So we all waited for him at a transfer junction on the Island, watching for him. As soon as he came off the bus, somebody spotted him. "There go C Allah."

Even seeing the hundred dudes waiting to beat his ass, he showed no fear as he came up to us. He had the heart of two hundred motherfuckers. I don't know what he was thinking, but there was no fear whatsoever on his face as he approached. He was 5 Percent, and I guess maybe he thought that since I was a Godbody, too, and a few others of the Wreck Posse were 5 Percent, that we wouldn't do anything to him. He walked right up to us like we didn't have the nerve to do anything.

No one said another word. We waited for a minute as he reached the crew. He came over to me and gave me dap. He went over to Love God and gave him dap. "That shit wasn't right, God. It wasn't right," C Allah said.

One of my friends, Looney, started it all by punching C Allah in the face. And just like that, all of us rushed him. To his credit, he fought a few of us off, but he couldn't fight a hundred of us. Once he realized how many of us were out for blood, he ran. He ran to the ferry and we chased his ass onto the boat. He chilled by the police for the whole ride, so we couldn't do anything there. We just lurked nearby, salivating, waiting to exact our revenge.

Police escorted him off the ferry to the subway. Once he went downstairs, the cops went back to the ferry and we caught him downstairs waiting for the 1 train to pull up. He hopped on, but we jumped right on after him. We climbed all over this motherfucker and took him down, just pounding on him, and there were so many of us he couldn't do much. If we'd wanted to, we could have hurt C Allah really bad, but we just gave him a universal beatdown. That's where you just use fists and maybe your feet on someone; no knives, no clubs, no guns. You might feel like you wanna die when we got done with you, but you aren't gonna.

He took his lumps and never came back to Park Hill again. He spent his whole life in jail except a couple years here and there, and he's currently in on a thirty-year murder charge. By the time he comes home again, I'll be an old man with grandchildren.

Funny enough, seventeen years after his beatdown, I last saw him in the studio with Ghostface Killah when he was making *Ironman*. Ghost has always liked troublemakers because he's a troublemaker himself. He's just not happy unless he's stirring things up, so he and C Allah fit together like two motherfuckin' peas in a pod.

But I left them crazy street dudes alone for the most part, mainly because they were too hardheaded about most things, and

I couldn't keep getting involved in that drama to help keep things cool.

My hood had its fun parts, but we felt stagnant when we'd just chill around the way for too long, so we'd go out and hit the clubs. We stayed up in Union Square back then. We were some serious party peoples growing up. We used to go to all these clubs in Manhattan. At those parties is how this became solidified as "hip-hop." We used to get fresh and go to Red Parrot or Red Zone or Latin Quarter, Zanzibar or Sensations, Palladium, and especially Union Square. All the major clubs where anything was popping, Staten Island had to be there. Union Square was my spot—'cause it was so big, it was like the mecca of the music scene at the time.

The world was ours. We were going all over the city to the hottest clubs, rocking the latest fashion and gold chains. It was like a drug in itself to be able to cop whatever clothes you wanted, roll a hundred deep to the club so that you're practically invincible, and get attention from the ladies.

We might beef among each other, project to project, but we still stuck together when we went to Manhattan. We'd all meet at South Ferry, then jump on the train and head straight to Union Square. It'd be Park Hill, Stapleton, West Brighton, New Brighton, everybody.

Now, keep in mind we were still strapped, 'cause you had to be. We were wearing jewelry, rope chains, grilles, designer clothes, brand-new shoes, the works, and no one was gonna take any of it from us. But the clubs didn't want anyone bringing guns inside, so me and Raekwon would stash our nickel-plated .32 caliber pistols in rat holes we found in Union Square Park.

We'd be in the clubs a hundred deep. We'd be so deep, other dudes would think we were from Brooklyn. It was a mix at times, 'cause you'd have a hundred Staten Island guys going to the

Square, and when we got there we would merge with a hundred more from Brooklyn we knew. Now there was two hundred dudes rolling together.

We'd be up in Union Square doing our thing while Doug E. Fresh would rock the house. Union Square was hip-hop all the way. They usually had a hip-hop artist who was hot at the time performing there, and then Kool DJ Red Alert was on his equipment, known as the wheels of steel. He and Chuck Chillout would be switching back and forth on the turntables.

I remember seeing Eric B. & Rakim when they first came out. I also got a chance to see Big Daddy Kane, Biz Markie, and even DJ Jazzy Jeff and the Fresh Prince all rock at the Square when they first came out. Later on, we caught LL Cool J and Run-D.M.C. at Madison Square Garden; that concert in particular was off the fucking chain. I was a part of hip-hop history, even back then as a shorty rocking out at the clubs.

You know who I didn't get to see back then? KRS-One! The night he performed "The Bridge Is Over," during his feud with MC Shan, that was the only legendary night that we didn't make it into Union Square. We were on the line, waiting not so patiently, when a mob got into a rumble right behind us. A few people got stabbed up in the melee, so they shut the door down right as we got up there and said it was too packed to let anyone else in. Then someone called the cops, and we all got thrown against the wall and searched. Luckily we got out of the area with no arrests added to our rap sheets, but I was mad we missed that night. No one knew it was going to be legendary like how it was, but you just sort of felt it—we all knew we missed something big that night. Even so, Queensbridge gave birth to Mobb Deep and Nas, so they were still representing.

I saw all the other greats, though. That's why I can close my eyes and still see Union Square filled beyond capacity and everybody is on the dance floor in Dapper Dans. Peoples in their Polo

or Louis Vuitton or their Coca-Cola rugbys. Spot-Bilt was popping, door knockers, slacks, Ballys, big chains, big rings, cameos,
Benetton sweaters, gold frames, Gucci links—it was a beautiful
era, and I'm grateful I was able to see all that up close.

I can still see the girls from Queens looking flawless. Queens
always had the baddest girls back then. This was during the whole
Salt-N-Pepa (and the beautiful Spinderella) era, so that was the
flavor, and Queens had it locked, at least to me. Their hair was
impeccable, mad feminine, but still mad tough. Everybody I knew
wanted a Queens broad.

Other clubs had different vibes. For example, when we went
to the Red Parrot, we had to dress up, put on the dress slacks and
silk shirts. It was more elegant there, so you had to dress the part,
too. Red Parrot was where the stars often went, too, so some nights
we would see Keith Sweat, we'd see Mike Tyson or Wesley Snipes.
Red Zone was where they filmed the movie *Juice*, with Tupac and
Omar Epps. Now, I didn't like Latin Quarter all that much, 'cause
of the vibe—it was too hood, too Brooklyn.

It would get funky in the club. We did a lot of chain snatching,
too, but once in a while Staten Island would get caught out there.
My man Jahking, who later bodied (killed) somebody, got his
chain snatched at Union Square right in the crowd. The funny
shit was the Brooklyn dude who took it realized it was fake and
threw it right back at him. He caught a murder charge later on,
and is jail right now.

In the clubs was also where I learned how to dance. I'm a
dancer, believe it or not. I used to dance when I was a kid. I was
one of the best dancers on Staten Island. Not the best, but one of
the best. I used to always get beat by the gays. My man Brucie
was—I ain't callin' him gay, but Brucie was one of the fucking
illest dancers on Staten Island, too. But I used to go to all the clubs,
all these motherfuckers. And Brooklyn dudes be doin' dances
uptown, Harlem dudes be doin' that. I learned all the dances.

Whenever I'd bust a move on the Island, I'd hear, "You should be a fucking dancer" all the time.

As we got older, we started wandering farther outside our neighborhood, jumping from one project to another. Fort Greene, Castle Hill, Polo Grounds; we'd always be in the 'jects. Sometimes it was for a party at their community center, or you might go just to chill with some dudes you met.

If you go to any of these projects, though, you best know someone who was local. That was the only way to keep from gettin' robbed when you were in a different hood. Because your team wasn't going to outfight or outgun a whole housing project. You needed those inside homeys. If you didn't have that secure, then don't even bother going to a different project. Unless, of course, you knew for a fact that the dudes there were pussies.

When I started venturing out into different parts of the city, either by myself or with friends, I quickly learned NYC was pretty much rough all over. New York of yesteryear was not safe anywhere. You could be in midtown and get robbed. You could be on the Upper East Side and get assaulted. Muggings, assaults, rape, you name it.

As for the subway? Man, the trains weren't anywhere near safe. You had to be careful every time you got on. You couldn't ride in the last car, or you were almost good as robbed. You had to sit in the first car with the conductor, or in the middle car. Not that they could really do much but call the cops if something jumped off, but it was better than a nonstop beatdown in one of the other train cars, with a grand finale of getting stripped of whatever your assailants deemed valuable. And even if you sat in the "safer" cars, you still couldn't sit too close to the doors because someone would yap your purse, chain, hat, or whatever and hop off the train as the doors were closing, leaving you robbed and moving in the wrong direction—away from your assailant.

Some kids would get robbed or beat up and become too afraid to step outside. That was weak. You had to take your lumps and come right back outside. You had to show them you weren't soft, and that a little beatdown didn't faze you at all. No one was going to keep me from going all over my projects, all over Staten Island, or all over any other part of the city. Especially with all the bad-ass girls New York has. How you gonna be hiding up in your house on a beautiful summer day with all them fine things out there?

I remember we used to troop to Jones Beach a lot in the summer. That was my first little taste of walking up to girls and trying to bag numbers. I would come back with like ten phone numbers, all girls from Queens, Long Island, the Bronx, and other places I rarely got to go to. Eventually, when I got my first car, a Volvo 740, we'd stay in Jones Beach just chilling and trying to kick game to females all day.

Even before my Volvo, we would always be on the hunt for fly shorties and parties and just good times. Sometimes the shit ran smooth and we'd get in and out of a party in a strange neighborhood without any incidents. Most of the time, though, there was going to be some drama.

One time we were out in Coney Island at least twenty, thirty deep. I had the best of the best of the Wreck Posse with me that night: Psycho, Budda, Chaz, Real, Herb—we went out there with fighters. And since we were coming out to see one of our people, Shawnee, who'd just moved from Staten Island to Coney Island, we weren't scared to come into their 'jects. Man, these dudes got mad as hell because we went out there fly as fuck. Sheepskins, gold teeth, Pumas, and all that fly shit.

When we got up in the buildings, these dudes tried to formulate on us. We weren't suckas by any means, plus we knew they were scheming on us because we did the same thing when UFOs were in our buildings. Now, if they had just taken the time to get to know us, it all would have been cool. But they got all twisted about our group coming in and possibly takin' what they thought was theirs.

I didn't go out there empty-handed, mind you. I didn't have a hammer on me, but I was carrying two big-ass shanks. And when those motherfuckers started swarmin', I pulled those two big motherfucking knives out of my coat. I was like, "Yo, all you dudes ain't gonna just stomp on me like that. I'm gonna take at least two or three a you with me."

Suckas or not, we couldn't win against the whole project. We were only there for a little while before we literally got chased out of Coney Island with what looked like a hundred dudes on our heels. It felt like *The Warriors* in reverse, because we had to get back home from Mermaid Boulevard with this mob of goons after us.

Sometimes, though, the people we would go see in different hoods had so much pull we didn't have to bring guns or knuckle up or anything. One time we were visiting my man Fresh up in Castle Hill. Him and his man Boo and the rest of them dudes were maniacs. So we up in the projects, and I had a lot of jewelry on, and not even one motherfucker tried us. Not one. It was because Fresh and Boo had them projects locked down. The other criminals in those projects wouldn't even look at us wrong or look at us to scheme. Fresh and Boo had so much pull, just being with them was protection enough. The hierarchy was strictly enforced, so no one got out of line.

I could go up in Lafayette Gardens in Bed-Stuy and be good, too, because of my man Jamal. Or I could be around St. James Place, and my uncle Matt and them would make sure no one fucked with me. The more land we conquered, the more people we met that could plug us into new things and more people.

And knowing the right people could potentially save your life.

Once, Raekwon and me went to downtown Brooklyn after we got our Summer Youth checks to buy back-to-school gear and new kicks.

Summer Youth was a city program where they put kids from the neighborhood into jobs for six weeks during the summer. It was a good program because I didn't have to rely on my mother for money for the summer.

You'd sign up, and then you'd go to P.S. 57 and they'd read the list of everybody who got jobs. But everybody who wanted a job didn't always get one. There was only a certain number of jobs, so everyone who signed up couldn't get 'em. I don't know how my mother finagled that shit, but I always got a job every summer. I guess it was 'cause I was a responsible kid. When I worked as a counselor for the YMCA, I was always there on time every morning, putting my work in every day, and I guess that was a reason why I kept getting jobs.

One summer I had the YMCA job. Another summer I worked for the park department pruning trees and cutting them down and all that. We cleaned up things, we went around the neighborhood, I babysat kids. I did all that and more, and I got my little two hundred dollars every two weeks, which was really good money back then.

The Summer Youth program also refined my work ethic. Whether it's bagging groceries or Summer Youth jobs or slingin' packages or layin' down tracks, whenever I knew there was money to be made somewhere, I was always on it, and I always put all my work in, every time.

But once we had that cash, it was gonna get spent. So that day we were at the Albee Square Mall, and I noticed in the window reflection that some Brooklyn thugs were behind us, trying to scheme on us.

Now, if you were around NYC in the eighties, you knew about the crazy robberies that happened in Albee Square Mall, on the corner of DeKalb and Fulton. Brooklyn dudes always had that reputation for taking shit from whoever the fuck they wanted. It was heightened around the mall, though, because people from all over were shopping there. Because of that traffic you also had stickup kids from all over Brooklyn.

We walked out the sneaker spot, and some dudes tried to snatch our bags. We fought back and held our bags so they weren't able to get them from us. We remembered their faces, though.

Sure enough, that same motherfucking night, Rae was in Brooklyn with one of our peoples, Jaime, and met the kids who tried to rob us. Jaime straightened them out. "Yo, man, this my peoples. This my man. They good, they my peoples."

"Yo, Jaime, that's your peoples, son? Pardon me for that, man. We didn't know."

They all exchanged handshakes and laughed it off. No harm done. Rae came back and told me what happened, and I couldn't believe what a small fucking world it was.

After that, we had no problems in downtown Brooklyn anymore. But we would still see those same kids snatching bags and robbing people, but they always ran right past us now that they knew we were cool with Jaime. They were always at it. You'd see them posted up looking up and down the avenue for victims and come-ups. They were like predators scoping out a watering hole. That was their office, on DeKalb and Fulton, Atlantic Terminal, Fort Greene. Some Gods would be building, some civilians would be shopping, some kids would be hanging out, and the jack boys would be catching juxes.

Brooklyn, yo, you gotta love it.

# 6.

## CRACK HITS THE HILL

When crack first hit Staten Island, Park Hill was still a community, albeit a dysfunctional one. At first there was more than enough money to go around, and the fiends weren't completely desperate yet. Heroin and base had done some ravaging in the community, but my hood was still relatively unified.

Then the hood went straight to hell.

For those who don't know, freebase and crack are the exact same thing. It's simply cocaine that's free of the hydrochloric acid added to powder cocaine (cocaine hydrochloride). This purified version is much more potent and addictive.

*Crack* is street slang for freebase. It got that name because the cooking process breaks it down into its purest form, turning it into a solid form that looks like little chips of paint that cracked off a wall. Hence, crack. The fastest, most powerful way to get high on crack is to smoke it. Powder cocaine is smokable, but people prefer to snort it rather than smoke it.

Keep in mind there is no difference in the chemical makeup of powder cocaine and crack—it's the same drug, just one is more pure than the other. However, penalties for crack offenses are more severe because our government decided to create what is known as the War on Drugs. So all the thousands, maybe millions of people (such as myself) convicted and sentenced for a crack offense got an enhanced prison sentence because of drug terminology, not facts. The federal statute penalizes cocaine hydrochloride and cocaine base the same, and this hasn't changed since 1914, when cocaine became illegal to possess, no matter what chemical form it was in. The government introduced mandatory sentencing for crack offenses simply because crack was more popular among poor people.

The whole drug game just seemed to come into the hood outta nowhere. In the early seventies, it was all about cocaine. Coke was for rich people. When freebase—a purified, smokable form of cocaine—came around, it was still a plaything for the elite in the late seventies. By the time the eighties rolled around, regular working-class people were smoking freebase.

In the early eighties, there was a huge glut of powder cocaine from South America, which drove the price of coke way down. To maximize their profits, the dealers flooded the inner-city neighborhoods with crack, which was simple to produce, cheap, and could be sold in smaller quantities to more people. And when it hit in force, the neighborhood went straight to hell.

Before the epidemic, as a kid, my day was always planned out. I'd wake up, head over to the grocery store, and bag some groceries. A good bagger could clear five or six dollars in a couple hours. After that, I might hit the corner store, maybe hit the arcade, then head to the pond out back and make some mud cakes. From dawn till dusk, we were always moving, always active. By the time we'd come home, our clothes would be a dirt farm—we'd be covered in it; our tongues would be red from candy; our hair would be messed up—all signs that we'd had a good day.

Next thing you knew, fucking dreads—Rastafarians, typically

from Jamaica, but also some folks from Guyana—were comin' out of nowhere. Illegal motherfuckers were poppin' up everywhere, and drugs were every-fucking-where, too. What the fuck just happened?

There was so much money floating around, the temptation would just suck you in, especially if you were poor. Crack took advantage of the community, of the fucking dirt poor who had no food in their refrigerator—I'm talking about having *no refrigerator* at all, having to put the fucking milk outside on the windowsill in the winter so it gets cold. Roaches, mice everywhere. Roaches in your cereal box. Welfare. Hard cheese. You-ain't-got-shit poor. You're-living-in-the-projects-and-your-mom's-a-crackhead poor.

The drug game is the last stand for survival, where you have nothing else on the streets. You don't even know what the fuck you're doing. You don't have an education. You don't have a job. How you gonna eat? Welfare pays three hundred dollars a month—what's that? You can't live off that. You need to do something to survive. That's what hustling provided. It's a subculture that regular people with jobs and who are middle class just don't understand. They just don't understand poverty on that level. That's where I came from, that's where motherfuckers in my neighborhood came from. We clawed our way up outta that shit.

Think about it—if you can make thousands upon thousands of dollars in just one hour, would you turn that down? You put that shit in the hood, and I can make ten fucking thousand in thirty fucking minutes. What would you do?

And it was *everywhere*.


I was about fourteen when I first really got into the game. By that time I was too old for playing in the back of the building, and my Summer Youth pay was long gone. I couldn't ask my mother for change for ice cream anymore, or even for fresh school clothes.

Material stuff is so enticing when you don't have shit. It's not that we were even materialistic like that, but when you've got old-ass clothes and last year's boots on in winter, it's hard to have a righteous attitude. My mom provided the bare minimum, but that was all she could afford. If I wanted to get fresh and have some money to eat, I had to come up with my own plan. And since things I wanted were out of her budget, the fastest way to get them was to hustle.

The dreads came to my hood wearing fly shit like Fila suits and gold chains and gold teeth, while we were dead broke. They were making money and driving flashy cars, and they would come up to a guy smiling, flashing those gold fronts.

The very first dread I worked with, Dusty, had his gate at 55 Bowen. "Yo, red mon [because I was so yellow]! Yo, me wan' see if you wan' work in the gate." When they said "work in the gate," that meant working in the drug spot. Simply put, a drug spot was an illegal store that sold drugs. It could be set up anywhere on the street; in an alley, on a corner, or even in the lobby of a project.

So I was like, "Okay." I didn't know a goddamn thing about selling drugs, all I knew was that I had to get me some of that money they were always flashing.

The list of reasons why not to sell drugs is endless, but I ran through it in a few seconds and accepted the dread's pack. Even with all these deadly factors, I decided to hop in the drug game.

My first time in the gate, that shit was spooky. It was a little hole in the door, and people would shove their money through the slot and demand their drugs. This was at the top of the crack game, so these motherfuckers were pulling like a hundred thousand dollars in a matter of hours. There was so much traffic coming to this fucking spot. Every few seconds there'd be a knock at the door and some fiend asking for some shit. The constant knocking was making me nervous.

To make things worse, I'd already started smoking woolies, so

I was extra paranoid. Woolies are a mixture of weed with coke or crack rolled up into a blunt or joint. Before the dreads brought blunts into America, we were all just smoking joints. But the Jamaicans brought Fronto leaf (a dark, wrapper-grade tobacco leaf) with them, and rolled the weed in that, and when you couldn't get the Fronto leaf anymore, you started cutting open Phillies. So Jamaicans were responsible for the blunt sensation.

Anyway, I was too paranoid in the spot that night. I couldn't relax. Everything about the situation had me on edge. Thing is, I've always had a little sixth sense, though. Dudes always used to say, "U-God can see the cops coming over the top of the Hill," as they were on their way to raid us. This particular time, there was so much traffic coming through and so much money exchanging hands that I got really nervous. I could just feel it—I had to get the fuck up out of the spot. A part of me was trying to ignore the voice in my head telling me to get out; the hungry hustler part of me wanted to ignore that voice and keep right on clocking (working) out of the gate.

Soon my inner voice got the better of me, and I knew I had to go. So I shut the spot down and locked it up. Me and my man Choice packed up the drugs and the money and we walked outside. I barely got around the corner, and here come the police with the battering ram, pushing me out of the way to raid the spot. I remember one cop yelled at me to get out of the way as they charged right past us. I watched them run right to the spot and smash in the door I'd just come out of.

When I got back around the way, the dread I'd been working the gate for saw me and came over to get the scoop on the raid. "Red mon! I thought you was in the gate when the cops rushed!"

"I had to get out! Shit was just too hot, dread. I could just feel it," I told him.

He asked me where the money was, and I gave him the mad

stacks of cash we'd clocked that day. He broke me off a little bullshit three hundred dollars.

After me saving all that cash and work for him, and he only gave me that little punk-ass three hundred, I was mad. This drug game was for chumps. Almost getting arrested and shit for that bum-ass three hundred dollars?

*Fuck the dope game!* I thought.

There weren't many other options out there at the time, though. So at fifteen, I decided to get a little nine-to-five job at the Statue of Liberty with Method Man. They hired Staten Island dudes because we were right by the ferry. We then had to take another ferry to Liberty Island, but I guess the bosses figured we didn't mind the ride, since we were always taking a ferry everywhere anyway.

Meth and I worked that job for almost two years. It saved my life in a lot of ways. It helped me get on my feet. During that time, Meth and me also got real close.

When we did click and started hustling together, Method Man really started coming into his own. He wasn't just talented at hustling, either. That boy had already produced a beat on a little Casio and rapped over that shit. He named the song "Panty Raider," and it was a smash in our hood. He made another one called "My House, My House." I had it on repeat in my tape deck even back then.

We were both writin' at that time, kicking around ideas together when we weren't mopping the floors and hauling garbage and doing all this crazy shit for Mr. Hill, our boss. We used to write rhymes on the back of coasters, just sitting in the back of the shit on garbage detail and writin'. We'd pick up these little paper coasters to write on, and one day Meth said, "Yeah,

C.R.E.A.M.: Cash Rules Everything Around Me." He started tagging everything with that acronym—the project walls, Dumpsters, train cars, whatever he could find. I remember when I said that should be a fucking hook; we made that fucking shit up way back then. True fact: The title of Wu-Tang's first hit single started with Meth and me sitting at the Liberty Island garbage detail.

I wasn't making enough money there, though. Even though we'd steal cases of soda, we'd steal camera film and resell it on the street and skim money here and there, I just wasn't making enough money. Plus, we were stealing so much the owners started getting wise to us. Before they fired us, I quit. That was the last regular job I ever had.

I've always wanted to go back and see Mr. Hill, 'cause we did a lot of shit we weren't supposed to back in the day. Now that I'm older, I respect the business hustle and the business-minded way Mr. Hill was thinking. I do feel a little sorry for doing him dirty back then.

I was seventeen when I came back to the streets after the Statue of Liberty job. And I came back hard. I met up with my Puerto Rican man, Bright, who lived in either 185 or 225 Park Hill, I can't remember which.

It seems like a no-brainer now, but at the time not many black kids thought to have a Puerto Rican emissary when you went uptown to cop cocaine in weight. Bright spoke Spanish, and he took me uptown to meet the connects, the coke distributor who wholesaled base to the street dealers. That was how I first met my connects. They were pretty heavy. In the drug game, I learned there's always somebody bigger and heavier out here. It's best to not even try to be the biggest. That's a setup for a lot of drama and disappointment.

Supposedly, my connect was the one getting BMF (Black

Mafia Family) their shit. He was supplying them for years, I think. I found that out years and years later, of course, but I definitely wasn't surprised when I did find out. Simply put, they had access to a lot of coke.

They sold me my first brick for seventeen thousand dollars. I had some money saved from my Statue of Liberty job, and I hustled up the rest on the block. I came up from an eight ball (one-eighth of an ounce) to seventeen stacks (one stack is one thousand dollars). Back in the day, you could get an eight ball for a hundred dollars. You chop that up, cook it, and you can sell that for two hundred dollars. Then you'd go buy more coke, chop that up, cook it, sell it, you make four hundred dollars. That's how you flip. You flip from two to four to six to eight, twelve, sixteen, twenty-four, and you make your motherfuckin' way.

I chopped that eight ball to three hundred dollars. The three hundred went to six hundred dollars. I kept flipping until I could cop the quarter key, also called a "big eighth." Then I really started to flip, and got to half a man, then to a man (a full kilo). You kept flipping and flipping and flipping. The thing about it is, you could make that money in four or five hours easy. I went through my two hundred, boom, fast four hundred, boom, eight hundred, and so on. In two weeks I'd be up to seventeen stacks.

The whole time, for the two months or so I was out there hustling up the money for a brick, I wore the same pants every day. I'd be out all night, then up early in the morning. I'd change my socks and boxers and just throw the same shit on and go back to hustling. I scraped up every dollar I could in those days getting to that brick quota.

The first rule of hustling is to stack your money, as in you don't spend it. You don't spend no bread. You eat, maybe cop a pair of Timberlands so you don't get cold, get some T-shirts to be hustling in, and you save the rest, every last dime. Every day you hustle, but you keep saving that bread until you reach that quota.

I reached that goal, and I was good. I took my seventeen thousand dollars right uptown with my man Bright to see my connects. Once I met them, I didn't want for nothing after that. Once I got good with them, they just loved me. These dudes were taking care of me. Because of them, I always had it, and I didn't have to worry about having it, either.

I was also too smart to have to do all that sucker shit the rest of these fools were doing building up territory and all that. Like I said, I'm the ambassador, so I didn't have to do horrific things for territory. I had three or four different territories rocking, and they made up one big territory.

See, the whole thing about it is, you got the kingpins, you got the workers, and you got the enforcers. That's how that shit works. The enforcers don't do nothing but come in and clear the block of dumb fucking dudes. The workers come in and hustle. They get all the bread, they make sure the money's rocking. The kingpins go back and forth with the heavy shit—they bring the bombs in, they take the money, they keep it moving.

It was easy after that. I could just come back to Staten Island and mark up whatever I got. I'd have like half a brick just for selling weight. Without even leaving my house, I could make twenty-five hundred dollars in a night or two. Then I'd run back uptown and get back on the clock.

"Yo, I need another one of them thangs."

"I'm flying uptown right now. I'll be back by six."

That shit was a steady flow of traffic. I learned about the importance of that traffic. Customers didn't have to cop heavy, but if enough of them cop, you're gonna make a lot of money. And that's how it was for me at first.

The whole situation, the reason why it was so easy, it was about convenience. It was convenient for me to come outside and make that type of bread. That's why I was able to get over the poverty level. We weren't broke no more. We weren't struggling. Even though it was wrong, I could provide and also go to school. I was hustling and going to high school. I couldn't have a regular job. It was a choice: either go to high school broke and struggle along every day with no food in the refrigerator and starve, or hustle and go to school eating steak and eggs and all that fly shit in the fucking refrigerator.

And again, just because I was doing this to survive didn't mean I was going to fully embrace the criminal lifestyle. Yeah, I was committing a felony every time I sold drugs, but it wasn't one that, if I got caught for it, I'd never come home again. I still recognized those lines that marked going too far and took care not to cross them—although I came real close more than once.

I was hustling with the 26 Mob from the 260 Building in Park Hill. It was me and a bunch of dudes from my neighborhood and New Brighton. This was my first crew of young hustlers. We were really just learning the game as we went along. We would watch some of the older hustlers and listen when they came around to drop some knowledge about the game.

There was this one dude, Barry Blue, that we all wanted to be like. He was a bit older than us and doing it big. We would try and soak up some of his wisdom and emulate his style. The crazy shit about Barry Blue was the way he got killed. He got shot up on this block in Staten Island that was historically known for drugs. Sadly, dudes getting killed on a drug block wasn't very dynamic. What was dynamic about Barry Blue's death was that he died the exact same way his father was killed, doing the very same thing on the very same block. Two generations living the same life, going out the same way. Can you imagine? What are the odds of that?

Back then it didn't really strike me as odd. Most of us were going to live and die hustling on this block. You had to accept that cold hard fact, or else you were just lying to yourself.

I also pulled Meth into drug peddling so he could make some money to keep himself fed and clothed. He had lost his job, had gotten kicked out of his house, and was going through a really rough time. He'd dropped out of high school, and back then there were very few opportunities for inner-city youth. Often they ended up with their back against the wall and would do what they had to do to survive.

Meth's transition from the nine-to-five grind to the street was rough. When he first came out on the block, he couldn't make a sale to save his life. At first he had to fight to boost his clientele. To get his stripes up, he had to fight to show motherfuckers he wasn't weak. I told him, "Yo, dog. Dudes ain't gonna respect you unless you stand up for yourself out here." Remember, at the time, he was still going by Shaquan, his 5 Percent name. Dudes pulled guns on him and all that fly shit, but Meth stuck through all of it.

Meth also had to learn how to deal with the fiends and the shit they'd try to pull to get their fix. Hustlin' on the street was insane. You'd have the sneak-thief dudes who'd try to boost your stash. You'd have the women who'd proposition you for a hit.

One day, this familiar fiend rolled up. Meth came over, the fiend rolled his window down, and Meth put the crack bag in. Instead of paying, the fiend slapped the crack out of his hand and started drivin' off while Meth was hangin' on to the car door! Finally he had to let go and went rolling down the street, all scraped up and shit. He definitely lost the sale that time.

But after going through all that drama, by the time it was all said and done, every time Meth came out, he would shut the block down. You couldn't even get a sale off when he was putting his work in. Maybe after he was done, you could get your little money, but while he was there, all the junkies were reporting to him for that shit. All you could do was wait until his stash ran out and he had to go back upstairs for more. Even then you weren't guaranteed a sale in his absence.

He started winning because his clientele was up there. About two or three weeks into the game, he started taking over. Me and him was Batman and Robin on the block. We'd come in and we would just shut it down. We'd make our couple stacks in a couple of hours and be out. Then it was back to the crib to smoke weed and whip up some more work while Meth would write rhymes. This transformed him into the rapper we know as Method Man. He incorporated the street life into his rhymes, about guns and drugs and all that, because he was living that experience to the fullest.

We were scooping up so much money, there was nothing left over for the other dealers. You have to understand, there would be a dozen dudes out on the block, all selling crack against each other. But Meth and me were the only ones who partnered up— all these other guys were hustlin' solo.

We would do all types of shit on the block to make our stacks. We would double-team customers, with me at one end of the block and Meth at the other end, so no customer could get by us. When he was dealing out of a car, I was hustlin' from a building. It was crazy. It got to where we could feel when the fiends would rush for their fix, and we'd be there, givin' it to 'em.

Saturday mornings between six and eleven thirty were killer. Like six in the morning to eleven thirty was off the fucking chain, just fiends lining up around the block. Then around noon to 2 or 3 P.M., it would slow down to trickles. Then around 5 P.M. to 1 A.M., it'd be poppin' all night long, just rush rush rush rush, crazy traffic comin' through, bombarding us. Then Sunday would slow down, so much that you might not even get one sale that day. But on Monday, they'd be back again.

It also always got busy around the first of the month. That's what the Bone Thugs-N-Harmony song "1st of Tha Month" is about. That's when the welfare checks arrived, so the fiends would come out 'cause they had money to spend.

That's the hustlin' rules right there. Now, the weed dudes didn't have to do all that. They're on a twenty-four-hour-a-day, seven-day-a-week grind, morning, afternoon, night, that's non-stop traffic, slower than the crack fiends, but steadier, too.

Coke and crackheads didn't move like that. When it was too hot, for example, the fiends didn't come out for the shit. There were certain times of day when peoples were sleeping, and they weren't coming out for that.

It got to where we were dominating the block so much that the other dealers had to call the police on us. The police weren't stupid; they knew people were selling, they just didn't know exactly who was selling, or how much. We'd hear 'em driving down the block and they'd be on the loudspeaker, calling people out.

Police used to call Meth by his government name: "Clifford, what are you doing with your money?" Punk-ass Elvis used to call him Shaquan. "Shaquan, what are you doing with your money, Shaquan? You look like a bum all the time."

The police really underestimated us. They thought we were just some dumb thug street kids. They had no idea what we were up to, we were so far underneath their radar. They knew we were out there doing what we were doing, but they had no idea we had seven, eight grams in the fuckin' house, that I was droppin' packages in five neighborhoods. We weren't flashy, which is exactly how I wanted it to be—if I popped up on their radar, then they would have come after me with everything they had. They also didn't know we were in the studio trying to get out of the goddamn game, too, but that's for later . . .


I learned all I could about the game. I still remember who taught me how to cook crack and freebase shit up. I got so nice with it I could cook half a kilo in a pot and lose maybe three grams at most. But before I got that ill with whipping work in the pot, this junkie taught me how to do it. It was my man Choice's (RIP) mother. She was a real coke connoisseur.

"U-God, I'm gonna teach you how to cook that shit up. Pay close attention now."

See, basically you cook the cocaine to get the shit out of it. By the time the kilo gets to New York, it's already been stepped on, cut with other ingredients to make the drug go farther. So you gotta cook it. In the process of cooking up that shit, you add baking soda. Baking soda clears out all of the impurities in cocaine. That's why crack is so powerful and potent.

Anyway, she was the one who taught me to cook, but she was so meticulous with her shit she'd cook it ounce by ounce. I've got thirty-six ounces to cook, and she wants to cook each one individually. But I picked up the overall process from her, and soon I was doing a quarter key at a time, and then a half key. Eventually, I was cooking the whole kilo at once.

One of the techniques she taught me was that after I'd cooked the shit up, I would drop it in ammonia. The ammonia would clean out the remaining impurities. Then I'd let it dry. And my goodness, Lord have mercy, them fucking fiends used to go crazy for that shit. By the time I was done, fiends were smoking the purest shit on the block.

"U-God, my ears are ringing. What the fuck is that you just sold me?"

"I need two more, U-God, I need two more." They were going crazy.

We had clientele so loyal that they'd walk right past anybody else to see us. It helped that I'd give my old babysitter some free work spreading the word about our shit. And all that was because we had the baddest crack. And that was due to that technique Choice's mom taught us.

"Dip it in ammonia!"

"Dip it in ammonia?"

"Dip. It. In. Ammonia."

I dipped it, then dried it, and my tester blew it. We always had someone test a batch before we would put it out on the street. Man, she started clicking and talking all crazy. She couldn't sit still. That's when I knew we had some serious shit.

My babysitter would see me coming from way down the block after that, and start flagging me down from far away. I used to give her some free joints on occasion. I gave them out here and there because there were a lot of dudes posted up on the block, so you had to make sure people knew you had that killer shit so you could steal other dealers' customers.

We would take other people's customers almost guaranteed once they tried our shit. We were getting our shit off in Park Hill, plus I was in other projects, too. That's when my diplomatic immunity really started coming in handy. I could drop off a ten-thousand-dollar package in New Brighton and another one in West Brighton, and come back and scoop my cash at nine that evening. I had about five projects in Staten Island clicking. While other thugs were shooting it out with each other in the projects, I'm just sliding through different projects, humble and quiet, to see my mans so I can hit him with this package and move on. I was making like ten thousand dollars a day easy. Well, I wouldn't go so far as to say it was easy. It wasn't easy at all, really, but the drug game did feed me for a time.

I did put in work when I was hustling, though. Five o'clock in the morning, I'm eating my breakfast. Get ready to go out in the streets when the sun comes up at six. Why? Because that's when all the fucking fiends come out. That's when everybody trying to get their fucking drugs. The big rush is early in the morning. You have to get up early to get them. So, you're out there at six o'clock in the morning. Drug dealers are not lazy. You get up early doing all this shucking and jiving. Now from six to one o'clock, I ran through at least eight thousand dollars' worth of shit. By time one o'clock came around, I'm chilling for the day. I don't want to come outside the house anymore. I'm going shopping. I'm gettin' fly. I'm getting ready for the night. I'm goin' out on the town and having a good motherfucking time.

There were a few times that, for different reasons, there were droughts. When droughts would hit, the Island would get even more crazy. We'd have to go uptown and get coke that was stepped on with B12 or other adulterants to make it go farther, aka garbage. The whole Hill would lose clientele because we were pushing garbage. All the fiends would be over in New Brighton or some shit copping their work. I might have a package in Brighton, so maybe I'm still getting a little piece of that, but it was slow in Park Hill.

News of drugs, bad or good, travels fast. Your rep for having some killer shit is only as good as the last fiend who copped. And if you got a bad consumer report, shit could get slow. Packages ain't moving. Dudes getting desperate and mad. Then we'd be able to score some raw uptown again, and we'd be back clicking, the Hill flooded with junkies like it was supposed to be.

We survived a few droughts, and I began moving up the hierarchy. My good connects had me doing more and more consistent business. The coke was regularly good now, and with the ammonia technique, our clientele had us bringing home competitive salaries at the very least. Especially for some high school kids who had been getting wedgies from the Avenue Crew in our younger years. The Baby Crash Crew and Wreck Posse were all grown up now.

We also saw a lot of older dudes we respected succumb to drugs, though, and that made us feel funny in a way that we were making the drugs work for us, not the other way around. It still boggles my mind that we were young dudes still in our teens and had grown men taking orders from us. We had the vision and the strength to be leaders, I guess.

———

People think selling drugs is easy money. That's why so many are willing to try, and then they get killed in that shit. They think you just gotta come outside your building and post up and as long as your product is proper, the shit will sell itself.

Let me tell you straight up—it's not easy.

See, the drug game, when you're really *really* in it, is nothing but heartache and frustration. These punks thinking they selling drugs because they're doing a couple of hand-to-hands, or moving a little weight, they're not doing anything.

Full-time drug dealing is *hard*. Harder than regular working people can ever imagine. You need to have some trustworthy workers and a connect, and you need to know when to fall back and when to go hard.

You had to break down the weight accurately.

You had to make sure the packages kept moving out on the streets, every day.

You had to have clientele.

Your product had to be up to par, or the junkies wouldn't come back.

You or your workers had to be on post almost all day to ensure your clientele kept coming back to you.

You had to watch your workers, to make sure they weren't shorting you or dipping into the package.

You had to watch your back for the fucking police.

You had to watch out for informers trying to set you up for the police.

You had to watch out for crackheads setting you up to get robbed by the stickup kids.

You had to watch out for kidnappers trying to snatch you for ransom.

And you get very few second chances on the streets. You fuck up once, that's your life. You make one mistake or false move, and you could get hurt or killed or end up in jail with some serious time on your head.

And Staten Island was just a totally different hustle to add to all the other variables you had to factor in. For one, you had a lot of white people coming through copping eight balls and things, so you could move a good amount of coke. You didn't have to just pump capsules all day.

Besides that, though, when I would go uptown to see how my mans and them were hustling, they'd sell these big ol' tall caps for five dollars. Uptown, you move so much and so fast that you're gonna make a profit anyway. You're only making a certain amount of profit there, though. If you came to Staten Island with that same cap, you're gonna make ten times as much. That makes things worse when competition comes into play.

It's fucked up when you think about it, because even though me and my friends and other crews were making money off base, things got bad in our hood, like savage. Not in their hoods, rarely in their hoods. It's like the line in *The Godfather* when one of the dons says they should sell drugs only to the "dark people" because "they're animals anyway."

Very few people were unaffected by drugs in some way. Even if you didn't sell or use drugs, you might have had your bike stolen by a crackhead or your crib burglarized or maybe your uncle sold your Sega Genesis. One way or another, you were caught up in the storm.

And, of course, with more drugs came more cops. That's just the natural order of the drug trade.

For a long time, the police were getting at the wrong people in my hood. They were running up on the older dudes, thinking they were the kingpins who had the projects clicking. But it was us, the fifteen- and sixteen-year-old dudes, who had all the bread.

Once it became known, they sent their *21 Jump Street* cops in. By that time, we were already moving on, already on our way to doing something else. We were rhyming. I was in school. I was always moving.

One thing I always had was respect for law and authority. That's another reason why police never really fucked with me on the Island. They respected me. They knew I was jingling—just not the level I was jingling on.

They were always watching me, seeing me do this shit. I tried to keep the building clean, no bullshit goin' on. No empty vials in the fucking halls. Swept the shit up, kept it clean all the fucking time. You got to keep your shit right. And whenever I saw the heat, I left.

I never served to any pregnant women. I helped the elderly upstairs with their groceries, their food, their clothing, whatever they needed. If they needed me, they called me from the window, I'd go and help them. If anybody needed some money, I gave them bread. That was my ritual every day. They respected me for that, I guess.

It's a double-edged sword to be known on the block, though, because both the stickup kids and the cops know who you are. I'm sure police knew who I was, but for whatever reason they would hop out to run up on other motherfuckers, and they almost always ran right past me. Officer Delpre, he ran past me all the time. Gallo, Pistol Pete, Elvis, Hopkins, Collins, Marshall. They'd run past me a lot when they blitzed. I think that's due to the fact that I tried to not always be on the fucking block. If I was hustling, I was in the building. I didn't wanna always be seen. You're there every day from noon to night. You think they don't know who you are?

As far as bribing cops, I got approached a couple of times—I can't say the officer's name, but I did get approached by one—but he didn't know how to approach me. As I got older, I realized he wanted to come to me and ask because he liked the way I moved. Like I said, as soon as I saw him, I'm gone.

Another police dude, he looked like Rocky from the movies. He used to lurk in the bushes all the time. Always be in the fucking bushes. I'm the only one out in the front of the building, and he's in the bushes. He looking though the bushes and shit, and I don't move. I was doing my thing, but he was in the wrong area if he wanted to find my shit. He's always in the wrong area. He kept doing the same shit every day.

One day, he dropped a brown paper bag on the ground with nothing in there. I didn't pick up on it until I said, "Damn, this dude wants me to drop some money in the bag." He wanted a couple grand. That's what he wanted, but it didn't go down like that. 'Cause once you feed the devil, he will never go away.

One day when I was fifteen years old, I was enjoying a day to myself and didn't have any drugs on me. No gun, either; I didn't like to carry unless I was working or if I was in a vehicle. All I had were some brass knuckles I kept around for emergency brawls. I was coming back from uptown, driving through the hood, and I got caught while trying to park my car.

I remember that day clearly because I'd rented a Ford Taurus from the Africans at the cabstand around the corner. We were mobile from our early teens because there was this crew of Africans that used to rent us cars on their credit cards. I remember sideswiping a few parked cars while learning how to drive. By our mid-teens, though, we were whipping them shits all over NYC. Yeah, I took a few side-view mirrors with me once or twice, but by the time I took my road test, I was whipping that shit like a pro. Well, usually, anyway.

Now, you never drove your car *into* the drug zone or parked it there. It was one of our rules, because there was so much surveillance going on. You parked on the outskirts, and then you walked into your projects. It's all just part of the certain rules and regulations you moved by.

I'm making a turn to park my shit, and the fuckin' cop sees me and pulls me over. Now, I looked a lot younger than I should have looked behind the wheel, 'cause I thought I was the shit. I had no license. The car wasn't in my name, and I later found out it was reported stolen, as well as being rented on a stolen credit card, and was the subject of a hit-and-run investigation. I had no idea of any of that, or that I wasn't even supposed to be driving it because of its record.

I wasn't dirty, either. I wasn't carrying any drugs or guns. I didn't have anything but my bankroll and my brass knuckles. Two fucking things I always carried was the BB: bankroll and brass knuckles.

I had on all red Polo gear, red pants, red Gucci sneakers, three gold fucking rope chains, heavy as a motherfucker, and about five thousand dollars in my pocket. I was comin' back from uptown and chillin' with my peoples, so I was dressed to a fuckin' T that day.

The cop walks up to the car. I didn't have a license, so he gets me out and searches me. Finds the brass knuckles and the five K. He puts me up against the fucking car. I'm standing there, my hands on the fucking hood. He puts everything on the hood.

"I'm going to have to take you in."

"Okay. Lead the way."

Soon as the cop took his eyes off me, I grabbed the money and jetted. I didn't care about the car because it was rented from the Africans. I just took off runnin'. There was a straightaway that went all the way down to the 'jects. All I had to do was reach the buildings. If I could make it there, I would disappear like a fart in the wind.

He took off right after me. He was right on my tail, but I knew if I could make it to the projects, I could disappear on his ass. So I cut through the basketball courts. I'm tearin' across the courts with the police right on my ass. I'm running, running, running—almost got this motherfucker beat.

I come around the corner with him right on my tail, there's two behind me and two in front of me. I Allen Iversoned, crossed over on the two in front. In other words, I did the shaky leg on them, made them fall on the floor. You learn how to do these things playing tag as a kid, so you shake them. I faked out the cop so hard, I think he injured his knee. Later, I saw him with a scraped-up face and bloody knee.

I laughed over my shoulder at them and kept bolting. Shouldn't have gloated so much. Some Good Samaritan stuck his damn foot out and tripped me up while I ran past him. Boop! I crash to the ground and get smothered in police. The cops were on me in a second, hitting me with their walkie-talkies and kicking me. They tried to kick my teeth out, but I was able to protect myself. They still fucked me up pretty good, though.

They took me to the precinct and booked me; I was all bloodied up. I got accused of grand larceny (basically driving a stolen vehicle); I got assault on a police officer (the pissed-off fallen cop with the bloody knee and face); all these charges are on my public arrest record. I would have gotten away completely if it hadn't been for that Good Samaritan. I could've gotten away with it all if it was just no driver's license.

Back then, getting caught driving without a license just got you a fine. It's a whole other story now. The funny part was that when I actually went in to get my real driver's license, I had to pay off twenty-five hundred dollars in parking tickets and *still* had to wait two years for my suspended license to be granted, even after passing the test and everything! All because of the tickets I got while learning to drive those African whips as a teenager.

Instead, they charged me with grand larceny, which fortunately was a misdemeanor back then. I've got all this shit on my fucking record to make me look more dangerous than what I really am. Lucky for me, I was a minor with no previous record. I pled out to the grand larceny charge, they dropped that bullshit assault charge, and I wound up with a weekend in the Manhattan Detention Complex, otherwise known as the Tombs, and 150 hours of community service. I had no lawyer representing me—if I had, I probably could have gotten the whole thing dismissed.

So I get out of jail and I do my community service. Soon as I come home, I walk up the street, and the African dude named Bengali who rented me the car is out there in his little silk shirt and gold chains looking all slick.

"Yo, dog, you rented me a stolen car!" I told him.

"I didn't know, man—"

I broke his fucking jaw. I just punched him dead in his face with my brass knuckles and told him, "Man, don't ever disrespect me like that again. Don't you *ever* rent me a fucking stolen car! If you gonna rent me some shit, then rent me some shit that isn't stolen! Now I got possession of stolen shit on my record!"

Last I heard, he wound up doing fifteen years for heroin possession, then came home and died of AIDS.


I witnessed a lot of great escapes from cops on those streets. There were three types of runners in the hood. What I mean by runners, I'm talking about Jesse Owens, Carl Lewis–type runners. You had the slow, galloping steady mover—that's how I move. I'm slow to accelerate, but once I get my stride, you aren't catching me. Then you had the semifast pace. And you got them Carl

Lewis-fast, gone like the wind types. What I mean by Carl Lewis is the ones that run like lightning the moment the pistol sounds off. They got that speed that when they take off, you just forget about it, you aren't gonna catch them, period. Then you have runners like my man Kaze, who went zero to sixty like a fuckin' Ferrari.

Method Man had speed. Back in the day, he was a jack-in-the-fucking-box. I used to call Meth the "klutz genius" on the basketball court, because he would trip and do some shit and it would still go in the basket. Now, mind you, Method's a tall motherfucker, about six foot three, but he was fast as fuck. He had the Carl Lewis speed, too.

I'm Batman, he's Robin. Just because I'm small, and he's bigger than me, that don't mean nothing. One day we were standing in front of the building, as usual. We dealing with our usual one-two step, trying to get our money for the day, and it just was mad police flying up and down the block. It was just hot that day. We didn't care. We didn't believe in hot because when you're a hustler, you don't give a fuck because you know your customers. You had to practically have a photographic memory. You had hundreds, even thousands of different customers, and you had to recognize every single one of them. I knew every one of my customers on sight. To this day, I might recognize someone from back in the day. If you didn't keep tabs on your clients, you were gonna get busted fast. Undercover agents would try to come up and buy shit from dudes all the time, but they'd tell 'em to get the fuck outta there.

Now, one of the rules I had—this is another reason why certain police probably respected us dudes—when it was hot, when I saw certain po, we would shut it down. We left. I would just leave. I would give them they space and let them go. This day was a different day, for some reason.

Anyway, Meth had this long deep-green Polo coat. Long one,

down to his knees. We used to rock real long trench coats back in the day.

One day we in front of the building. It was crowded out front. Dudes were hustling, fiends were running around, and Lounger Lo, the building's practical joker, was there as well.

Something you should know about Lounger Lo, aka Lounge. First, he's Cappadonna's brother. Second, this dude was the hands-down slang king motherfucker of Staten Island, and made up a lot of the terms the Wu kicked. Lounger had slang for every fucking thing under the sun, he was a walking slang dictionary. If you heard him talk, unless you were from Park Hill, you wouldn't understand a word he said because he speaks in all slang.

I rep him because I knew where he came from: *Jelly,* or *jell-t,* means to move in a sporadic motion; *darts,* that means rhymin' with precision; and *bungee* means we're about to get up outta here, we're about to bungee out of here. *Politicking* means talking to someone else. All that is Lounger, that's Cappa and Lounger and their family's shit. Cappa's notorious with slang, too, but that shit really comes from his brother.

The "Ooh" Building and all that, that's also Lounger. They called it the Ooh Building because dudes were coming out of there like, "Ooh," or lit the fuck up. That's the Ooh Building. Yeah, another one. Ooh, Ooh.

You just had to sit down and listen to him talk. You'd start saying shit like, "I'm at the store. I'm about to jell-t. I'm a bungee over here and bing. Pop a little. Yeah. We gonna do that." Ninety-nine percent of the slang that came out of New York City came from that dude's mouth. Most people don't even fucking know it. And he's never stopped, either, he just keeps coming up with new words and new terminology every day.

Anyway, Lounger would yell off the roof, "The cops is coming, the cops is coming," and the cops wouldn't be coming. He'd cry wolf all the time. We used to hate him for that.

But that day, for some reason, he was doing the opposite. In other words, he'd say the cops coming, the cops ain't coming. Then when he ain't saying nothing, the cops're fucking coming. Fucking asshole.

Anyway, this was how connected me and Meth were. We were so in tune with each other back then that he could read my thoughts from across the street. I'm serious. All I had to do was just look at him, and he could tell by the look on my face what to do.

So we in front of the building, and I used to get these, to this day I still get these little chills, like a *whoosh!* I get like a *whoosh* inside of me. I can't tell you what it is. It's almost like Spidey-sense. It's like a spiritual feeling when trouble's coming.

All I knew was that things were happening. Weird shit was going on. So I stepped off the curb in front of the building. Something was just telling me to go. Soon as I'm stepping off the curb, both the cops and the TNT, the Tactical Narcotics Task Force, are pulling up. They only show up when an undercover agent makes a buy with marked money. And they brought the whole team out that day.

Meth is dirty as a motherfucker. I turn around and look at him and give him the eyeball. I didn't even have to say a word. Carl Lewis in motion. He was gone. He didn't even waste time looking around, he just knew to book 'cause I gave him the eye. The moment I turned around and looked at him, he did the Dark-man. You just saw his fucking green coat go flapping into the fucking building.

By the time he got inside, the police were coming through the back and in the front. He made it past these motherfuckers and made it up in the staircase and got rid of the shit and came out the side of the building.

He was like, "Woo!" He was like, "Yo, yo, dawg, I read your mind!"

I just grinned and said, "I know you did, man. I know you did."

The Africans renting us whips helped us out a lot. We were mobile now. We could get uptown easier to cop those drugs. We could get around the city more just in general. Now we were meeting dudes in different hoods and just conquering land. Every weekend we'd be out and about. The block would be a ghost town. This shit was like a real nine-to-five for hustlers. On the weekend, we didn't really want to hear about junkies and all that shit. Of course, whoever stayed to hustle on the block on Saturdays and Sundays was gonna get all that paper. Because we were all off the clock out trying to bag numbers and ride around and smoke weed, the crackheads would be lining up to see whoever was out there in our place.

During all this time, running back and forth uptown and going to different projects to drop packages, I still managed to keep going to school. I went to McKee Vocational High School. To attend I passed an entrance exam, like an aptitude test or whatever. It was a specialized school, and I did more than well enough to get in.

As I got older and started hustling more, I still stayed in school. I realized I didn't have to be in the streets to get money. I was giving dudes packages, and they could have my money moving while I was in class. I'd get up at eight in the morning and put those packages in the street. By three o'clock, when I'm home from school, they were finished. So I'd just collect my money after school and put more packs out.

Then it was upstairs to do homework and be back either late that night or early in the morning on my way to school to collect my funds and replenish the packs. Same routine, day in and day out. I'd let the hard heads who just wanted to be home and un-educated get rid of those packages for me while I was in school. I knew those dudes weren't ever gonna be shit anyway, because they just wanted to lay up and sell drugs all day. Never go to school, never leave the block. They were happy just doing what they were doing.

We'd all hustle on the block, but I never liked being on the block all the fucking time. I didn't want to be known like that, by the cops and the nosy neighbors and snitches, especially since I was doing mad dirt. Anyway, aside from school, I didn't want to be out in front of the Hill all day. Not when there was so much of the city to explore.

On weekends, we'd go uptown to cop more, or we'd drive out to Brooklyn to the weed gates and cop some good greenery. We'd go to an area of Bedford-Stuyvesant called Hancock. The whole block would be lit up with Rastafarians and Jamaicans. Or we'd go uptown to Edgecombe Avenue and get a chicken bag, which was like you'd pay twenty dollars, and get fifty to sixty dollars' worth of weed. It was so competitive up there that the dealers had to sell that much product for cheap to make sure their customers came to them. It was so damn much weed over what you'd usu-ally get, and you could bring that back to the Island, break it down, and flip it, too. We made good money for a couple of train rides. There were all types of ways to come up, and we tried damn near every last one of them.

7.

## IT'S YOURZ

A successful drug dealer knows how to invest the money he's earned. You had to have money in the stash for bail and lawyer fees for your mans who got knocked. You needed extra re-up money in case you took a loss, so you still had dough for the next round. I just made sure my bills were paid, made sure my people were all right. But I always knew there were rainy days right around the corner. My workers were getting knocked by the police here and there, and packs would get lost or confiscated, or your spot might get robbed. There was so much to learn, and learning by making mistakes usually involved spending money to fix them. Especially when you're out there doing dirt. You had to protect yourself and your crew when you're out there doing wrong.

However, we were also a bunch of punk-ass teens with all this income. So, with the excess we had, we'd rock the flyest threads and dope jewelry, Polo rugbies, rope chains, Gucci kicks, Cazals—all that drug dealer chic was at its apex in the crack era. We set social and fashion trends back then that are still emulated today.

Also, I was getting around more, making more moves around the city, and I had to look the part. I was rocking Gucci, Polo, and some butter-soft shit. Any ill concerts I could get tickets to (we could just bum-rush the show), I went, because I had money for it.

And as soon as that brick flipped to forty thousand dollars again, I would put aside my expenditures money. I would splurge on some stupid shit, but most of my dough went right back to my connect to cop more coke and to keep the block flooded with no lapses during the re-up period. I was striving to perfect my hustle so it was a fine-tuned machine with no glitches, and I was able to stack up a good amount.

I learned about finance through trial and error. When you get successful on the street, no one teaches you about finance. They don't teach you about taxes, they don't teach you about IRAs and tax write-offs and budgeting your finances and balancing your checkbook and giving yourself leeway for certain things. You get a certain amount of money, you could go on vacation, you could buy a car. Just because you got ten million dollars don't mean you go out and buy a five-million-dollar house. You buy a half-million-dollar house. You live below your means, but you're still wealthy. Being rich is not necessarily making a whole lot of money. Being rich is having your bills paid off and being able to do the things you want to do when you want to do them.

Of course, working on the streets is a whole different set of problems than a legitimate business. First of all, you aren't dealing with taxes or Social Security or any of that shit. You're dealing with fucking ornery, crazy fiends and schemers. You have no protection, and you can't call the cops. You can't call the cops when you get robbed. You got to handle that shit the best way you know how to handle it. That's why I said nine out of ten times, instead of shooting or stabbing or hurting some crazy motherfucker, I'd rather just delete them from my life. I just said, "I ain't fucking with you anymore." That hurt them even more because really, I had the bank. Those guys didn't have shit. I saw it from the banker's perspective. The bankers don't give a fuck because they the ones shoveling all the money. If you fall through on your loan, they don't give a fuck. They're just not fucking with you anymore.

I put myself on a budget way back then, due to all the variables of the drug game. That was a good lesson when I started getting this rap money. A lot of rappers with a supposedly bigger name than mine are out here broke. Not me. I've always saved my money since the drug game, and I've always lived well within my means. I'm not gonna go the club to throw fifty thousand dollars in the air. Fuck that. I'm not into all that, and I never was.

See, if you got a fucking couple of million dollars in your pocket, you have all types of motherfuckers jumping out of bowls of rice and all types of situations just to get some from you. Friends you grew up with, people you ain't even seen in twenty goddamn years coming at you behind the scenes, and just doing a whole bunch of scheming. It's just how the world is.

About this time, my mother's years of hard work were starting to pay off. She had gotten a few promotions, and things were getting better for us. It was too late for me, though. By the time she was getting it together, I was too grown up—she'd find my guns and crack and other wild shit. It meant a lot to her that she was getting off welfare and getting herself situated, and I wasn't going to fuck it up for our family. I can't blame her at all.

The last straw was when she found fifty thousand dollars and two kilos of coke in our house.

I was seventeen at the time. I said, "Ma—"

She said, "Lamont, what the fuck?" That's when she kicked me out. She said, "You too heavy. You got to leave."

I wouldn't let my mother go down for none of my shit. That

wasn't happening. Fact is, she didn't even know how heavy I was. And just like that, I was out on the street.

In fact, when Wu-Tang first broke out, my mother didn't believe it. She thought I was still out there selling drugs. She didn't believe it until I brought home a gold album. I put it in the living room. And now she believes it.

So I moved in with Method Man, into an apartment across the street from Trackmasters, where we lived with a fucking sneak thief cokehead. That spot was fucked up. The heat never worked. There was always a little crack and/or money missing from there. You couldn't leave anything in the refrigerator either, cause anyone who came through was always eating up whatever they could find.

We also had a dog named Samson, a Rottweiler. He started out real nice when he was young. As he got to his fucking full size, he started shitting like a dinosaur, just everywhere. Basically, it was a hellhole. That particular apartment embodied the struggle we were going through at the time.

But there was still music. There was always music.

There were times when Meth and I would be on the corner, pretending it was a stage and we were putting on a show in front of thousands of people. We would dream about getting out of the streets, flying around the world, getting a crib in L.A., meeting movie stars, getting with women, the whole lifestyle. At the time, our self-esteem might have been in the toilet, but we just knew we were going to lift ourselves out of that situation. But first came putting the work in, because without it, we weren't going anywhere.

But we kept our moves discreet, partly because we didn't want to set ourselves up for disappointment. Also, it was best to move in silence with all the crabs in the barrel surrounding us. The few dudes on the block we did tell about our plans thought it was all bullshit, anyway. They didn't take it seriously.

We had to keep that shit secret because motherfuckers treated you weird. Even when I was in high school, people would be like, "What are you doing?" when I'd have my headphones on making rhymes. "Writin' rhymes?"

"Yeah, man, I'm writin' rhymes."

"You ain't EPMD. You ain't Big Daddy Kane, man." Those were close-minded motherfuckers. I bet you they sittin' there like "Oh shit" now.

Method Man was really serious about it, though. He had entire songs, verses, and choruses in place. Out of all of us, Meth and ODB were more serious about rapping and entertaining. When it came to entertaining, they were the best. That's why they were so advanced. Their dedication to their respective crafts was very real.

Even with all the other dudes around, Meth always stood out. I knew he was going to be great, even when his self-confidence was lacking a bit and he didn't believe it himself. But as he developed his rhymes, I started to see his talent grow and realized he shouldn't be hustling and ducking cops on the block. I wanted him away from that so he could focus solely on the music. He'd already done a lot of shit to hold us down in the streets, so he had earned his respect.

But in order for Shaquan to truly grow into Method Man, though, he needed to focus on his writing. To do so, he had to step away from the asphalt jungle, and in turn I had to step it up in his absence. I took care of him so he wouldn't have to be in the streets.

"You know what, man?" I told him. "You just sit there and write. You do your thing while I cut this half a brick over here," I said. I used to cut a fucking joint up, right in front of him.

I'd be sitting there cooking up all this fucking coke, and he'd be pacing around the room writing his rhymes and reciting them to himself until he had it down, then he would rap that shit to me. Or he'd just be sitting there doing his rap, eatin' his sandwiches from this fucking corner store. He'd have his headphones on, getting busy. He'd write them, and then slide off and do a studio session sometimes. I'd be whipping work in the pot, nodding my head while he kicked his verses. His rhymes were crazy.

One afternoon we were kicking it, me chopping and cooking, and him writing, when "Method of Modern Love" by Hall and Oates came on the radio. Of course it's got that great refrain: "M-E-T-H-O-D-O-F-L-O-V-E" and we're just doing our thing, and that's when it came to us, and we knew "M-E-T-H-O-D-M-A-N" was here to stay!

That's always been a gift of ours, transforming thoughts, acronyms (like C.R.E.A.M.), and slang, and providing the right energy or mind-set that can turn a simple concept into something much bigger, whether that be a rap name or single title that would become a worldwide hit.

In fact, Meth was responsible for coming up with what the acronym W.U.-T.A.N.G. stands for: *W*itty *U*npredictable *T*alent *A*nd *N*atural *G*ame. We were acronyming everything at the time: "Cash Rules Everything Around Me," and all that, and certain things stuck, and certain things didn't. But given that we were also heavily influenced by martial arts and Asian kung fu movies and all that, the name Wu-Tang seemed like a natural fit.

Even when my drug game was at its height, I always kept in mind that I was just trying to make a fucking living in a fucked-up situation. I was content with my small operation, making enough to get by and taking care of my peoples.

But with all that, I was still learning about the game. Anything you do, you should study it extensively. I'd hop in my Volvo 740 and go check out my contacts uptown, not even to cop drugs, just to observe and learn from the way they were hustling there. Plus, it was an escape from Staten Island. I got to see how other hoods hustled, how they dealt with the heat and the stickup kids and all those headaches. You had to learn the latest tricks the cops and the junkies were pulling, or you'd be their next victim.

When my operation was running full-bore, I had about twenty people working under me. Then I had to shave it down because some dudes were fuckin' up. I shaved it down to about five or ten people. I got better output when I downsized, because I wasn't dealing with so many crazy motherfuckers anymore. I ran my operation like fucking IBM.

The ones I cut were users who were fuckin' up and sometimes not coming back with money. They didn't respect the structure. So I let 'em go with no hard feelings, but no second chances either. I looked at it like, "Okay, you fucked up, so you got to go. You ain't getting no more bombs or money from me ever." Now, I know dudes that killed motherfuckers for stupid shit like that, just to maintain their reputation. Reputation isn't everything, it's only gonna get you in trouble. "I gotta reputation to protect, I gotta protect this legend I've built on the street, so if you cross me, I'm gonna come back on you and hurt you to protect my rep."

I know a dude who shot another guy to protect his rep, and now he's doing thirty years. Ego combined with anger will fuck you up every time. There's hundreds of dudes in jail right now kicking themselves in the ass over shit they pulled to protect their reputation, wishing they could take it back.

But you're always gonna take some shorts. It was the cost of doing business, and you just had to deal with it. Like I said, people eliminate themselves. For some apparent reason, as a youngster I already knew that. You didn't have to shoot anybody. I told dudes, "Man, you don't gotta shoot anybody that owes you fucking money. You just don't fuck with that dude no more." Whoever's doing good, you stick with those. Whoever fucks up, they fuck up. You just don't fuck with 'em no more. Leave them alone. Ain't no second chances. You only get one. 'Cause I know if you fuck up once, you gonna fuck up again and again and again. You gonna keep doing the same damn thing. You're a dummy, and I'd be just as dumb to trust you again.

Some people I grew up with, they were hard-core shooters doing all type of dangerous sucker shit to get turf. They wound up snitching on each other and they killed eight dudes, they got eight fucking bodies, and all wound up in a big conspiracy case and all type of shit. Today, they got nothing to show for it but jail time.

Some motherfuckers just wanted more money. The more turf you covered, the more money you were getting. That's why we said the 160 was our building. Then there was 350 and 55 Bowen. There was 141 and 260. There was 280. These are notorious drug buildings, and 160 was our building. That's where the majority of the traffic was coming through, 160 and 260. Before that, it was 55 Bowen when Dusty and the dreads had brought the first wave of drugs into the neighborhood. After they died off and got locked up, and their entourage got locked up, we took over.

I had three buildings. I had 160, New Brighton, and West Brighton. I was doing more than good enough to get by. We were eating. We didn't know what to do with the goddamn money, but we were eating. 'Cause we were giving the money right back to the coke man. Go buy some more coke. Buy more product. Buy some gifts, you go eat, get a car, pay your rent, pay your bills, then you give the rest to the fucking man again. Try to re-up again.

At first, it was all cool. Making this money. Doing what we got to do. Doing whatever. Then I just got tired of it. I just got tired of dealing with the guns, the carnage, the people. I got my diploma from McKee Vocational High School. I graduated. I graduated because I didn't want to be a drug dealer my whole life. I didn't want to have to be looking over my shoulders for police, stickup kids, junkies, robbers, hateful people. I just got tired of that shit.

Years later, I would tell dudes who were fighting over buildings and shooting it out over drug blocks, "Why are we fighting over these buildings? We don't own them. None of this is ours. Watch, there's going to be a day when ain't none of us even going to be out here."

Sure enough, you drive past those buildings now and there's nobody there. Nothing. It's like all them dudes got shot, murdered over drug buildings, and nobody even owns the building. Dudes are in jail and others got killed all trying to claim the building, and not one of them could lay any type of real claim. It was all over nothing. It all meant nothing.

At the level I was at, I went through all types of shit. I almost died probably about five times. After I cut peoples loose, some tried to get back on me. It happened all the fuckin' time. One called the police on me. Motherfuckers shot at me. I've been kidnapped. Literally. The killer shit was just missing me, or I saw it coming and avoided it, or shit happened and it was just that close.

Once, I almost got killed because I was in the wrong territory. Like I'm the ambassador, right? I was supposed to let the locals know I was in town, but me trying to be on some sucker sliding-under-the-radar shit, they didn't know I was there.

I was up on a spot, getting it clicking. It was the first stages of a new territory for me to make money. I'm there doing my one-two stepper, in the bathroom counting the day's take. Got my gun on me. Junkies running around the apartment out front, making a whole bunch of noise. Fucking house is noisy all day. Then all of a sudden, it just stopped being fucking noisy. I didn't pick up on the shit. I'm like, "What the fuck? It's quiet out there." I'm sitting on the toilet, contemplating what's going on. I got my nine, I got my shit. The door is closed, and I'm counting my money.

Something told me to shoot through the fucking door, but I

didn't listen to my fucking instincts. I open the fucking door, four men run in with guns. They got me cornered in the room, and grabbed me and started beating me in the head with pistols. Boom, boom, boom, boom. Gave me a hairline skull fracture. I still got a skull fracture from that shit.

They beat me up, tried to knock me out. Dude's like, "Yo, where's the drugs? Where's the drugs?" I gave them everything I had on me. He was like, "Nah, this ain't it." So he threw a blanket over my head and put a gun to my head. After he put the gun to my head, he clicked it back and said, "Man, I'm goin' kill you. Where's the money and the drugs?"

I said, "Yo, dawg, I gave you everything. I don't have anything else." Plus, with the fucking blanket on, I can't see, I'm blind. I got a gun to my head, I got a towel over my head. I thought I was a dead motherfucker.

I'm sittin' there. One of the dudes is like, "Yo, man, we should take him with us."

The other thug's like, "Nah, nah, nah."

Other dude was like, "Yo, you know what, man? I got respect for this dude. You'd be in there cryin'." I hear him talking to his friend. "You'd bend like a little bitch," he said. "You'd fold like a little bitch."

I'm sitting there listening to this shit. I'm amazed this whole shit was going on. So he cocks the pistol and says, "Yo, you know what? Count to ten, man."

I said, "Then what?"

He said, "Don't worry about it. Count to ten."

So I'm sitting there. I'm counting. I hear the door close. Those dudes just fucking leave. I come downstairs. I'm all bloody and all that shit. My man Each, he used to run the projects, he was like, "Oh, shit, dawg, why the fuck didn't you tell me you were upstairs, that was you? I know the dude told me there was some guy upstairs selling . . ."

I was like, "Yo, dawg, where's your man at?" I knew who had set me up. I said, "Where the fuck is your man?"

He was like, "The dude didn't tell me it was you."

I said, "I know he ain't tell you. I told him to tell you I was here." I said, "I'll be back, man."

When I came back, I was all blacked out, getting ready to kill this motherfucker. I'm in the bushes, blacked down head to toe. You can't see me. I'm the ninja squirrel. I see the motherfucker who did it. He don't see me. I waited and I waited until the guy got real close up on me. He was with my man Each. I guess Each must have known, because he was with the dude real hard.

I jumped out on the guy, ready to blow his fucking top off.

Each jumps in front of him and says, "No, don't do that shit, God. I knew you was coming. I knew you was coming. You're real mad. Just for real, man, just forget about it. I'm sorry. It didn't mean to go down like that."

I said, "Yo, man. You lucky little bitch. My man in front of you. I'm gonna see you."

He was like, "Oh, shit." His face dropped. His fucking bitch face just dropped. He knew I meant what I said.

I was calm afterward. In fact, I kinda forgot about the whole situation. I let the shit slide, but then my man Each got murdered. They killed him, too. The dude that set me up, he ran off. He ran off like a little girl when Each died, because he knew his protection was over, and if I ever did see him again, it would not go well for him.


Of course, there was a downside to all that easy access to drugs. We all did that shit in the fucking hood. That was part of growing up in the projects. We smoked dust. We smoked bowls. We smoked crack. We did mescaline. I did all types of fucking crazy shit growing up. We didn't know any better.

Me and a lot of my crew smoked woolies, a mixture of coke and weed packed into a blunt. At first it was some fly shit to be doing, some baller shit, because you needed money for the weed and the crack, so it was like rich man shit. Soon, though, some dudes couldn't kick the habit and got turned out. That shit was addictive, and since we had the money and the access, there was no regulating our use of it. Luckily for me, I was able to stop.

I can remember the last time I smoked woolies. It was New Year's Eve, and me and a few of my crew had a rental car for the night. We decided to go uptown to Edgecombe Avenue in Harlem to get some weed.

We kind of like lightweight bum-rushed the spot. Not fully, but we just pushed our way in, and dude was only in there with his girl. He had all the coke and weed out on trays.

There was too many of us, so we started getting sticky fingers. We wound up taking mad coke and mad weed. We were so hyped on getting fucked up for New Year's that we drove over to the West Side Highway underneath some overpass. We rolled up all the windows and were smoking that shit up. I shit you not, we musta smoked about twenty or thirty motherfucking cocaine and weed blunts. It was real smoky in the car, and my throat was burning. I don't remember much after that.

The next morning, I woke up back at my place, and my throat felt super raw and closed up. I had a headache and felt mad sick. I thought I'd OD'd. I didn't know what the fuck was going on. I couldn't get out of the bed, and I couldn't even talk. I looked over on the table, and there was still mad coke left. Just looking at it got me disgusted. I felt so sick from just having that shit around, I got up, grabbed it off the coffee table, and threw it out the window.

After that, I made a commitment to never smoke that shit again. I was constantly smoking and getting high. I was addicted. I made the conscious decision to not do that anymore. I have supreme willpower with that. Right now, I have the willpower to say, "No, that shit is poison. That shit is no good." Like I said, I chose money over that shit.

Let me tell you one thing about me; I love money more than I love anything in this goddamned world, except for my family and my babies. I love money more than I love drugs, women, all of that. I'm addicted to money. I like to have it. I like to spoil the people I love. I will never touch no cocaine or none of that shit ever again. I am straight weed, alcohol, and that is it. Money, weed, that's it. I've stuck by that shit for the rest of my life.

Once I kicked the woolies, my health started comin' back. Before, my face was all fucked up. I was sunk in. My belt was on its last hole. After I made my decision, my weight started coming back. My face started coming back. My pockets were bigger. I had more money. Got a car. I just started doing more and more better for myself.

Some of my peoples didn't have that willpower, though, they became addicted to smoking crack. They started smoking the pipe. They graduated from that to something else. They stayed on that plane and continued on that downward spiral. Life is harsh in the ghetto, and sometimes you get caught up trying to escape it. I bet there's a lot of clinically depressed people in the hood, people with a lot of unresolved issues who can't afford any type of therapy. That's why the drug trade is a billion-dollar industry. Millions of folks looking to self-medicate. Even the dealers on the streets, who were supposed to be stronger than that, would succumb to coke. Just trying to maintain and hold shit down can have you wanting to get blackout high.

Meth had some trouble kicking that shit. He was going through a lot of trials and tribulations, especially at a certain point in his life. We were all smoking woolies, and he was no different. At the time, Meth couldn't kick it. He couldn't stop. Even when the rest of us stopped, he couldn't kick the habit. Dudes started looking at him funny, like he was a junkie.

Eventually, he started rocking real heavy with me, and he got up off that shit. We weren't angels after that, but he cleaned himself up. We were both still dirty street ninjas, but we were just trying to better ourselves and our situations and clean up our acts more.

Woolies became the demise of a lot of hustlers. Like my man Choice. I used to always wonder why his paper always came up short when I hit him with consignment. Then I found out why— he was upstairs smoking woolies. We always broke even, he never turned a profit. He would be with his wife upstairs all day, smoking crack and fucking. Like that was the life for him, he couldn't be happier. He had a little bullshit apartment, he was getting his dick sucked every day, and even made a few babies and all that. He just wasn't thinking about his future. He was content with some woolies, a woman, and an apartment. That's why I had to just stop fucking with him. I like dudes around me with some ambition.

Because it's easy to get caught up in the petty shit, the nickel-and-dime drug money, and feel like you've made it. Especially coming from where I did, where just making ends meet was an accomplishment. I made sure, no matter how clean my Gucci sneakers were and how much gold I wore, that the drug game was not the be-all and end-all. Not by fucking far.

So I kept pushing for more.

# 8.

## CASH RULES EVERYTHING AROUND ME

I made it through a short misadventure in Sacramento in 1988 when I was seventeen, and got rushed out by the Crips and the Bloods with just two thousand dollars left from my original six-thousand-dollar investment. Once I got back, I was jingling in no time. That was the extent of my out-of-town drug capers—I'd learned that if I was gonna make a fortune, it'd have to be right here in Gotham Fucking City.

Sometimes it got to be too much for us young black men to handle. I remember once when we were going through some particularly hard times in Park Hill. Raekwon was suffering through his trials and tribulations. He was growing up and clashing with his strict mother. And then there was the issue of being a poor black kid in the city. He was so stressed over his situation and the hardships he was dealing with day in and day out that he stopped writing rhymes.

We were all in the hallway at 160 selling. We called it One Six Eww, 'cause it was grisly, like "Eww." Don't remember why Rae wasn't at the gate in 225 that day.

There was a lapse in the crowd of customers, so we were kicking our rhymes to one another, passing the time like we usually did. We all spit new rhymes, as always. You couldn't come out on the block with the same rhymes day after day. That was like only having one outfit to wear to the club every night—your peers would notice, and you might even get clowned (made fun of). So we all kicked fresh new rhymes daily.

Rae, though, kicked a rhyme he'd already kicked the last two or three times. That meant he'd put the pen down. I didn't say anything at the time, but later, when it was just him and me, we talked about it.

"Uey, I'm over this rap shit," he told me. "Kicking freestyles ain't helping us get money. I might as well just secure this paper, nah mean? I'll rap if I got time for that shit."

"You can't stop though, Rae," I said. "We gonna do this, bruh. This music is going to be our way out of all this drug shit."

"Nah, Uey. I'm just trying to keep my workers in order and keep these fiends coming. I'm not thinking about rhymes right now. That rap shit ain't going nowhere. Look at RZA. He back in the hood, just like the rest of us now. Even if you get on, you still end up back in the projects."

When we rapped that "Cash Rules Everything Around Me," we meant that shit to the fullest. Rae wasn't trying to put all his eggs in the rap basket. He had to make money to eat, and he'd rather never rhyme again than starve. Technically, he was right. But I wouldn't let him quit. I kept telling him that this shit was going to materialize for us. I felt it, I just always felt it in my heart. I always knew somehow that we'd be running all over the world with this rap shit. I believed from the bottom of my heart that the Wu-Tang Clan was going to take us out of our hell.

Because of that, I wouldn't let Rae put his pen down. Not my brother. I was basically on top of him all the time. "Keep writing, keep writing," I told him. "Keep writing, keep writing." I'd yell out the window at him, "Hey, you write any new shit?" He'll tell you himself that I pulled him back into rhyming when he got too caught up in surviving day-to-day.

In the end, he kept writing. At the time, his rhyme heroes were Kool G Rap, Big Daddy Kane, and Rakim. You can tell from Rae's criminology style that he's heavily influenced by G Rap. Rae was in the streets so much, he could take the details of drug dealing and being in the streets to a new level of detail. G Rap and Melle Mel invented that type of rap, with the mobster references and drug dealing and all that fly shit. Rae took that style and added to it because he was seeing so much of it day to day. And because of that, he was ready when it came time to spit those rhymes with RZA.

He wouldn't have been in shape mentally to do "C.R.E.A.M." if I hadn't been a real friend to him and encouraged him to keep going with that rhyming shit. I don't give a fuck what anyone says—I was the one who pushed Rae to keep rhyming. He might have still gotten on, but the thing is this rhyming shit is like boxing. You have to mentally stay in shape.

I wrote every day. A paragraph, a rhyme, whatever. You have to exercise your mind. Even back then when we were on the block, if we would have succumbed to just keeping our thoughts on the day in and day out of the hustle, we would have never sharpened the part of our brain we use to be creative. But we did, and now look—Raekwon is credited for starting that crime rhyme genre of rap more than Kool G Rap is, at least the updated, modern version of it. All the Mafia references, the aliases, that was something Rae drew heavily on from Kool G Rap and from the time he spent in the game.

Also, we grew up on Staten Island around Italians and hearing certain names. So when it came to time to write a rhyme, I guess that's what Rae drew from. And it was successful. So much so that Rae pretty much birthed a genre of rap after *Cuban Linx* hit the streets. After that album, everyone had a mob-sounding alias.


Our dreams of success seemed so far away that we didn't know if they were ever gonna come to fruition. We didn't know the Wu was going to be so influential at the time. It was so easy to get disheartened when we were running around in the streets like animals, shooting it out with other crews over money. Stickup kids were everywhere. Gates were getting robbed. And sometimes you had to put your creativity and imagination and any other aptitudes you possessed on the back burner to ensure self-preservation. We were all dealing with this fucked-up reality. And it's not just creativity. It's book smarts, too, that eventually take a back burner to the hustle and the grind.

I didn't let it, though. I learned how to hustle drugs, but I was still in school. I didn't want to be a drug dealer. I was happy with two bricks or three bricks. These other dudes, they wanted a hundred bricks and to be Pablo Escobar and shit. I didn't want to be Escobar. The street will have you chasing something completely different than what you got in the game for. At first, things in the streets had us doing shit just to get some food in our bellies and clothes on our backs. We got that done, and even managed to pile a little bread.

I was always looking for a way out of the streets. The block wasn't going anywhere, I realized that early. Those dudes I had hustling for me and other dudes on the block, they had no education. They thought drug dealing was the life, and they weren't looking toward their future. They weren't thinking about going to school, education, or trying to better themselves, they were just trying to sell fucking drugs.

When I picked up my money from them, I told them this wasn't the life, it wasn't anything to be glorifying. Their parents or whoever was raising them wasn't implementing that need for education like my moms was. They didn't listen, though; they were hardheaded little sons of bitches with no drive or ambition, they just wanted to sit on the block and sell drugs.

You see, knowledge is infinite. And if you're not open to obtaining new knowledge, then you're only gonna go as far as what you currently know will take you. Am I open to acquiring new knowledge? Yes, I am. Is everybody? No, no, no. Sometimes ego gets in the way of trying to learn new shit, because you may think you already know something, that you know all there is to know about a topic. But if you're a real 5 Percenter, a real Godbody, you're a sponge, you're always learning.

If there's one lesson I would tell the young'uns of today, it's that the drug trade is *not* a permanent lifestyle. It's not for you to sit there and make a living and think you're gonna last ten years doin' this shit. The drug game is not for you to live that life for the rest of your life. It's for you to get in, and if you're trying to buy some other kind of business, that's what you dump your money into. Then you make the transition from the streets. Once you piled up enough bread to get out, you dump it into a legal business, and then you cut off all ties with the connect and walk away—that's it, you're done. It's as simple as that.

But these dudes get into the game and get sucked in deeper and deeper. Some of those dudes back in the day, the Escobar-emulating motherfuckers running ten keys, that was close to a million dollars they were making on the regular. The smart move would have been to take that million and do the *Godfather II* hustle, get into some kind of legit business and leave the street grind behind. Say, "I'm done with this shit," and walk away.

But the problem with a lot of motherfuckers was that they couldn't get out of the game. They got caught up in the life, and they couldn't stop—until they got busted or shot down.


Going to college made me realize like, "Yo, man, there's more out there than just the projects." I was in school from probably like twelve in the afternoon to six at night. That schedule exposed me to a different world; it allowed me to see other things. I was meeting new kinds of women, friends, etc. People from Queens and

Brooklyn, and meeting other motherfuckers who weren't drug dealers. They were kids. Just regular kids going to school, and it was beautiful. It was nonthreatening, and I liked it. I was at the Borough of Manhattan Community College working on my bachelor's degree. I actually met AZ, who later joined the Firm, and a couple other dudes from around the area: PI, Blizz, Jamal (from Lafayette Gardens), Lil' Kim, even Puffy.

I used to love going to school, even though my focus was kind of fucked up because I was still street poisoned. Women were a distraction, too. But I still came out of there with about a dozen credits. If I had kept going, I'd probably have my degree now.

I was transferring from BMCC to LaGuardia Community College to study mortuary science, but by then I caught my case and had to drop out to do my time. I went to school up until I got locked up, though.

Believe it or not, I was gonna be an embalmer. That's what I wanted to do. All that fucking carnage I saw and death and all that, all them fucking bullet wounds, that wasn't shit for me to handle dead bodies. To this day it's nothing for me; I can go in, see the corpse, the shit don't even faze me. Certain things that'll quease a motherfucker out just doesn't bother me.

I got the notion to be an embalmer when my cousin Jimmy died, which is a crazy fucking story. One day, my grandmother called me up. "Lamont, you gotta go to the Bronx."

"For what?" I asked.

"Jimmy's not calling me," she said.

"So what? What happened?"

She said, "I don't know. We gotta go, that's all. We gotta go see what's going on."

We get to the house. On the door there's a letter from the ambulance. We were like, "Oh, shit!" But there's nothing on it about which hospital he went to, just that the ambulance was there. We don't know what the fuck is going on, where he's at, nothing.

We open the door to his house. Grandma's got the keys. We smell piss on the bed. Look through the house trying to find out anything. Can't find him. We asked the police where the nearest hospital was at. He gave a list of the five hospitals in the area that might have taken him in. Fine. We started driving around to all of 'em.

When we get to the first one, my grandmother said, "Yo, you gotta go downstairs in the morgue." She tells me to go get him, go find Jimmy.

"Don't worry 'bout it, Grandma," I said. "I'll go down to the morgue." They had babies, adults, everybody in this goddamn cold chamber, just rows and rows of square metal doors with bodies behind them.

Once she knew why I was there, the attendant stood next to me and let me start looking for Jimmy. I started pulling out racks—metal shelves on rails that you could pull out—checked the body, and slid it back in. Racks on racks of people. John Doe. Jane Doe. John Doe. Kids. Infants. I'm pulling one after the other. I'm pulling back babies. I'm pulling back medium-sized kids. I'm putting them back in. I can't find him. We went to all five hospitals. I went through the whole day looking at dead bodies.

Afterward, I'm just sitting there like, "Wow. Oh, shit! Now what?"

"Okay. You know what? We gonna go back and check the first hospital we went to," my grandmother said.

The morgue lady had the white jacket on. I had a white coat on, too, 'cause it was freezing in this refrigerator. I'm pulling out rack after rack after rack. Literally, hundreds of unclaimed John Does. Finally, after about an hour, I pulled one rack in the back. All the way in the back back. Under three motherfucking bodies. Cousin Jimmy. I pushed the plastic down to his face and said, "Oh, there he is."

Turns out he had a heart attack in his house. Somehow he got to the phone. He got up in the ambulance. The ambulance people came and got him, but they didn't take his ID. When he gets to the hospital, he didn't have any ID, so he became a John Doe. He passed away in the hospital, and they had no idea who the fuck he was. That taught me to always have my identification on me, and to make sure my elders always carried their ID at all times.

My grandmother was happy that Cousin Jimmy had been found. I was a bit traumatized—not from the adult bodies, but the babies. I talked to the coroner dude that's handling it. He said, "Man, this happens every day." Two-, three-year-olds that their mother dumped in the Dumpster. The Bronx was just chewing them up and spitting them out.

I was blown away. I didn't realize that every hospital has this. Every hospital has a fucking morgue underneath it where it has people in the refrigerator. They discard all the clothing. They got a box on the side, just full of all the dead people's clothes. John Does and all that.

That shit might fuck somebody up. Once you see carnage and cadavers, the effect of life and death, somebody get shot in the face, all that shit, you change. Literally, you become a bone man. We're all just bone men. We ain't nobody. We're so fragile. It's crazy how people act so tough and hard and like they're so invincible, when everything around us can kill us at any time.


By this time I was nineteen, the Rastafarians had faded out because they'd all gotten locked up or killed, so the Hill was ours. You have to understand, we felt like Park Hill was our land. We had a right to do whatever we wanted on our land. We'd grown up from little toddlers to grown men there, and taken the beatings and all kinds of shit, and we were still there standing and growing. Park Hill was ours because we all had made our claims to hold it down; we defended it, spilled blood there, and knew every inch of it. We didn't own a single inch of it legally, but we still felt it was ours.

And I got my percentage out of that motherfucker, too, make no mistake. Even so, there was a whole bunch of other motherfuckers out there doing way more than what I was doing. You had dudes up the block, you had dudes down the block, you had us. The whole neighborhood was drug infested. When I wasn't there, someone else was always keeping the traffic coming. That's the reason why it was money in the streets. It was simple economics; without supply and demand, there would be no customers.

That was a regular thing. And occasionally, outsiders would come into our hood trying to get money. It would start with some Brooklyn dude coming through the projects to see some girl he knew. She'd let him in the house. Then he'd see us making all this money running up to cars pumping our cracks. He'd see us in the hallway counting our stacks of fucking cash, and then he and his crew'd want a piece.

He'd run back to his neighborhood, wherever he's from. "Dudes're getting money on the Island."

"Oh, word, we gotta see about this."

Eventually, we would run them out of town. Queens, Brooklyn, they came from everywhere. But we'd run them out. Sometimes, though, they'd hurt a couple of us in the gun battles before they left town.

Thing I learned about that was you have to stop outsiders as soon as they come in. If someone comes into your territory, you can't let 'em linger. You have to act right away, get 'em out of there fast. We let a couple of motherfuckers just linger and a lot of dudes got hurt or killed because of that bullshit. We learned the hard way that you have to be proactive when repelling invaders.

One of the dudes I knew got shot in the eye with a MAC-10 by an outsider who wasn't even supposed to be in our hood. The guy who got shot wasn't my peoples, we had our little beefs and never really got along, but we were from the same hood, so I felt bad when he lost an eye over some Brooklyn dudes trying to invade our turf. We should have handled the intrusion off the rip.

Sometimes I can't even believe I made it out alive. So many good dudes I know passed away on the same block in front of the same building that I was in front of daily.

I remember seeing this kid get hit right in front me. I was in the barbershop getting my hair cut. I was with my man Blue that day. There was another dude named Mike there, a real smooth-faced, dark-skinned dude. He wore gold-framed Cazals and was always really quiet. He was also a stone-cold killer, an enforcer for the Rastafarians pumping crack in my hood. He always showed me love, so I didn't know this guy was a fucking maniac. At the time, I was very young, about fourteen or fifteen, and still wet behind the ears.

I'm in the barber's chair, just minding my business. Suddenly we hear a MAC-10 spitting. We hit the floor just as the shop window burst. After a second it got quiet, so we ran outside the shop to see what happened. I still had the barbershop bib on.

The guy Mike shot was a notorious stickup kid, thief, robbin'-ass motherfucker. I didn't know his name, but he went by the street name of Beatbox. He got hit, and within seconds, collapsed right in the street. A couple minutes later, his neck swelled up, his hands, his face, everything. He was just lying there swelling up like a balloon. He went from living and breathing to a swollen, bloated corpse in less than a minute.

By the time the police came and covered his body with a blanket, the whole hood—little kids to grandmothers—had already peeped the body. It was some scary shit.


I carried a gun from the age of fourteen to twenty-one, until I got locked up. It was necessary. Guns started popping off everywhere after crack came.

Greed came into play, and when the money would slow up or get low, wars would break out over territory and prices and connects and snitches. Shit just got crazy—people were trying to control their territory and would do whatever they had to do to keep it.

Our neighborhood became nothing but a meat factory—straight butchery. Maniacs running around, sticking up people, popping rounds off every day. Motherfuckers getting shot down in the street. At its worst, people were getting hurt or killed almost every day. A lot of people dying. Park Hill soon got the nickname "Killa Hill."

That's when I started carrying, which was illegal as hell, of course. When you're young, you don't even think about trying to get a registered firearm. Them motherfuckers would've looked at me like I was crazy if I said some sucker shit like that.

But it was always fucking drama on the streets. You know how many times I had to flash or pull my pistol out? Once I had to back a couple guys down who tried to rob me on the A train in Brooklyn.

"Shorty, whatchu got in your pocket? Let me see that hat."

"Nah, man. Dead that." Out would come the .32.

"Oh, a'ight. You got that, shorty, you got that."

"I know I got that! Keep it moving, motherfucker!"

That happened more times than I can count. Dudes would just shrug it off and keep looking for another victim. Not gonna lie, there were a couple times I got caught without my getcha and had to take a few lumps, but overall I got out of most situations with my shit intact, gun or no gun.

There's three stages to flashing a gun: showing the handle in your belt as a threat; pulling the gun out; and finally, cocking the hammer. It usually only took one of the first two steps, but there were times I had to pull the hammer back to tell someone I wasn't fucking around—and I wasn't. Every time I drew my pistol, I was ready to use it, and the next thing you were gonna hear was thunderclaps. The rule in the streets was if you carried a gun and you drew it, you best be ready to use it.

There was a saying back in the day: "I'd rather get caught with my gun than without it." When you got caught with a gun back then, you only did six months in prison. That's why so many people were running around with guns, they figured they could do six months easy. That was nothing. Nowadays, you get caught with a gat, you're doing a three-year stretch.

Fortunately, I don't have to do that anymore. I hire guys with a permit for that now. I know cops who would love to pull that kind of security work. My protection is legal now.

During that era, there were mostly two types of criminals: the hustlers that fed off drug fiends and customers, and the wolves that fed off the hustlers. Usually they robbed drug dealers or drug spots, and that's how they made their money. They let you make it, then they'd come and take it. Pretty simple.

Another one of my peoples came to me with a plan. "Yo, man, I need to get some money. I need to borrow that hammer." So I gave him my nickel-plated .357 with a wooden handle, and off he went to stand by the weed spot.

His plan was to stick up customers at the gate or in front of 160. Dude was holdin' dudes up every day, catching multiple robberies. He was a robbing machine, and motherfuckers would come out of the building on ambulance gurneys with bullet holes in them. Fiends wouldn't give up the money, he'd pop 'em, simple as that.

Let me tell you, if a dude throws a gun in your face, just give him the shit. If somebody got the drop on you, you're getting robbed, so you give them whatever the fuck they want. Simple, plain as that. Don't be a superhero. This isn't reality TV, this shit is real. It's not worth your life, not worth your blood, not worth your hospital bill.

Of course, there was nothing we could really do about this guy, either. First of all, he was part of our growing up. He was a part of the hood. Second, the dreads in the building selling weed in the spot where he was robbing, they were doing illegal shit. Third, like I said, it was a drug-infested fucking area. It was a drug zone, where anything goes.

It just came with the territory. Who you gonna call—the cops? You can't call the cops on motherfuckers, saying I got robbed at the weed spot. You're not supposed to be in there copping weed in the first place. You're not supposed to be coming in buying crack, either. You aren't supposed to be there doing any of that shit. If you wind up getting shot in the course of that, you can't even tell the police that shit happened, so at the end of the day, they can't really do nothing.


As the drug game escalated, the regular little .25s, .22s, and .32s weren't cutting it anymore. I guess crooks still carried them, but they were more used as backup guns or guns to sneak into clubs.

Once things got really violent on the block, fully automatic weapons became the norm. The occasional one-shotter or pistol got overtaken by the omnipresent spray of bullets echoing throughout Park Hill.

It was war. Like for real war, complete with casualties, sanctions, and collateral damage. Just like when countries are warring, we were in an arms race, trying to get our hands on better weaponry than our enemies. TEC-9s were popular at the time. So were Uzis. But the baddest gun out there in Staten Island at the time was this chromed-out MAC-10. I shit you not, this gun was so pretty, it was like the Mona Lisa of automatic weapons.

That gun was legendary. It was used in so many robberies and homicides and who the hell knows what else. Everyone who saw it fell in love with it. It was the prettiest gun you'd ever seen in your life. Imagine the shiniest chrome rims you ever saw, but instead of rims, it was a gun. It sounds weird that an instrument of death can be pretty, but that shit was beautiful, straight up. Something about the power and the gleam of it. This gun was so shiny, it was like looking into a mirror. You could see your reflection in it. Just holding it, feeling that weight in your hands, made you feel invincible. It also made it really hard to get rid of.

It was just too damn sexy to get rid of. People would shoot motherfuckers with it and try to get rid of it, but it would always wind up in somebody else's hands. You'd hear about who had the MAC-10 through the street grapevine. So-and-so caught a robbery with it, or so-and-so shot at the cops with it, or so-and-so caught a body with it. It was crazy because no one wanted to get rid of the gun. Even though it was the dirtiest gun in the hood, people knew it had bodies on it and it was linked to mad robberies and shit, they would still take the gun and hold on to it.

Back in the day, usually if you committed a crime or popped off with a gun, you'd toss it. That way, whatever crimes you committed couldn't be traced back to you. Not this fucking weapon. No one was tossing that pretty little bitch, no matter how much dirt was on it. I saw it with one dude in the hood, then I saw it with this other stick-up kid from the building behind mine. I held it once, and only once. I remember it being light as a feather. Then I wiped my prints off and gave it right back.

Every so often a new gun would come into town from Florida or Virginia, still in its original box, with the cleaning kit and all that shit, but the majority of guns were obtained from janky guys. Real sketchy dudes, so you had to take what you could get. Hell, a couple times I ended up carrying pistols that had been police guns. I had revolvers that had police serial numbers on 'em. That's how grimy New York was.

And you didn't know if the gun in your hand had been used in a murder or robbery, you didn't know anything about that, and you didn't really care. Plus, we were young—I sure didn't know any fuckin' better. Remember, we didn't know anything about registering a firearm. Also, we were black, we weren't gonna get any legal shit done that way anyway.

I didn't care where the gun had been or what it was used for, because it was protection. If I wanted to go to Brooklyn, I needed a hammer to hold me down, 'cause sure as shit I was gonna be robbed in Brooklyn. If you had a coat, or sneakers, or a chain, there was a 90 percent chance you'd get boosted in Brooklyn—that's just how the neighborhood was. It was the Wild West out there—in the dark days Brooklyn alone would post something like a thousand homicides a year.

This was the era of Bernhard Goetz, who was the epitome of what was going on. He knew what everybody knew—everybody was carrying. Dude had gotten robbed so many times that he just got tired of the shit, and ended up shooting four alleged muggers himself. You ride the subway late at night, you're gonna get robbed, it was as simple as that. There were no cops on the subways.

All praise to Dinkins, Giuliani, Bloomberg, 'cause they cleaned that shit up. They shut Forty-second Street down, they came down hard on guns, including pumping up the jail time.

And we recycled guns all the time. I remember after my man popped all those people by 160, he gave me my .357 back. I then loaned it to another dude. The gun was dirty as fuck, but he held that shit down anyway. He needed it because he was out there rocking for me, and dudes from my hood didn't really know him like that. They viewed him as a foreigner. So they got at him while I went uptown to get some more of the raw.

A-Train was supposed to be holding him down, but that didn't happen. The gun I loaned him didn't do him any good, either.

He got shot up in front of 160 and dropped my hammer. They shot him the fuck up and left him blamped up [shot] in the gutter, trying to hold his guts in.

Incredibly, someone else picked the gun up and gave it back to me when I got back on the scene. Can you believe that, like an asshole, I actually took the gun again? Thinking about it now, I can't believe I was so stupid.

Eventually, my .357 saw its last days on the street when my man Shakia asked to borrow it. We were outside as always when the scooter cops rolled up on us. Everybody ran, except for him. I don't know why he didn't run. The cops patted him down, found my burner, and locked him up. That was the last time I saw my chrome .357 or Shakia. To this day, I don't know what happened to him.

Then one day, shit got really weird.

Me and Method Man were chilling in front of the building, doing what we do. The dread that ran the weed spot in 160 came outside. He was pissed because that dude was bringing mad heat to his spot by sticking up and shooting people.

Now this Rastafarian, his name was Fire, was a for real voodoo witch doctor, with dreads down to his ankles. He came downstairs and started smashing bloody cow kidneys against the walls of the building. Just holding them in his hands and whipping them on the walls. It was my first time coming across that voodoo shit, so I didn't know what to think.

"Yo, Fire, what the fuck you doing, dread?"

"Red mon, the fuckin' buildin' is cursed, mon. Too much blood! The buildin' is cursed! Too much blood spilled!" He did his little prayer and said some other shit, I have no idea what he said. Then he went upstairs. When he came back down again, he had a bowl of candies in his hand.

"Red mon, take the candy and eat it. No demon spirits can touch you in front of this buildin', mon. Nothin'. No one, not even police."

I took the candy, a red Jolly Rancher. Not sure if it worked or not, but here I am still to this day. I made it out from those buildings, and I can think of more than a few situations when I was supposed to have been blamped up. I didn't believe that shit until a couple things happened that made me think twice.

The first situation was late night, probably at like two in the morning. We called that time from one to four the "scary hours." Now, I don't like scary hours. There's still fiends comin' through, but those are still scary fuckin' hours; it's dark, it's pitch black, dudes would get robbed, you could get shot in the back of your fuckin' head for your package. Stickup kids would wanna shoot you; hell, fiends would rob you, shoot you for what you had 'cause they needed their fix.

Anyway, it's during the hours when nobody but the crazies are out and about. We're still trying to get money, but we should have known better, because it's dangerous at this time. So we have our burners stashed up and down the block.

There wasn't a soul out on the streets. Me and Meth are in the hallway. We hear something. A whistle from below us.

"Ay yo, who dat?" we called out.

No answer. I decide to creep down a few stairs and look around to see if anyone's in the dark down there. I did a silent ninja jump down to the landing. When I peeked around the corner real quick, there's three dudes with masks and guns sitting there, waiting to rob us. When I peeked out a second time to get another look, one of them saw me. He ran at me and pulled out his gun. I jumped to the first landing, and as I was about to run the rest of the flight up, he pulled the trigger. It clicked, but didn't fire. I laughed a crazy, triumphant laugh 'cause his gun jammed, then jetted up the stairs and took off with Meth.

Another situation was when we were at war with some dudes. I'd just come home from my first bid, and upon my return these outsiders from Queens were trying to act like we can't sell in our own projects, outside of our building. We didn't care, though, we still had to hustle.

So I was out there doing my thing when this dude who was known for busting his gun comes running up from across the street. He pulls the .45 out and tries to blamp me. Somehow, the clip falls out of the fucking gun. We both looked at the clip on the ground and before he could look up at me, I took off.

As I ran, I thought about the dread who gave me the candy and said I was protected from any evil in front of my building. Did his black magic prevent me from getting murdered? I'll never know for sure.

People might think Staten Island is the boonies, but it's far from it. The amount of traffic we had coming through those buildings back in the eighties was insane. We'd be in the hallways in 160 of course, but also in 141, which was like Grand Central station with the foot traffic. You could make some serious motherfucking money in an hour, I kid you not.

One forty-one was crazy, because you came into the building though the front, like you would 160. It had long corridors down both sides, at least a hundred yards long. Not sure if that was intended when they designed it, but we used that to our advantage to scope the cops coming. To make it even better, the exits had slam locks and couldn't be opened from the outside.

When the cops would blitz 141—which was pretty often, considering most of this drug war shit meant getting low-level drug dealers doing hand-to-hand and direct sales. Since we locked the back doors, they always had to come through that front door all the way at the far end of that corridor. All of them would come running in all funneled together and shit, tripping over each other's shoes. The only other option was to come in through a door on the side of the building because it didn't have a lock on it. But because of that, you could still see them coming if you were inside the building, and you had plenty of time to get away.

I'll never forget this one fucking time. Me and one of my project homies, we were up early. It was about 7 A.M., and we wanted to catch the morning rush. That was what we used to call it when the functioning addicts would cop a morning fix before they went to work. We had to lock in and be on point for them.

So you'd go to the store first, and get your bagels or turkey with Swiss or whatever breakfast. You eat that outside, and then you go into the hallway and you post up with your package. We had three different stash houses we'd run to in the building. Once we're done, you not gonna find us. I probably had about eight thousand dollars' worth of shit on me. All in a big-ass Ziploc bag like the reckless teenager I was, with a heart as big as New York City.

We were playing the west side of the building, watching the fiends coming in, make the corner, and then we serve them at the end of that hallway. No one *ever* left out the fucking back. We made them go right back out the way they came in, so no cops could gain access.

It was a busy morning as usual, so I didn't have a chance to keep track of my bread while I was making sales. Me and my homey were in the hallway just getting it, money's just rolling in hand over fist. Now keep in mind that he's doing his thing and I'm doing mine—we weren't partners or business associates or anything like that, we were just two dudes slinging in the same building. But there was so much traffic coming through, we didn't even have to cut each other's throats for sales.

After a bit of a slowdown, I decide to count my money. I got a bag stuffed full of bills. I'm counting the dough, straightening it all out so it's neat and there's less chance you'll drop some money or give someone the wrong change. But every so often, you have to keep looking up to make sure the cops aren't blitzing the building. You have to keep looking up. You *have* to. That's a part of the hustle—you can't drop your guard for shit. Not for one second.

Counting. Looking up. Counting. Looking up. Counting. Looking up. I finished counting my money. I looked up. Coast is still clear. I decide to take inventory of the Ziploc with my remaining work. I looked at what's left, and I was down to my last little bit. I must have had like two vials left out of eight thousand dollars' worth of shit. When I held it up to estimate how much was left, one of 'em fell to the floor. Just that one vial fell to my feet. I glance down the corridor again before leaning over to scoop it up. Nobody was coming.

Don't you know, soon as I dropped my eyes to pick the shit up, I looked back up again and police were flying at us through the gates at high velocity. Running full fucking blast down the corridor toward me and my homey. I got this big fucking bag, I got about eight grand in my hand.

Everything went in slow motion. I could see their eyes looking at the Ziploc of crack in my hand. They see it clear as day from the look on their faces. There was no stashing on them this time. We had to run. The *Chariots of Fire* theme song went off in my head, and we were out up the stairs.

I slid off, I took out the remaining two vials, swallowed them shits in my mouth as I'm running up the stairs, the police on my tail. I come around the corner of the staircase, and BAM!—the eight grand flies out of my hand all over the goddamn stairs. The police, soon as they saw the bills fly everywhere, those motherfuckers stopped dead in their tracks.

So, I'm going up the stairs. I dropped the eight Gs on the floor. *Boom.* They thought I was gonna leave it and keep going. Oh, hell, no!

I turned back around and started scooping up all my money off the floor. The two police officers didn't do anything—they just sat there and watched me collect eight fucking grand from the floor. To this day, I still don't know why they didn't bust a move on me right then and there, but they didn't. I just took the shit and put it in my pockets and walked upstairs to my other fucking spot. They didn't do shit. That's when I got on the radar. But they still really never bothered me, even after that.

We get to the house we used sometimes to escape and slipped in quietly. After a few moments, we heard mad walkie-talkies from the cops still running around. The crackhead who lived in the apartment came out from the back. When she saw us and heard the cops in the hallway, she knew the deal and just shut her face. We gave her a few cracks, and she got high while we waited for a couple hours.

We left the crackhead's apartment and ventured out. Cops were gone. The fiend threw our stash out the window to us, and we went right back to pumping for the never-ending stream of fiends in front of 141.

Although we made mad stacks at 141, eventually it got too hot for us, and we had to move our operation to 160.

Deck's mom was an angel; she used to hold us down like that at 160, too. There was many a time I'd be tearing ass up the stairs with the cops a few flights behind me. I ran to Deck's crib, knowing he wasn't home. I'd knock real quick and walk in.

"Hi, Miss Hunter. Is Jason home?"

"No, he's out right now. I actually thought he was with you."

"Maybe we missed each other. Listen, the police are chasing me, but I didn't do anything, though. Can I stay here for a minute?"

"Stay as long as you'd like."

She saved my life a few times that way. In a regular community, harboring a suspect running from the law might seem like the wrong thing to do, but not in most projects. Most of our neighbors were okay with letting us hide out for a while. You had certain doors that you knew was open in the building. In every building, I would have somebody's apartment to run to. Each building I went past in the projects, I said, "Okay. Mrs. So-and-so is in there. Mrs. So-and-so is in the building." Why? Because that's where I grew up at. They knew I'd hit them off with some cash, or they'd known me since I was a kid, and they just loved me.

Most of them were used to the drama anyway, because there was always something happening on the block. There's just too many different personalities all crammed into one restricted living space for things to ever be chill for very long. You just had to be on point for whatever the day might bring. Cops might blitz. Stickup kids might try to jack you. A jonesin' fiend might flip out. You just never knew.

There was some funny shit that would go down in the midst of all that carnage. Like this one time, this fiend approached me and Meth while we were selling. He didn't have any cash, but he wanted two dimes of crillz (crack) in exchange for a sheet of acid with a picture of a skull and crossbones. Meth figured it was a good trade, so he did it. I said, "Man, you are fuckin' crazy!"

He took a few tabs and offered me one. I declined the offer, saying, "I ain't trying nothing with a poison sign on it!" and continued serving fiends. Pretty soon Meth starts feeling the acid, he starts tripping and crawls into some bushes.

Meanwhile, the stash was getting low, so I decided to head uptown to get some more. I went all the way uptown to Harlem, which takes about three hours round trip. I saw the connect, got what I needed, and came all the way back to Staten Island. When I got back, Meth was still in the bushes. A three-hour mission, and upon my return he was still in the bushes. I was like, "What the fuck? This dude's out of his goddamn mind."

I went over to him and asked, "You all right?"

He looked up at me. "Nah . . . I ain't all right . . ." Whatever effect that drug had on him, it had him stuck in the bushes.

I grabbed him to pull him out of there, but then he took off like a shot down the block. I had to literally chase this mother-fucker down, laughing the whole time. We got around the corner, got some water into him, tried to flush that shit out of his system. I told him, "Yo, man, don't ever take that shit while you're hustlin'!"

Just another day in the projects.

9.

ENTER THE WU-TANG

Through the peak years of hustling and partying and getting fresh, we never lost focus. Most people don't realize that the Wu-Tang Clan was eight years in the making. We were hungry to be creating, focusing on our art, while other Escobar-emulating motherfuckers were running ten keys.

My friends all felt the same way I did. RZA, Raekwon, Ghost, Meth, we all had one thing in common: we wanted to be stars. We wanted to be fucking rappers, to get our music out, make money and be rich and famous, and we wanted out of the fucking ghetto *immediately*.

Didn't know how we were gonna do it. Didn't know how it was gonna happen, but for some reason, we just always knew it was gonna happen. I just always knew, and Meth knew, and Rae knew. We were all certain, we just *knew*. That's why we were able to do what we had to do, 'cause we were all going in the same direction toward the same goal.

Besides, by this time I was nineteen and tired of the game. It didn't help that dudes were falling like flies in the drug game, either. I was trying to get off the streets entirely. I was still in school, but looking for something more than even what college had to offer as a way off the block. Music turned out to be the vessel that took me and my cohorts away from the ghetto violence we grew up around.

---

Ever since the Baby Crash Crew, we were always rhyming and making up little songs together. That didn't change when we started hustling in front of the buildings of Park Hill.

At the time, I wasn't really rhyming seriously yet, but I was the beatbox guy in the hallway for other dudes to get their own shit off. It was nothing for me to beatbox for people, because that got me my rhythm, which gave me certain things, like beat coordination as well as improved physical coordination, that other motherfuckers didn't have.

I'd beatbox for Cappadonna and Raekwon while they caught wreck. When RZA came along, we started taking our beats and rhymes more seriously. I already knew him as the DJ from the Stapleton block party. By 1989, he'd moved out of his mother's place and got his own apartment, which was actually his family's old apartment that he sublet from his mother (in the city, once you get an apartment, you *never* let it go). He'd also moved away from DJing and started making his own beats. He was getting serious about the rap game, and so were we.

The nights I got tired of ducking the cops and dealing with junkies and stashing guns around where we were posted up and keeping an eye out for any potential drama that might pop up— those were the nights I'd go to RZA's place. Even though it was in Stapleton, another project just like ours, when we were at his crib, we didn't have to worry about all the shit going on back in Park Hill. We could concentrate on what really mattered: our music.

I'd walk into his building and take the elevator up to his floor. You could hear the beats and smell the weed before you even stepped into the hallway. The door was never locked at RZA's joint. Stapleton apartments were like that. First off, there's not much to steal, but also, who's gonna try anything up in RZA's pad with an endless cycle of hood-ass, slanging-ass, gun-toting individuals coming in and out all day?

Now, I was still hustlin', so I'd walk in wearing all fly shit, new sneakers. I was strapped back then, so I'd take out my gun and put it on the glass table near where Ghost would usually be sitting. RZA, on the other hand, wasn't hustlin' like that, so when I came on looking fresh, he'd be smelling like a goddamn onion. We used to call him "RZA Radish" back then, 'cause he never wore deodorant.

We'd bring our forties and weed and whatever else and just write and rap and listen to beats and build for hours and hours. RZA's brew back then was Brass Monkey, a premixed cocktail of dark rum, vodka, and orange juice. Ghostface and RZA were living together at the time, so they'd be eating ramen noodles and watching kung fu flicks. For a while, those two were like me and Meth, on some Dynamic Duo shit. RZA and Ghost would just be in that crib all day long, eatin' Oodles of Noodles, watching kung fu movies, and making beats on a little four-track recorder.

I'd walk in and the beats would be blasting. Dudes would bring the mic cord out onto the terrace and be rhyming. Sounds fancy, but it's far from it. Like I said, the Stapleton 'jects looked like jail facilities. The terraces looked like the tiers in prison. But we'd have the mike out there, and weed be blowin', and the Brass Monkey be flowin', and everybody was just getting high and throwing darts (rapping). It was a getaway from the drama, a way to transcend our surroundings and the day-to-day grind.

RZA's crib was our first studio, and that four-track was our first real equipment. That was our lab. When you have a whole bunch of possessions you don't do anything with, you don't have anything. When you got that one piece of machinery that you really master, though, that enhances your art. A lot of motherfuckers don't know how or don't have the discipline to just stay right there, in that chamber, until you've mastered it. They move on too soon, and lose that potential mastery and end up losing themselves altogether. That's the struggle of being an artist. You can't keep coming out with the same shit, but you can't lose yourself, either.

With RZA's four-track, we kept making bangers. At the end of the night we'd leave his place with a tape of what we'd done. We'd go back to Park Hill, listen to our songs, and critique our shit more. We'd compare ourselves to other people and their verses and just sharpen one another's steel. Then we'd write even more rhymes to improve our lyrics, some of us working harder on it than others. Meth was really working on it harder than other dudes.

One night, while working on one of our first original Wreck Posse cuts, "I Get Down for My Crown," Meth wrote a verse from which a portion would later be used by Ghost on one of his biggest hits, "Cherchez La Ghost."

Once Meth laid this verse down, I went into my rhyme books and put down my verse, and Deck came behind us and laid down the last verse. RZA even sampled the flushing toilet and added the sound effect to the joint as well. It was the first song that we laid down and felt good about as a group.

Back then we would dub tapes and pass them off to other brothers in the hood. That's how you used to do it back in the day, you'd make a bunch of tapes and pass 'em around the project, and it would spread through word of mouth.

Next thing you know, everybody in our fucking neighborhood had the shit. Then that person would take it to another project, and someone there would take the shit and listen to it and they'd dub it and take it to another project. Next thing you know, everyone in the 'jects was jamming "I Get Down for My Crown."

That song right there was an epiphany. We noticed when we did our first couple of songs together, they came out kinda hot. Meth, Deck, and me did a couple of other songs during the early days of fucking around with RZA, like "Let Me Put My Two Cents

In." We were EPMD babies and Public Enemy babies, Big Daddy Kane babies and Rakim babies. We just incorporated all that into our early little sounds. We would record 'em on tapes and listen to them and critique ourselves.

Once we got on those beats, when I first heard my voice over the music on tape, it seemed like the dream was even closer to being real, like it was something tangible that we could touch. 'Cause we weren't just rhyming and beatboxing in the project hallways anymore, we were actually laying down vocals now. And even though we were still wildin' in the streets, that dream of music saved us from getting too far gone.

Once we got a taste of hood success, RZA kept recording more joints. Deck put down a solo joint called "This Ain't Your Average Flow." That joint was crazy good, and it became a hood anthem.

When we started going to RZA's on the regular, we started seeing who the MCs really were. Here comes Rae getting on a song. Then Genius is up there. And here's Ol' Dirty, who RZA said was his cousin. ODB and GZA were both RZA's family, and they'd come through our hood fairly often. In fact, GZA lived in Park Hill for a little while with his family before they dipped to Brooklyn. They'd come see RZA in Stapleton, then they'd all come up to the Hill to smoke and drink and rhyme. Every so often we'd take a break from hustling to join them. RZA's place was a sanctuary.

It was there that a whole team of dudes, some I knew well, some I'd only met once or twice, came together to form something that would never be duplicated in rap history. A crew with similar upbringings and perspectives, but radically different ways of conveying their individual viewpoints. That was the genesis of the Wu-Tang Clan.


Around this time, some of us were already attracting attention from New York record labels. Warner Bros. signed Genius under their Cold Chillin' label and released *Words from the Genius* in 1991. RZA also did a joint, as Prince Rakeem, with Warners under their Tommy Boy imprint and released the *Ooh I Love You Rakeem* EP in '91.

I thought we were really on when RZA and GZA got their individual record deals. When that happened, we thought it was about to just happen for all of us. The industry had other ideas, though. RZA and GZA ended up flopping because their labels were trying to make them something they weren't. Both of them had bangers on their albums, but the CC execs went with "Come Do Me" for Genius. At Tommy Boy, they settled on the "Ooh I Love You Rakeem" single. It was obvious the labels were trying to re-create the success of artists like Big Daddy Kane and Eric B. & Rakim.

That's got to be the worst feeling in the world—being an artist with no real creative control over your art. Labels at that time were trying to get that crossover popping. They wanted something that took the grit out and made their music a little more accessible to the mainstream. A record about having mad girls or inviting hoes to fuck was the label's idea of what could make them money. They passed up on two of the illest lyricists that ever rapped because they were trying to fit them into a box that was all wrong for them.

When their deals went south, RZA and GZA both came back to the hood. We'd all been sharpening our swords all along, ready for any opportunity. We were beyond ready when RZA came and got his wolves. He knew we were where it was at. We kept rhyming over RZA's beats and building our skills. It started coming together really well. The core members started formulating and conspiring on songs together. It started from humble beginnings; the recording started off real small. Then, gradually, dudes started putting in work, putting in work, putting in work. RZA and GZA took what we were doing and enhanced it.

Unfortunately, some guys who should have gotten in at the ground level of the Wu-Tang got taken out of the game before they could even get started. Cappadonna was one who, if things hadn't gone the way they did, might have played an even bigger part in the formation of the Wu.

His rhyme style was amazing, really ahead of its time. I remember this talent show/rap battle that was going down at the Wave. Cappa destroyed everybody to win that battle; even RZA and GZA were no match. He just ate everybody. He melted the mic that day, rapping over "Impeach the President." GZA, RZA, and Dirty didn't stand a chance. It was Cap's hood, plus he was rhyming about shit that people from that hood could relate to. All his references were Park Hill related. I was right there with him. The crowd was unanimous in its choice.

Then Cappadonna got locked up. He was in front of the building one day, and this dude called Boo-Yay ran past him with the cops chasing him and dropped a package at Cappa's feet. The cops ran down on Cap and pinned the drugs on him. It really wasn't his stuff—the cops locked him up for somebody else's shit. That's why he said in one of his rhymes, "They locked me up. / They said it was mine, but it was Boo-Yay's stuff." Cappa wound up doing three years for a crime he didn't commit.

That shit fucked me up. Me and Cappadonna used to hang out pretty much every day. He was the rapper to my beatbox, my rhyme partner. Knowing he was innocent didn't help instill any faith in the justice system. The hood was like that a lot, though. There was so much wrong shit going on all the time, the chances of being caught in the wrong place at the wrong time were pretty good.

When Cappa went to jail, I had to move on with my life. I started going down to Stapleton more with Method Man to see RZA. Years later, when Cappa came home from prison, he got caught up in some other shit charges and got sent back. Altogether,

I think the system took eight years of his life. Because of that, he missed getting on *36 Chambers* entirely.

I became an adult while he was locked up. That's just how that is. You come home after being away for a few years, dudes are different. I'm driving a car. I got big gold chains on. He didn't even know we were going down to RZA's house and recording. People didn't know we were doing any of that shit at the time.

But they were about to find out.

## 10.

## TURBULENCE

To this day, more than twenty-five years later, I wish I'd never gone uptown in the summer of 1991. I was twenty years old.

It all started one afternoon with one of my dealers: "Yo, I need this package, bruh! I'm losing customers."

"Damn, I just came from uptown yesterday. Why didn't you see me then? You know how fast shit's going right now."

"I didn't have all the bread, right? Just hold me down. Go see your man."

"He's not around today. I'd have to see someone else."

"Do that, then. For me, bruh. I need this."

So I headed back uptown to hold dudes down. Again. This time, though, I fucked around and went outside my connect, and this guy hit me with a bunch of wack-ass pharmaceutical shit. When it came back, it wasn't what it was supposed to be. I remember getting so pissed, mostly because I should've known better than to fuck with these dudes in the first place.

So I grabbed the burner. I don't know why, I guess I can only attribute it to being angry, but I also grabbed the crack to show the bullshit connect it didn't cook up right. Dumb, dumb, dumb.

Me and this dude Mitch hopped in the Pathfinder and drove uptown. I spot the guy who sold me the bad coke on the block right away. His name was Jesus. I pulled up on him. My original plan had been to hop out the Pathfinder, give him the shitty crack, get my money, and then give him the bullet.

I hopped out. "Yo, you ain't right. You know that shit you sold me was garbage. Gimme back my money!"

"Nah, man, I—"

"YO! Don't play with me, dawg. You 'bout to catch a hot one. Now gimme back my bread!"

"O-o-o-okay. Wait here, I'm just going to the stash upstairs."

Mitch was talking to me from inside the whip, trying to get me to chill. I'm halfway to getting in a right mind-set and realizing what the fuck I'm doing is stupid. Next thing I know, the cops have surrounded the car. The scumbag connect who I copped that bullshit from ended up calling the police on me!

Now, I knew the deal. Whenever you get knocked, you keep your mouth *shut*. You don't say shit, 'cause *everything* you say will be used against you. Not until you've seen your lawyer or Legal Aid. It's not easy for some people, though. People get jammed up, and right away they get mad nervous. If you're doing dirt, you got to keep a cool head. Can't fall for that bullpen therapy, getting jostled from holding cell to holding cell while the cops scare you about how much time you're gonna get. A lot of people get shook, and try to get chummy with the cops, and end up saying more than they need to say.

They tried to flip me, too, of course. Basically, they wanted me to tell on all the other drug dealers uptown. I was like, "For what? For what? To get out of my time and then I'll be caught up in all your little snitch shit and all this other shit for the rest of my life? Get the fuck outta here." I copped out to the first thing that they gave me—I knew I was guilty, so why would I take it to trial?

Let me tell you something; people are always talking about snitching. But in order to be a snitch, you've got to actually see a motherfucker do something with your own fucking eyes. You've got to literally have it done in front of your eyeballs in order for you to know what's really going on. Nowadays motherfuckers go by what somebody else said or what somebody else think they said. I got a problem with that because I'm from an era where, "Nah, man. I didn't see that dude do shit because I didn't see him do it with my own eyes." Fabrication is a motherfucker. "Oh, shit, yo, I heard this . . . I heard that . . . I heard this . . ." If you didn't see it with your own eyes, shut the fuck up. Just stop it. You got to see it with your own eyes for you to even be a part of the equation.

It turned out that my man Mitch said more than he needed to and ended up implicating himself—I found that out when I saw his statement later on. I'm a stand-up dude, and he knew that. If I get caught doing something and I was doing it, I'm taking the charges. I'm not going to have my man who was riding with me all jammed up in my shit. I know what I'm into. I know the risks. I'm gonna handle it by myself. My word is Bond, as stated in Degree 1-11: "Have you not learned that your word shall be Bond regardless of whom or what? Answer: My word is Bond, and Bond is my life, and I will give my life before my word shall fail."

So I took the rap, saying as little as possible in the statement. Mitch was going home anyway. He knew he didn't have to say shit to the cops. But that bullpen therapy is a motherfucker, and he talked.

I also learned a big lesson when I spoke about my case with my lawyer. It turned out that *everything* I said to the court-appointed Legal Aid defense attorney while I was behind bars would be used against me. Unless you already have your lawyer on deck, it's unlikely you'll be able to contact him in a timely fashion, as the police don't have to give you a phone call.

So, like most people in jail, I was anxious to see a lawyer, so when the Legal Aid lawyer called my name, I talked to him. The Legal Aid lawyers all work for the city. Whatever I said was supposed to be used by him to help my case. But if you fire the dude, he'll turn over the file to the same officer who arrested you!

Anyway, as far as I could tell, he ended up turning everything I said over to the D.A. From that experience, I learned it's best to not say shit *ever*. To *anyone*. If you get a Legal Aid lawyer, just tell him, "Get me bail, or get me the fuck outta here." Don't tell him what happened, don't tell him *anything*. Get your bail set, or your R.O.R. (released on your own recognizance), and just talk to your own lawyer. Don't tell cops *or* Legal Aid shit, because anything you say will be used against you in court. I can't stress that enough.

Basically, it's the police's job to lie and try to stack as many charges up against you as they can, even if those charges have nothing to do with your original case, in hopes of making *something* stick to you. Your lawyer's job is to knock each lie, each charge down. And if you don't have the money to pay a good lawyer, you're fucked. The public defenders don't have the time or the focus to really work on your case.

This is why there's such a divide between the public and the police. I respect the cops—I'm a grown-ass man, I want to respect the cops, but how can I when they don't respect me back? It has to go both ways. I know too many people who went to jail on trumped-up charges and lost eight or ten years of their life before they got an appeal and got back out. And they can't get that time or money back—it's gone forever.

So if you're guilty—or even if you're not—and you don't have the resources to fight it, if you get jammed up in that kind of situation, it's often not worth going to trial because they'll railroad you either way. They'll nail you, and you'll spend the rest of your life trying to file an appeal, which you also can't afford. And if you're guilty, you might as well take the plea—take the first offer they give you, and handle that shit the best way you can. Because you won't be able to get out of it in a trial. The courts will chew you up and shit you out right into prison.

But there's always some dumb motherfucker who thinks they're so goddamn clever, they can outsmart the court. It *never* happens. One of my peoples from Brooklyn—his name is Blizz—got it in his mind that we needed a professional mixing board to do some recording shit.

So this motherfucker went to a studio, tied up the two dudes that were there, stole the mixing board and put it and the two dudes all in a U-Haul truck. The guys he tied up got free and called the cops. He got caught with them and the board on FDR Drive and got locked up for grand larceny, kidnapping, and some other shit.

Blizz was a repeat offender who'd just gotten out after doing three to six years. Even with that and all the new charges, they offered him a plea bargain of eight years. But that wasn't good enough for him, so he took it to fucking trial—and blew up his sentence to thirty fucking years. He thought he was so smart he could outsmart the courts.

Another guy I met in my cell in Manhattan House. He told me how he was taking his case to trial, and was already facing thirty years. Now, at that time, he looked like me, just a regular young man.

Fast-forward two and a half years; I ran into him again as I was coming out and he was coming in. Dude had blown his trial, got sixty years. Now, his whole head—face, hair, everything—had turned stone gray. Last time I saw him, he'd looked just like me, good skin, jet-black hair, just another brother in the system. Thirty months later, he'd turned ash gray from everything he'd gone through.

The most important thing I learned from reflecting on that experience is that like most people, I make bad decisions when I'm angry. I got angry once and made a decision that cost me my freedom, and I'm still dealing with its consequences more than twenty-five years later.

Who in their right mind would travel with crack and a gun to a coke block in Harlem? I didn't need to bring the package back to the connect. But I was so angry I just wanted to grandstand on him a little bit before I plugged him. Now the cops had me on a weapons charge *and* criminal possession of a controlled substance. Dumb, dumb, dumb.

Back then, a gun charge would only get you six months on Rikers. That's where the whole "I'd rather get caught with a gun than without one" mind-set came in. We had guns on us like it was part of our uniform. However, "metal attracts metal": In other words, cops knew when you were carrying by the way you walked. If I wasn't holding heat, the cops would glide on by. If I was holding, they would do a U-turn and roll back up on me. That's when I had to run.

I could've been home in six months. But because I got caught with a controlled substance as well, I had to cop out to a one-to-three for possession. I copped out because I was guilty. I'm not stupid: I was carrying a gun; I was holding drugs. Just gimme the deal, and I won't waste your time.

They actually wanted me to go to trial, where if I was convicted, I could wind up doing five to fifteen. There was no way I'd go that route. "I committed the crime, I'm guilty, what's the offer?" When you're *not* guilty, that's when you take it to trial. But I'm not stupid, so I pled out and got the one-to-three. If I hadn't taken that, the next offer would have been two to four years. You do the math. The police wanted to put me away for the whole fifteen if they could, but I wasn't gonna give 'em the satisfaction.

Even then, I was lucky to get busted where I did. The crazy shit about Manhattan, it was more lenient with coke charges than Staten Island. Staten Island will bury you with any type of drug shit. That's why I *never* got locked up on Staten Island. I got locked up uptown in Harlem. That's why I only got a one-to-three for three and a half ounces of coke and the gun. If I'd gotten caught on Staten Island, I probably would've done two to four years. Maybe five.

While I was at home waiting for sentencing, things almost got worse. In order to pay my lawyer, pay for my bail, and pay my everyday bills, I was posted up in front of 160 hustling harder than normal. I knew I had to get money since I was going away for a bit.

This motherfucking fiend Dupreme came up on me around the building, asked me for some shit. At the same time, he dropped a stem on the ground, and before I can blink, *woop woop*—the cops pull up.

I had the pack in the toe of my sneaker. Not a crazy amount, but coupled with my standing case, it's enough to send me away for a good while.

"What're you doing out here?"

"Just waiting for my girl."

"Bullshit. You're coming down to the precinct. We're gonna strip search you." They bagged both of us. My heart dropped down to my stomach. But I was cool. I didn't panic, I just played it smooth.

We get down to the precinct, and they're searching through my clothes as I take them off. They're turning my sweater and coat inside out looking for something, anything.

"Take off your sneakers."

I thought I was done for. I sat down and took off my sneaker, but the bomb was so wedged in there, it just stayed stuck up front. Off straight instinct, I shoved the sneaks right under his nose. He turned away, and I chuckled like I was enjoying putting my funky, hustled-in-all-day shoes in his face.

"Drop them on the floor," he said.

I dropped them on the floor and by the grace of God, nothing fell out. I kicked them to the side and took the rest of my clothes off.

"A'ight, get your clothes and those funky-ass sneakers of yours and get the fuck outta here." I grabbed my shit, they wrote me a little summons for loitering in front of the building, and I bounced. When I got out, I ran my ass off to the cabstand and got the fuck outta there.

Later I saw Dupri, who had gotten locked up with me, and who, I found out later, had ratted on me in the first place. "Yo, God? What'd you do with that crack? I thought the cops had you for sure!"

I just looked at him like, "Yo, you a fucking idiot." I took my shoe off and peeled the crack from the front of my shoe.

When he saw it, he was like, "Daaaamn, God! I cannot fucking believe you still got the shit! You are the luckiest motherfucker ever in the whole fucking world!"

I couldn't help thinking about the Rasta who'd given me that candy. He'd said nothing could harm me in front of the building or in it. The cops had overlooked the crack. Maybe the voodoo shit was real. Either way, I figured I'd best stop pushing my luck.

On April 17, 1992, I was convicted of criminal possession of a controlled substance.

When I got charged, I had to turn myself in. The judge said I had to come back and be remanded. That's a fucked-up feeling, when you know you have to walk into court and you're going to jail. People were telling me not to report to the judge, that instead I should just go on the run.

That's some bullshit. You can't run from shit in life, especially if you're gonna be living the street life. You have to accept that there's gonna be dues you have to pay for making fast money. All that money you're making and jewels you're flossing (showing off ) comes with a price. Those dues come in the form of robber-ies, death, and, of course, jail. I figured if I just did my time now, I'd get out fast enough. Probably one of the smarter decisions I've ever made.

And the really crazy shit, looking back on it now, even with all the trouble it caused me, in the end I'm kinda glad I got locked up. I feel the Lord was intervening on my behalf, working in his mysterious way to get me off the streets before I slipped into be-coming a true Savage. He always had bigger plans for me, that's how I always looked at it.

But at the time, I remember feeling like I had no idea what was going to happen to me. If I was going to make it out of this okay, I had to pay real close attention so I could learn how to go to jail, how to bid and come out the other side in one piece.

11.

## ON THE INSIDE

Before I entered Manhattan House of Detention, I'd never been to real jail before, at least, not for any longer than a week. As much shit as I did on Staten Island, I never got locked up out there. I got arrested once in Harlem, when I went to go plug the connect who gave me the bad coke, and another time when I got caught in Times Square with the stolen whip from the Africans and did the weekend in the Tombs. That was small shit compared to this.

I had to learn the jail scene in a hurry, though, because that was going to be my reality for the next year at least. Of course it was tough at first. Your first time in jail, you don't really know how to bid. I didn't know anything about touching the phones or how to earn respect from the dudes controlling the yard. I had to learn all that shit fast.

Prison is by no means like it's shown in the movies, but I learned so much about human beings there. My time behind bars was a really insightful look into the human mind and spirit. There's no school like jail. Everything is stripped away. You can't hide behind your guns or your hood or your crew or your clothes or even your rep. You're gonna get tested, and you better have the right answers, or it's curtains for the rest of your bid. When I was in there, that's exactly what it was like.

I didn't like those Manhattan House motherfuckers I was with. They were too boozy and soft, just a bunch of sucker-asses. They had strayed into being Savages, as stated in Degree 1-2: "Why did Mussa [aka Moses] have a hard time civilizing the devil in 200 B.C.? Answer: Because he was a Savage. A Savage is a person who has lost knowledge of himself and is living a beast way of life. Civilize means to teach knowledge, wisdom, and understanding to the human family of the planet earth."

Now, me being a civilized man in jail, that's what the Supreme Mathematics did for me. Being that I had knowledge of self, it kept me from being a Savage in pursuit of happiness.

That wasn't going to stop the Savages from banging into you, but it also made you aware of what you were dealing with. You were dealing with a person who was an 85 percenter: dumb, deaf, and blind. A slave to mental deafness and power, who did not know himself, did not know who he was, didn't have any teachings, and was ignorant to himself. Who was locked in mental bondage, stripped of his own language and identity. He did not know that, so that's why he was living a beastful way of life. Those in the hood who don't have knowledge of self and who don't really know themselves can also stray into that self-destructive mentality, because knowledge of the self helps you and prevents you from becoming a Savage.

Having 5 Percenter knowledge put me on a different wavelength. When you get your degrees and become a 5 Percenter, you deal with refinement. That's part of the culture, it's called power and refinement. That means that you have the power to do shit, but you also gotta be refined, which means you gotta be clean—your drawers, your mouth, your hair, your nails are well done, and your sneakers are clean. Everything is good. You ain't walking around all bummy, smellin' like a derelict, robbin' motherfuckers, doin' stupid shit, and not taking care of yourself.

But I learned things inside jail, too. They put me in both anger management classes and Narcotics Anonymous meetings. Both of those programs served their purpose, because they made me realize certain things about myself and my relationships both to my anger and to drugs.

Now, as a dealer, I didn't feel like I had any addiction to drugs in a user sense. And because I wasn't a user, I argued with my drug counselors all the time, like, "Why the fuck am I even here?" But once they pointed out that I would hit the streets and start slinging again as soon as I got out, I heard what they were laying down. The program helped me to realize that I was addicted to the money from the drug trade. The twelve steps of NA really helped me to see my addiction to drug money for what it was, and how it was controlling my life:

1. We admitted that we were powerless over our addiction—that our lives had become unmanageable.
2. We came to believe that a Power greater than ourselves could restore us to sanity.
3. We made a decision to turn our will and our lives over to the care of God as we understood Him.
4. We made a searching and fearless moral inventory of ourselves.
5. We admitted to God, to ourselves, and to another human being the exact nature of our wrongs.
6. We were entirely ready to have God remove all these defects of character.
7. We humbly asked Him to remove our shortcomings.
8. We made a list of all persons we had harmed and became willing to make amends to them all.
9. We made direct amends to such people wherever possible, except when to do so would injure them or others.

10. We continued to take personal inventory and when we were wrong promptly admitted it.

11. We sought through prayer and meditation to improve our conscious contact with God as we understood Him, praying only for knowledge of His will for us and the power to carry that out.

12. Having had a spiritual awakening as the result of these steps, we tried to carry this message to addicts, and to practice these principles in all our affairs.

Same with the anger management program. I know I probably would have seriously fucked someone up or killed someone if I hadn't learned how to approach situations I found myself in differently. The steps of this program go along similar lines as the twelve-step program from NA:

1. Think before you speak
2. Once you're calm, express your anger
3. Get some exercise
4. Take a timeout
5. Identify possible solutions
6. Stick with "I" statements
7. Don't hold a grudge
8. Use humor to release tension
9. Practice relaxation skills
10. Know when to seek help

Both of these programs set me on a very different path as to how I would handle situations in the future, which I'm grateful for, because my life would have turned out very differently if I hadn't gotten control of myself. Once again, once I had that knowledge of self (to know thyself), I was able to use that to move forward and better myself.

But as soon as I walked into Manhattan House, dudes were getting fucked up. One guy got hit in the face and blood was spilling all over the place. I just shook my head and took my blanket and my belongings into my cell.

The next day, I wanted to touch the phone, but they were all taken. I quickly learned I had to make my calls early in the morning, when everyone was still sleeping. Even that first day, though, I saw people get beat up and cut for the phones. That link to the outside world was vital to a lot of people. I realized this was gonna be a problem. Can't front, I was more than a little stressed about the phone situation.

People in jail are always getting moved around, though. Some thugs got moved, so I tried to get their slot time—a certain time of day that you've made clear to everyone is your time to be on the phone—but some dude pulled out a razor and chumped me for the phone. I was shocked, completely taken aback. I wasn't ready for all that. It kind of threw me off balance, so I just backed down.

But then this older dude showed me how to handle that type of situation. The guy who pulled his blade on me tried to intimidate the older dude the same way.

"Watch this, Light." Everyone called me Light because I was light-skinned. "I'm a show you how you handle this."

"You dead on that slot time, homey!" the razor guy said.

"A'ight, young'un."

Soon as the thug with the razor turned his back, the older guy grabbed the mop wringer and hit him upside the head. The dude with the blade thought he had the upper hand, but the moment he got too confident, the older dude laid him out.

The COs came and packed the dude with the razor up and took him out of the house (jailhouse). Because whoever gets wounded has to pack up and leave. That's how jail goes. If you fuck around and get hurt, you're the one that goes to the infirmary, and then the guards move you to a different housing unit. The dude who hurt you is chillin' back in the house. You have to move to the next cellblock and start all over again, learning who controls what and getting in good with the right people.

Anyway, after the old man finished his call, he returned to drop some wisdom. "Don't worry 'bout a dude backing out on you. Just worry about how you retaliate behind that shit. Sometimes they gonna get the drop on you. You might have four guys pull knives on you. If they ain't poking you up, though, it's really bullshit. And as long as you play it smart, you still rocking. As long as you still here standing, you can catch them out there. Don't let them dudes punk you like that, but don't let 'em pressure you into a dumb move, either. Just play it cool 'til you see your opportunity."

I had a few real gangsters like that coaching me in jail. You had to handle yourself a certain way, and I learned fast. It helped that I got cool with this Dominican dude named Panama. He was like MacGyver with a banger (improvised knife). He could make one out of anything. He could make a blade out of a plastic bag. He'd melt the plastic with hot water and scrape it against the wall for hours, and the next morning he'd come out of his cell with a blanket wrapped around his new knife. He'd walk right through the metal detectors, because the blade was plastic, but it would still fuck you up if he banged you in the gut with it. A plastic knife is just as pointy as a steel knife, it will stab the shit out of you. If you got banged in the gut with a plastic knife, you were going to the infirmary, no doubt.

That's how Panama made his money in jail, selling knives to inmates. On the shakedowns, the COs would come in with the metal detectors. They'd flip your mattress over and turn your cell inside out, looking for weapons and contraband. But if you knew

how to hide it in your mattress a certain way, they weren't find-
ing shit.

That happened to me once in Manhattan House, too. Luckily
for me, my man Chuck, who I grew up with and who was one of my
best friends, was a corrections officer there. He wasn't on my dorm,
but he came down in the middle of the night to make sure I was
good. Because I knew him, he was able to move me around inside.
Like the one time my cell got tossed by the Riot Squad. They're
supposed to be looking for contraband, but a lot of times it's just
an excuse to fuck with an inmate. They'd flip your mattress, destroy your shit, tear up pictures, do whatever.

Anyway, they ripped up some of my pictures of my baby boy,
and when I tried to stand up for myself, they beat me and tossed
me out of my cell in my drawers and nothing else. Afterward,
Chuck got me moved to the top floor of the cell. I called it the
penthouse, 'cause I was now on the top floor. Life was better there,
too—less shakedowns and attention from the guards overall.


Panama and I got shipped out from Manhattan House to Rikers
Island at the same time. Rikers takes convicts from all five boroughs, so you never knew who you'd be rubbing elbows with once
you got inside. Now, you were gonna run into somebody you know,
because nine out of ten times you go into the can you know someone who's already there.

Rikers Island is dangerous for many reasons, but the worst shit
about it is that you're serving time with dudes serving minimum
time right next to stone-cold killers with life sentences. Even if
you're just serving a drunk driving charge, you're thrown in with
all these guys with murder, assault, and robbery charges. I was
shitting fucking bricks.

If that wasn't bad enough, when we arrived I realized I was getting housed in the notorious Four Building, known as Four Main

House of Pain. There was Four Main, and the other hard-core criminal building was the HDM, known as the "House of the Madmen." Both units are legendary on the streets of New York City.

When I got there, it was quiet. When inmates are quiet, it's due to tension, not peace. I walked into the cell and threw my bag down, then came out and looked at the phone. There's only one phone for forty or fifty inmates. It's swinging ever so slightly, almost like it was mocking me. I needed to use it because I wanted to get my packages—things we couldn't get on the inside, like clothes, money, letters, magazines, soap, pens and pencils—schedule visits, and talk to my girlfriend. So I'm sitting there watching it and wondering whose it is.

At that point, I'd been in jail long enough to know that no matter what jail it is, somebody's running the phone. I didn't want to make the same mistake I had in Manhattan House, so I tried to peep for who was in charge. Problem is, I can't pick him out. I'd also been in jail long enough to know only a goddamn fool would touch that phone before knowing what's going on and who's who. You could get killed over that phone, and a lot of guys have been hurt doing stupid shit.

There were three dudes in leather jackets in the back of the dorm—they had the entire jailhouse on smash. Everyone in there was scared to death of these guys. A three-against-one situation is not good. This is a true *Art of War* situation: how to get what you want with minimal risk to yourself.

Five Percenter knowledge comes with both physical and mental refinement. Like I said, you have the power to do things, but you're not going to go rush out there wildly. You're gonna approach it in different ways. You're gonna think it through and plan and refine how you approach things.

In jail, those Savages would normally come up and just stab you for the phone. That's how a Savage generally operates. You got the phone, he wants the phone, he gonna cut you in the face for the phone. Instead of talking or making a deal, they just gonna put you down. That's the only way a Savage knows how to get what they want.

So, I gotta figure out a way to not get in that situation. I had some weed on me. My boo, she helped smuggle in some weed for me, sewed up about twenty-five cigarettes in my jeans. So instead of me having to punch or stab a motherfucker, I light up some marijuana. When I do that, motherfuckers went, "Oh, who got the weed?" The very same Savages were goin', "That fuckin Light got that. Oh, U-God got the weed?"

It ain't nothin. I gave a dude a lil' piece of joint. *Boom*—next thing you know, I got phone time. I ain't got to worry about any suckers here. Soon I was in the back with them, playing Crazy Eights and chilling and having convos about life in the streets, our cases, and just bullshitting.

How you move in certain circumstances is basically brainpower, it's basically the mentality I mentioned earlier. That's what the degrees and the 5 Percenters shared with the next generation. That stuff gave me the ability to think things through without having to use violence all the damn time.

Sometimes, though, violence was inevitable when you're dealing with a Savage.


I saw Panama a few days later on the chow line. "Yo, chico!"

"Yo, what's up, Panama?"

"You need a banger, chico? You need a knife?"

"Nah, I'm good."

"You sure? I got one I made special for you," he said.

"A'ight, fuck it, I'll take one."

Panama passes me a long, crazy-ass ginsu through the bars separating our jailhouse dorms. My entire jail squad saw that shit.

They saw the size of that knife, and that gave me more respect and leverage.

When it came time to leave Four Main, I left a lot of my things behind for my dorm mates. My Walkman, my radio, sweaters, socks, pants, envelopes, food. I always did that throughout my stay, since I couldn't bring any of it with me. When it was time to get transferred, I'd leave all my shit for those who held me down. That way I would go play the yard and see twenty or thirty of the dudes I'd left some shit for. They'd all show me love in return, and it gave me a rep that I was cool, that I was good. Again, though, in jail and to a certain degree the streets, you can't show just kindness, because it's always taken for weakness. Unless you show you're not a punk. Best way to show that is through loyalty.

Like my man Jolly. This lil' dude weighed about 130 pounds and was about five foot three, but he had the biggest heart I've ever seen. He came into my dorm while I was still in Rikers. I had already been down for a minute, or two months, so by now I wasn't really sweating the phone. After a while, you stopped caring so much about staying in constant touch with the outside world. 'Course, calling home wasn't always bad, either. When I called home, there was only certain motherfuckers I could talk to. For instance, I had my girlfriends, my son's mother, my man Jay, Method Man, and Hope. Those were the half-dozen motherfuckers I could talk to.

See, the problem is that most of the time the phone gets you in trouble, with you worrying about what's going on outside while you locked up. You just gotta know how to do your bid. You have to know how to occupy your time from the moment you wake up to the moment you go to sleep. You wake up, you might work from six in the morning to noon. Then from noon to five you might go to the gym. Then from five to seven you might go to the law library. You might go back to the gym from seven to nine. You head back to your cell, watch a half hour of television, then do about five hundred or a thousand push-ups, shower, and go to bed. You gotta keep yourself active, you gotta read books. Once you occupy yourself like that, the days just fly by.

You also don't get involved with the gangs. You just keep to yourself, and you deal with it. Me, I just came to a point where I didn't give a fuck. I didn't want any part of the outside world, so I left it alone. I learned all that baggage is just too much to keep track of and worry about. Just let it go. It's worth the peace of mind.

Now, I still called the outside from time to time. "Yeah, I need my package." But I didn't give a fuck about what was going on out there in the streets. I got to where I was only needing about ten minutes on the phone, that was it.

I remember this huge motherfucker came up in the dorm once. I thought it was gonna be drama, because dudes usually want the phone right away when they come in so they can talk to their peoples and let them know where they're at. And this guy was brolic, so I thought he was going to come in and just start regulating. Dude didn't even get a chance to look around, let alone inquire about the phone. Jolly was already scheming on him.

"Yo, Light! Watch this. I'm gonna go get that chain."

"Whatchu gonna do?"

"Don't worry about it. Just hold me down." That meant he wanted me to watch his back. That's what Jolly said all the time, "Just hold me down, and I'm a hold you down!"

He went over to the dude and whispered something in his ear. I didn't know what he said, but dude took his chain off and gave it to Jolly. I thought the big dude was gonna pound Jolly's head in. But he didn't, he just gave Jolly the link.

Jolly comes back over to me with the chain. "Told you, Light. I told you I was gonna get that link, right?"

"Yo, dawg, what the fuck? What'd you tell this dude to get him to come out his chain like that?"

"Yo, I told him, 'If you don't give that chain up, my man Light over there is gonna kill you.'" He was talking 'bout *me*.

"You told him I'm gonna kill him? Awww, man. That's some punk-ass shit."

"But it worked, right?"

"Yeah . . . it worked, it worked."

I had to laugh. Soon after that, they packed us up and sent us to a different dorm because they had us on some gang shit. Any time you're put in a situation and you have to overpower other individuals, motherfuckers call the police on you, and you get your ass packed up. That's all it really was. But I was just trying to do my time, do my little drug counseling, and come the fuck home.

# 12

# HEADED UP NORTH

After Rikers, they moved me to a minimum-security prison called Camp Gabriels. Minimum security means no fences, and that shit was sweet. Everything was real lax. You could cook in your cell. You could get all kinds of shit from commissary, which was good, because I wasn't getting much from the outside.

See, people I took care of in the street didn't reciprocate the love when I was incarcerated. No visits from a lot of people I was holding down. No packages comin' up north. Not even a letter. Only people who sent letters and accepted my collect calls were Method Man, Jay, and one of the most reliable people I could depend on, a woman who was one of my top workers.

In jail, you need money. I didn't even need to see their faces if they didn't want to make the trip. I would've been happy if they would have sent twenty dollars. I didn't get a dime from nobody I took care of in the streets. It was a rough bid for me, and that made me understand the importance of having my own back.

Camp Gabriels was on New York Forest Preserve land, and we spent our days cutting down trees with a chain saw. I must have cut twelve miles of trees during my time there.

Afterward I'd go work out for a couple hours, have a late dinner, and go to bed.

I learned a lot about myself in prison. I learned what I'm capable of doing, and what I'm not willing to do. I learned that when shit gets funky, I'm gonna handle mine. Even in fucked-up situations, I'm gonna stand up and handle it. Because your size, rep, or whatever doesn't matter in jail. It's different in jail; everything is not about a fight, it's more about winning at any cost. Dirty, no rules, none of that. They'll throw boiling oil in your face and disfigure you. They'll squirt some flammable mixture on your hair and light that shit on fire. It's not about being the biggest or strongest. That one skinny, crafty dude might be the one to tear your head off. I've seen scared dudes doing their first bid beat the shit out of some thug with a jailhouse rep. I've seen the smallest guys take down giants.

After serving eight months overall, I made parole. In no time, I was right back on the streets, selling and shooting and ducking the cops. But I didn't stay out there for long.

Violating my parole for the first time turned out to be a blessing in disguise, because the Island got wild while I was away. Some new people, outsiders really, got into positions of power. Our hood had been infiltrated.

It started because some dumb-asses from our projects vouched for some outsiders. Then the outsiders turned on the ones who vouched for them as soon as they got in a position of strength. I don't cosign for you or even claim to know you unless I know your family. Not just the people you run with in the street; I want to know your mother, your father, your brothers and sisters, your cousins, your grandparents—if I can't trace your roots back, I don't know you. Just because I smoke a blunt with you one time doesn't mean I know you.

That's how you verify the peoples in your circle and make sure their shit is real. I'm not sayin' that knowing a dude's family is an absolute guarantee they'll have your back—you can know all this shit, and a motherfucker can still flip on you. Either way, you're rollin' the dice on someone, and you won't know how it turns out until the shit gets real.

So they were like, "Yo, help us out. These dudes took my gate and kicked me out the spot."

"What?! I thought they was your peoples?"

"Nah, fuck them dudes. I thought so, but . . ."

They used them, shook them, and set up shop. We had to get them up out of Park Hill. It wasn't gonna be easy, though. They had settled. They had apartments to run to and stash out in. They also had neighborhood girls holding them down, providing shelter.

These outsiders from Queens were trying to take over Park Hill, trying to tell us we couldn't sell in front of 160, our own fuckin' building. It was a war every day after that. Every time we stepped outside onto the block, we had to be extra on point. It was home, but because of the UFOs trying to pump their drugs and shoot at us, we may as well been on foreign soil at the time.

It got so bad that peoples were turning against each other, fighting over those damn buildings. One of the dudes we ran up against was named Uncle, which made me kind of upset because he had kind of been a mentor to me on the street, but he'd thrown in with the dudes trying to take over our projects, and he was causing lots of problems. So he had to go.

Me, Varf, Trey-8, and a dude named Chip were gonna hit the UFOs. We were all blacked out, masks on, gloves on, bulletproof vests, ready to tear up the building. I had the MAC-10, ready to go.

Again, I had just come home, and already I was caught up in the situation. We crept through the back of the building, and Uncle was sitting out in front of the building. We got the drop on him. He had no idea we were there. With four hammers among us, we could have blown him the fuck to kingdom come.

I was standing there with the gun in my hand, aimed at Uncle, finger on the trigger about to unload, when I had an epiphany moment. Every now and again, I'd see the light about the direction I was going—about the situation I was in and what I was a second away from doing. It's moments of clarity like those that I call "brain jumps," and often they've changed my life.

I looked around, saw Varf and the rest of the dudes with me, looked into their eyes, and realized I was the one initiating the kill! The others were following my lead; they weren't as into it as I was.

That's when I got this funny feeling in my body to not do it. It was like an angel came down from heaven and said, *"Lamont, don't do this. Don't do it."*

I eased my finger off the trigger and lowered the gun. The others looked at me and went, "Yo, what's up, man? What you gonna do?"

And I looked at them and said, "Naw, man, I ain't gonna do it."

So we slowly all eased up outta there and got back to the house, and I took off all my gangster shit while the others were all starin' at me.

I just looked at them, left my burner at Varf's place, and said, "I'm goin' home, man."

And that's just what I did—I went home, and I sat down and thought about what I'd almost done. I didn't go anywhere for the next two days, just thinking about it and thanking God that I didn't squeeze that fuckin' trigger. Because I know for a fuckin' fact that the rest of those dudes would have told on me, they would have squealed on me. I felt it. It wasn't the fact that they would have squealed on me; it was that I had been in that situation already and had a change of heart. It was like God came down and softened my heart, and I didn't squeeze on this dude. Every part of me wanted to, but the Lord would not let me pull that trigger. I could not shoot that fuckin' gun.

The ironic thing about it all was that Uncle ended up in jail anyway, doing a sixty-year stretch. He turned informant and was the neighborhood snitch. As for the dudes I was rollin' with that night, well, besides the federal cases against them, Varf ended up getting killed by the police; they beat his head in with a walkie-talkie. Trey-8 got shot in the face and died. Chip is still runnin' around here somewhere, I don't know where the fuck he's at nowadays. And I became a superstar rapper.

I still think about it a lot—how, if I'd pulled that trigger, I'd have done ten years minimum and would never have gotten on the Wu train. I'd just be another ex-con trying to survive.

It was straight madness at that point. I had just come home and was already in all this drama. The drug game was all fucked up and had been reduced to a bunch of smaller factions trying to knock each other off to come up. There wasn't enough to go around like during the height of the crack game. The glory days were gone, and everybody was doing bad. We were shooting each other over drug buildings that we didn't even own. They weren't ours. We didn't own the land. And today, you go back there, and there's nothing there. The building's still there, but no one's selling. It used to have a sign out front that said drug zone, now there's no drug zone there—it's over.

I look back out on it now and wonder what we were doing it all for besides survival. It sure wasn't the path to any kind of career. At the time, none of us had the mental skills to take that money we were making and take it out of the drug game, use it for something positive. What was it all for?

Like I said, repetition is a motherfucker, and my parole officer sent me back to prison for another six months for dirty urine. Looking back on that now, not squeezing that trigger was the best thing I ever did. God was putting me in the dugout again to keep me safe from all the shit going down in Park Hill and the rest of Staten Island. Still, it hurt to only have been back on the streets for less than a month.

So I was back inside. Brooklyn House to Rikers Island to Bare Hill. I didn't really care, though, because I had learned how to bid. I could do six months easy. Or so I thought. What I wasn't aware of was that when you get caught on a parole violation, you can't get no commissary, no visits, no phone calls. You can't send letters or receive packages. Plus, the state only gives you one set of drawers, one pair of socks, and two T-shirts. For two months, that's all you have.

Plus, I got sent up in the dead of winter, so I was freezing that whole time. And with no commissary, if I missed breakfast (6 A.M.), I starved. If I missed lunch (12–1 P.M.), I starved. If I missed dinner (4–5 P.M.), I starved. So I made sure to eat a big breakfast and big lunch, and then after dinner, I might try to sneak some dinner back to my cell. During those two months, my man Zeiss from West Brighton snuck me peanut butter and jelly sandwiches at night. And when I could finally access my commissary account, I hit him back up real good. I always paid back a favor from a brother who was looking out for me.

When I got busted, I had about twenty-five hundred dollars on me, which they put in my commissary account. But I couldn't touch it. No flip-flops, no lotion, no snacks, no smokes. I had nothing for the first two months but the three squares a day and some PB&J sandwiches. When I took a shower, I had to use the state soap, the bar kind called Corcraft (the marketplace name for the New York State Department of Corrections, Division of Correctional Industries), and I had no lotion. My skin was like sandpaper.

Once I got access to my commissary, however, life got much better. It doesn't take much to live well in prison; you can do it for about a hundred dollars a month. You could get rice and flour, and I'd use the flour to make bread dough. I could get cookies and cake, all kinds of meats and seafood; I could make hamburger patties. If you knew how to cook, you were all good. I'd hit up my man in the kitchen with a carton of cigarettes, and he'd get me chopped meat, which I'd add to pasta and make lasagna, complete with cheese and sauce, the works, in the oven.

After that six-month bid, as soon as I touched down, I was getting right back into the street life—and getting violated and sent back again.

It didn't help that my fucking parole officer hated me, too. Mr. Ortiz had a real lifeblood vendetta out for me. Especially after I told him about the Wu-Tang album. At first, he probably didn't believe me. He didn't know too much about music at that time. Now, when I ran into him after we became a worldwide phenomenon, and he saw me in designer clothes, driving a brand-new Range Rover, and owning a storefront, he got really heated. I kept it light, like, "Yo, Mr. Ortiz, what's up, man?" I could see it in his face, he was like, *Fuck you.* That's one time when living well truly was the best revenge.

But the douchebag kept punishing me for dirty urine. He knew who the fuck I was. He knew what I was doing. I kept catching dirty urines, though. He thought I was selling drugs, which I was. He thought I was using drugs, which I wasn't.

The dirty urine wasn't from smoking weed, though. Like I said, I was still selling, and I was chopping and cooking up half bricks of coke on the regular. If you handle cocaine with your bare hands, it goes into your bloodstream without you even knowing it. Your skin absorbs the coke. You breathe it in and it gets into your system. I didn't know anything about that. So when I took the piss test, I had traces of coke in my system. So I got sent right back.

After the first violation, I couldn't go back to the minimum security at Gabriels, so they sent me to Franklin, which was a medium-security prison. They still have my picture on a bulletin board up at Franklin for former inmates who made it out and became something. I'm one of those faces. I still get people who come home after a bid who tell me my picture's still up on that bulletin. They always seem almost surprised. They shouldn't be, though. I've been up there.

I've slept on those bunks. I was in that chow line.

I was in the weight room up there. I was in the yard.

I was in Franklin. I got sent there after coming home from and violating my parole yet again. I never did maximum security because I never got bagged for any more serious infractions like murder or armed robbery, or taking a case to trial where I knew I was in the wrong. Also, by then I knew I had a good situation to come home to, so I started to cool out a bit. Everything I was doing was according to a preconceived plan. I knew we were gonna sign the deal with Steve Rifkind and Loud. I was mad because I got caught before that went down. If I hadn't gotten caught, I'd have been on the first Wu-Tang Clan album more. My plan was to cop out as fast as I could, 'cause I knew I was gonna come home in time to make the record. I was home for two months and was working on Wu-Tang stuff with RZA.

I got back in time to record my verse for "Da Mystery of Chessboxin'." I also got to make it to the video shoot for "Protect Ya Neck." That video was major for us. Not only did Uncle Ralph McDaniels help RZA finish directing the project, he also played it on *Video Music Box,* which was pretty much the only outlet for raw-ass hip-hop and a bunch of young grimy Staten Island project dudes jumping around.

All praises due to Uncle Ralph. He's the most humble guy, and the gateway for many great things. Steve Rifkind called him up after RZA met with Steve and told him that Uncle Ralph was playing the video. Steve Rifkind wanted to know if he should sign the group. Uncle Ralph cosigned us to the fullest, and RZA and Wu-Tang Productions signed the deal with Loud Records.

Then I violated my parole and got sent back to prison again. I came home in six months and got to shoot the videos for "C.R.E.A.M." and "Chessboxin'." Loud Records was smart in shooting our videos all at once so they could just have all of them on deck, fully loaded and ready to go.

Then I got violated again for dirty urine from cooking up that shit and absorbing it into my system *again*. So I went up for six more months, then came home. Three times I got my parole violated over dirty piss, and each time they sent me back for six months. Eight months plus six months times three is twenty-six months. So I wound up doing twenty-six months out of a fucking one-to-three. Dumb-ass fucking me.

Every time I cycled through the system, I got more lost. I was getting more and more comfortable in jail, which is how the penal system gets you. They can hit you with all sorts of time, and you won't really care, because jail has become your element. You get that institutional mentality.

And when I was back on the streets, I was still carrying guns and wildin', so I couldn't focus on the Wu-Tang Clan as much as I wanted to. Even with what I learned about my addiction to drug cash in the joint, slinging was still the fastest way to make money on the outside. My rhymes were already taking a back burner

because I had to fucking feed myself. I had a baby on the way. I
had things I was taking care of every day. I was all fucked up in
the head, so I couldn't concentrate on rhymes at the time.

When I wasn't hustlin', most of my attention was on caring for
Meth. The first time I went away, I left him with about five grand,
and he could hit up my peoples anytime he wanted. Even when I
was incarcerated, my peoples were still hitting him up with money
just to keep him from dealing. I told them, "Yo, make sure he
doesn't have to be in the streets."

When I came back home, he was still struggling to stay afloat
with all of that shit, but he was still getting money from my
peoples. All he had to do was go to my peoples' house like, "Yo, I
need some bread and nicotine." They hit him up with the bread,
hit him with this, hit him with that. That's how it was.

I said, "You know what? Fuck it. My man who's focusing on this,
I'm gonna push him further." Meth was more focused than me,
so I made sure his life was comfortable while I was hittin' it hard
on the streets. That was basically my responsibility. You might not
think it was, but it was my responsibility to keep him out of trouble and keep him on a good path.

I'm proud of that, even though it meant I didn't get a chance
to really get my feet wet. I said, "I'm up here taking care of my
man so he can succeed." And all that stuff going down was why I
couldn't focus on my own music at that time.

During those years that I was bouncing in and out of jail, RZA
sat me down and said he wanted to have a talk with me. That talk
probably saved my life.

"Uey, what are you doing, man? You keep getting locked up
like this, you keep fuckin' around, and they gonna hit you with
some real time."

"I gotta get my money. I still gotta be in these streets scram-bling."

"Well, we getting ready to really walk this Wu shit. You gotta leave that drug dealing alone. You have to decide, God. Are you going to keep fucking around and getting locked up and doing bids, or are you going to come do this fly shit over here with us? The streets ain't goin' nowhere. Just give me nine months of your life, God. In nine months, if it doesn't work out, you can always go back to the street and do whatever the fuck you want. The street's always gonna be there. This opportunity you have right now, though, if you take it for granted, you're gonna lose out on it."

What he said made perfect sense. The block and the fiends in front of 160 weren't going anywhere. Selling drugs would always be an option if I really needed the money. But this rap shit was so much more promising. Of course, I'd rather be traveling the globe with my brothers, meeting the finest women, copping cars and clothes, smoking and drinking the best of the best, all the while getting paid and living out my dreams.

"You know what? Why not? Why the fuck not?" I had about forty or fifty grand left over in my stash. "I'm gonna live off this right here for a couple of months, and I'm not gonna call the con-nect no more." I threw all my burner phones and beepers away.

God pulled me away from certain things and situations to save me, and this was one of them. My time in jail did make me much more appreciative of things, too. In hindsight, going to prison probably saved my life, because the building we were hustling in front of got shot up that first summer while I was locked up. I would've been out on the block when that shit happened. Two good dudes got killed right in front of the building. I would've been there, too, and who knows if I'd have made it out alive.

That was all my prison time really got me; like I said earlier, if I could have avoided it, I would have in a heartbeat, because it didn't do shit for me. You don't need a rap sheet to rap. Prison time has nothing to do with making music—in fact, it wound up hurting my career.

So when the blessing came, I didn't take it for granted. I was down to work.

# 13

# WHEN YOU COME HOME

By 1993, we were all ready to go all out to make the Wu-Tang happen for real. All the Clan members had that hustler's mentality, because that's where we came from. Oli "Power" Grant, the executive producer of every Wu-Tang album and CEO of Wu Wear, hustled. John "Mook" Gibbons, our road manager, hustled. Even RZA hustled in Ohio at a certain point. Some of us might have been deeper in the game than others, but we were all going through rough times, scrapping and scraping for a meal. We were out there with grumbling bellies and worn-out sneakers, our clothes smelling like mildew.

All that negative shit we were going hard with in the streets? We put that same energy into something positive. Times were changing on the streets; the drug game was over, at least the heyday was. There wasn't much out there for street dudes like me and my clan. Luckily the seeds had been planted years and years earlier, and now they started coming to fruition.

That's another reason why it was easy for the Wu-Tang members to stick together at first: We had a gang mentality, or at least we did in those early days. We knew each other and all had a common cause, so it was easy for us to bond over that.

We had to work harder than ever, though. No free rides, no free money. I had to stop making five thousand dollars a day hustling and do something for far less. We sacrificed fast cash and the street life for the security of a career that we weren't even sure was gonna pay off, but we went for it anyway. We believed in what we were doing, so it was pretty easy to stop calling the connect for the re-up.

Besides, I was still making a little bit of bread during this time. We had shows here and there and got paid per diems from the record label, forty to sixty dollars a day. The label also took care of our recording expenses. So I just ate off my lil' stacks I'd saved, the per diem, and the little bit of show money we were getting here and there. We didn't have to do nothing but get on the road and go. So why not go somewhere farther than I've ever been and help make a name for me and my team?

We were young as hell: twenty-two, twenty-three, twenty-four years old. Our first road experience wasn't even on a tour bus. Mook would come get us in his car, an old, two-door Mitsubishi Scorpion, and we'd all pile in and drive for hundreds of miles to do college promos. We'd go from college to college. Sometimes it was just me, Deck, Meth, and Raekwon. The Four Horsemen. We would drive two hours to Philadelphia. We'd drive three hours this way. We'd do little showcases that led to more shows and more promo. It was all leading up to that album release. Eventually all that initial work paid off in more ways than just record sales.

Truth be told, it was awesome. I didn't have to worry about being hassled by the police anymore. I didn't have to worry about my product or stickup kids or junkies trying to hold me up anymore. I didn't have to go around strapped with a vest on anymore. I didn't have to constantly check my rearview mirror to see if the police were following us. Later on, we had the van, with a driver supplied by the record company to take us anywhere we wanted to go. I just got to sit in the back, smoke a little weed, drink a little, and chill with my brothers. I didn't have to watch my back all the time anymore, and while I would never trade that learning experience for nothing, touring was great because the pressure of the streets was finally off me.

In 1993, I made the choice to leave all that negative shit behind me. I got caught out there doing some shit, yeah. I went to jail, did my fucking time, came home, and changed my fucking life. I had come to a realization: *Yo, you know what, man? I'm going back to the old UG man, who was just doing for himself, staying to himself, staying out of trouble, but this time I know how to live. I know how to enjoy myself. I know what matters.*

I made that transition. The Wu-Tang Clan all made that transition. We're all just some street-hustlin' dudes who put in that work, and we made it.


When *Enter the Wu-Tang (36 Chambers)* came out, it took us out of the hood and into mainstream America. It felt like it all happened overnight, but, of course, we'd already been grinding for years. A lot of folks also don't realize we dropped a double-A-sided single ("Protect Ya Neck"/"After the Laughter Comes Tears") independently on vinyl via Wu-Tang Records, and that we hit the road and developed our own fan base long before we signed to Loud/RCA.

We'd always had an indie mentality from the beginning. Since we didn't pay for play on the radio, we hit the streets, tore clubs up, and blazed our own path like rock stars. Our stage show was what put us on the map—we were a spectacle. No one had ever seen anything like it before, a big crew of characters hitting the stage, spitting so lyrical with so much energy, bringing the ruckus raw and uncut, leaving crowds soaked and always wanting more! A Wu-Tang concert was a mind-blowing experience; it wasn't till much later that radio started showing us love because we were undeniable, and soon thereafter labels started signing solo one-off deals with various crew members.

And all the while, we constantly stayed on the road. It seemed like if the Clan as a whole wasn't touring, one of the members would drop something; guys were rotating on and off; two members would come home, the next guy would take off; it was non-stop. Money was moving so fast back then that when mistakes were made they weren't so hard to swallow, but unfortunately deals were put in motion without proper oversight. CASH RULED EVERYTHING AROUND ME! In our later years, this would bite us in the ass and cause conflict among my brothers.

Along the way, we definitely had some characters around us. Like Mook, RZA's cousin and our first road manager. He was around prior to our first album and was instrumental early on in our careers. The dude quit his city job as an MTA bus driver to tour with us, and he deserves all credit. He was with us every step of the way in those early years, every show, every mile. He didn't hinder, he didn't fall, he didn't say no. When it was time to hit the road, he would drive us for hours to those early gigs. He was also instrumental in our early promotion efforts and getting the word out about the Wu.

Mook was a one hell of a character. He didn't hesitate to get tough with promoters, he'd only take cash (it was C.R.E.A.M. 24/7 with this dude) at our shows, and he carried all the money in an old-school Crown Royal bag along with a .22 Special. If things got hairy, he would get us up and out of the situation. He didn't have a problem beating people up, either.

Quite a stand-up guy, and we loved him . . . until we found out he sometimes charged a little more than the standard 10 percent management fee to promoters. He'd have us perform at 9 P.M. on one side of town, then take us to the other side of the same town for another show three hours later. Mook didn't play by anyone's rules but his own—if he could make some money, he was all in. He'd split the door with the promoters, then break us off what he deemed was reasonable at the time, depending on the situation. It's not that he was a crook, just that he was a definite hustler, and at that stage of the game we appreciated having someone like that with us on the road. Mook still pops up here and there, and has worked for RZA off and on over the years.

Anyway, we were putting that work in, with everybody now on the road for several months at a time, traveling all over the country, staying in cheap hotels, getting paid little bits of money. Those hotels in the early days were shitty. I'm talking two or three rooms for nine motherfuckers. Some of us slept on the floor, some of us slept in the bed. But even that was better than hustlin' on the streets, and I wouldn't trade any of that experience for nothing.

But the early days were just crazy. There were times we got shot at on the road. Sometimes we'd go through all this drama just to make a hundred dollars for all of us. I went from making several thousand dollars a day to having to settle for a hundred dollars split nine ways.

Sometimes we wouldn't even make that much. We got chased out of certain towns. One situation happened when we were in Houston, Texas, where we almost got our asses handed to us. It was a Scarface (from the Geto Boys) town; he was real popular down there. The crowd wasn't really feeling us too much that night. We'd faced that type of shit before, though, so we just tried to thug through it.

We got onstage and immediately started getting booed and shit. Then we got into a confrontation with some dude who was shouting at us to get off the stage and bring out Scarface. Then he splashed RZA in the face with some water or something. RZA went "what the fuck" and splashed him back. That's when bottles started flying. One crashed by my feet. Next bottle hit RZA, but didn't break. RZA threw that shit back in the general direction it came from.

Two seconds later, the whole crowd bombarded us with bottles. Glass was crashing and smashing all around us. We had to run to the van. When we got there, motherfuckers started rushing it. I guess a lot of the dudes that had come to the show were members of a gang, and they surrounded our van. Shots were fired into the air and all that crazy shit. We damn near ran dudes over gettin' out of there. It wasn't the first time a show went south, and it damn sure wouldn't be the last time.

Us getting run out of town was only half of the story. The promoter only gave us one hundred dollars. It turned out it was a fake hundred-dollar bill. We nearly got the shit beat out of us, we got chased out of town, and we didn't even make a dollar. Remember, we had to split this hundred dollars between nine motherfuckers now. In the beginning, we couldn't get no money to split among each other. We had to wing all of that.

Chicago also didn't show us a lotta love in the early days. When we first came to town, motherfuckers were popping caps outside the venue at us. Then, when we went on, we were told to get off the stage. They were like, "Fuck y'all."

Funny thing, though—we didn't have those kinds of problems on the East Coast. That sort of shit went down primarily in the Midwest. To be fair, we hadn't broken those markets yet, but we had to step into them to see where our footing was at. Back in '93, rap was still fairly underground in the Midwest, so we wound up doing a lot of college radio, select nightclubs, record stores, anywhere that would have us.

And often there would be local artists that would make it difficult to break in—not directly, but because the audience was used to a different kind of sound. When we toured the South, we had to do "southern" remixes of our songs. It's much different now, with everything being global, but at the time, every state seemed like a completely different situation.

That was all fine, though, because we saw the bigger picture, just like when we used to hustle back on the street. We knew this was just like giving out some free samples to get the fiends to try it. And for every hundred places we performed at, maybe only twenty liked us, but we'd take it and move on to the next stop. Every day we'd link up and talk about what steps we were taking that day to carry out the master plan. And our trailblazing pushed down the walls for more New York and East Coast rap—Biggie Smalls, Jay-Z, all of them—to spread across the country.


RZA was smart when he was assembling the team in the early days. He needed responsible hustlers that he knew could do the job. That's just my thing. That's why I have a tattoo of sergeant's stripes on my arm, 'cause if you give me a job to do, I'm gonna do it to the best of my ability. And keeping nine guys moving in one direction took a bit of organization. But we all had the same goal: get out of the streets. RZA knew that, and that's why I give him credit for picking not only the best rappers on Staten Island, but the hardest workers from there to make up the Clan.

For example, in the beginning, when we had to do promotional tours, I was one of only five of the members riding out every day. At this time, other Clan members were working on their solo albums. RZA was working on his Gravediggaz project, Meth was putting *Tical* together, and GZA was working on *Liquid Swords*. They were also getting Dirty's record (*Return to the 36 Chambers: The Dirty Version*) together too, so the rest of us were on the road.

It was Rae, Ghost, Deck, Meth, and me. We called ourselves the Five Horsemen, and we walked that Wu shit every single day. We went from town to town, doing our thing. Just all that promo shit, a lot of shaking hands and kissing babies. We did hundreds of radio interviews. That's why I'm not the most famous in the group, but I'm still recognizable. My name may not be like Rae, Ghost, or Meth, but people see me and they know. Because I've put in that fucking work.

Besides solidifying our fan base worldwide, another plus side of touring so heavy in our early days was that we became known as a touring band. A lot dudes in the nineties didn't want to tour, because it's hard work. They just wanted to chill while their songs were on heavy rotation on the radio and do the glamorous things. Not us. We'd be twelve deep in a van sometimes, a bunch of funky motherfuckers stinking like armpits, but we laid that groundwork, and now we can always tour the world. That all started because we didn't take the blessing for granted after going through the rough shit on the streets and in jail. None of us did. We were willing to put in the work. And we're still touring to this day, still on the road getting paid.

That first go-round, though, we were still learning about life on the road and performing. We had already put out "Protect Ya Neck," and I had come home in time to do a lil' verse and be in the video. We toured on that for a while, then came back to NYC and put out "Da Mystery of Chessboxin'." Those two records sold a combined 150,000 copies, giving us our first wind. Then, after RZA, Power, and Divine secured our deal with Loud Records/RCA, we filmed the videos for "C.R.E.A.M.," "Da Mystery of Chessboxin'," and "Wu-Tang Clan Ain't Nuthing ta Fuck Wit." Those three were in the clip ready to be let off while we ran around the globe promoting.

RZA hadn't put those videos out yet, though, because "Method Man" was still doing its thing. That song was a lot of fans' first real introduction to the Wu-Tang Clan because "Protect Ya Neck" was so underground, even though it was selling well. *Video Music Box* played it. That was about it. We had to stay on the road to really keep the movement flowing. Meth's song helped usher in new fans while we were on the road. Loud also dropped a hundred thousand dollars of marketing money on us. They pushed our record hard.

And while we were on the road representing Wu to the fullest, RZA was finishing up *Enter the Wu-Tang (36 Chambers)*. But he told me since I had been fucking up, bouncing in and outta jail and shit, I was only on two and a half songs. "I see you working now, though, U-God," he said. "You keep it up, and you'll get much more shine on the next ones."

I wasn't even mad at the time. I took being on only a few songs for what it really was: a great opportunity. We had the Loud Records budget in place, so we were living on the road, sometimes staying in nice hotels, fucked-up spots other times. But we were getting around. And once Loud kicked in this van for us to travel with, it was a wrap. We were in there all day.

And there was absolutely nothing to miss back home. Once we left the street, we never looked back. Dudes in the street didn't know what we were doing, because we didn't brag about any of it. When we came back, and people started getting wind of what we had going on, there was some hate and jealousy. I came from hell all the way up, and when we were getting it together and trying to get up out of the hood, motherfuckers didn't believe us, didn't believe what we were doing. They didn't believe nothing. Why? Because they couldn't see nothing but what was in front of them.

That's a problem with a lot of people in the ghetto. They can't see nothing past the ghetto, so they can't fathom that there's a life outside the hood. I had been like that once, too—I couldn't see past the projects I was hustling in.

But by that time, we were already doing what we had set out to do. By the time we came back, people in the neighborhood, including the police, were surprised that we had actually pulled ourselves out, instead of getting ground up in the streets. They were like, "Oh, shit. These dudes went and actually did that shit."

There were some old friends that were happy for us and our success. Still, when we left the hood, everything left the hood with us. Clientele, money, everything left. We took all that somehow. We took all the energy with us, and Park Hill was never the same afterward.

Meanwhile, we just kept moving forward in full-time work mode, totally focused. We played Jack the Rapper and other festivals all over the country. Then we did colleges. So many colleges, from Miami all the way to Rhode Island and back again. After that, we did nationwide radio shows.

We did the Midwest, we did Texas, San Francisco, Los Angeles, Seattle, Virginia, Miami, then back to Hollywood, and then up to Canada. One day we'd be on a beach in Hawaii, and then next thing you know we'd be on a beach in Puerto Rico.

We did promotion everywhere we went. Promotion, promotion, promotion. It helped that we had serious marketing money behind us. When the record company saw how dedicated we were, they got more comfortable investing to send us places and get the word out.

As we traveled, we realized just how big the earth really is. People in the ghetto think the world is small, like the size of a pea. The thing is, being in poverty restricts you from traveling. It's like you're stuck in confinement. But the world is humongous. Hit Australia. Hit Europe. Hit Japan. Hit South America. You don't have to limit yourself to just your city, or even just your country. Look at us—we're loved all over the goddamn planet.

A lot of artists are still thinking they want to be on the radio. Don't get it twisted, radio is an endlessly running machine, and it requires an equally endless supply of songs to keep it going. And if you don't put yours out there, someone else definitely will.

But radio isn't the be-all, end-all, either. There are so many touring bands out there that never have a single fucking song on the radio and still tour two hundred dates a year, filling up stadiums, traversing the world. Especially now that album sales are down. People may not be willing to buy music, but they'll always be down to pay for the experience of live music. We were blessed to establish ourselves early in our career as a touring band.

At that time though, we weren't sure if all those promo tours were ever gonna pay off. All the work we'd been putting in, RZA's beats and know-how and our talents for having wild crazy styles to attack every track with, made us feel fairly confident that we were gonna win, that it was only a matter of time. Some days, though, we just weren't as positive as others. Even with all our confidence, ability, and drive, we could never see the future with 100 percent clarity—no one ever can. We just had to do the best we could, bringing it every single time, every single day.

I remember chilling on the beach in San Juan, Puerto Rico, with Masta Killa one day. We had come down for a show and had a few days before heading back to the States for the next go-round, including an appearance on *The Arsenio Hall Show*, so we were just sitting on the sand, smoking weed and talking. I remember that time because it was the last occasion we ever even contemplated not succeeding as a group.

Masta started off: "Yo, God, I really don't know if we ever gonna make it. All I know is I don't wanna go back to the streets."

"I know, Killa, that's why we gotta give it all we got," I replied. "There is no try, it's do or die. This shit's gotta take off, it's just gotta. We gotta make it, 'cause I ain't goin' back to the streets, either. I'm never goin' back."

While we were there, we were playing on the fucking Jet Skis and shit with Divine and General Wah, and I'm gunning it around in the deep water. Just four guys from Staten Island fucking around on Jet Skis. For some apparent reason—I don't know why—I thought the shit had brakes like a mountain bike. Jet Skis don't have brakes.

I decide to try to get closer to those other motherfuckers, right? I got too close to Masta Killa. I didn't know I'd accidentally hit his Jet Ski. He falls into the motherfuckin' water like a bobber from a fishing pole. He had his life jacket on, but I still didn't see him for a good five seconds. He was gone. I was like, "Oh, shit, this dude's gone."

All of a sudden he pops up. "Yo! Help me, dawg! Help me! Help!" Goes back down in the water. "Help me, dawg! Help me!"

I get over there and pull him out of the water. This motherfucker grabs me with the clutch of death. The grip of life! He grabbed me so hard the front of my fucking Jet Ski pops up on a wheelie. I was like, "Yo, dawg! We both gonna be in the water soon!"

It was some funny-ass shit, but to this day he still says I was fuckin' trying to kill him.


We did *The Arsenio Hall Show* when we got back from Puerto Rico. This was the black *Ed Sullivan Show* for us, and we were the Beatles, poised and ready to invade the mainstream.

The label had everything set up already, their publicity machine was in full motion. They already had the new album. They had the videos shot and ready to go. These motherfuckers had this shit really, really big. Everything we had done over the past year, the thousands of miles on the road, hundreds of shows and interviews and events, was ready to blow up huge.

The night we performed on *Arsenio* was crazy. We were all backstage, and we were all nervous, Rae, Ghost, Meth, everyone. Now, we were comfortable performing in general, but this was *Arsenio*, the hottest show going at the time.

When we first hit the stage, we all felt the love from the crowd right away. We launched into "C.R.E.A.M.," and when that money fell from the ceiling, that was it. We killed it. As soon as that episode aired, Loud Records dropped the video and the single.

Our sales were decent before that. We were hovering around 170,000 units. Once that shit hit the streets and people saw the video, we were outta there. Within hours, "C.R.E.A.M." went gold. We hit 250,000 units sold, then within a week we went to 500,000, then 700,000, then 800,000, and we were gone after that. It kept going, up to 1.2 million, then to 1.8 million. That's when we knew that life wouldn't be the same anymore. My old life was gone.

After "C.R.E.A.M.," the other videos came: "Wu-Tang Clan Ain't Nuthing ta Fuck Wit" and "Da Mystery of Chessboxin'." We got swept up in a whirlwind. We started doing bigger and bigger shows. We were able to make a living doing what we were doing. We did a tour of Europe. Everything changed, and we were becoming hip-hop royalty.

"C.R.E.A.M." is a true song. Everything Inspectah Deck and Raekwon said is 100 percent true. Not one line in that entire song is a lie, or even a slight exaggeration. Deck did sell base, and he did go to jail at the age of fifteen. Rae was sticking up white boys on ball courts, rocking the same damn 'Lo sweater. And of course, Meth on the hook was like butter on the popcorn. Meth knew the hard times, too, being out there smoking woolies and pumping crack, etc. That raspy shit he was kicking just echoed in everyone's head long after the song was done playing.

The realism on "C.R.E.A.M." is what resonates with so many people all over the world. People everywhere know that sentiment of being slaves to the dollar. Cash is king, and we are its lowly subjects. That's pretty much the case in every nation around the world, the desperation to put your life and your freedom on the line to make a couple dollars. Whether you're working, stripping, hustling, or slinging, whether you're a business owner or homeless, cash rules everything around us.

It's amazing how the song that depicts the harsh life in Park Hill is what ended up taking us out of that very same ghetto environment. That song was just so real, so vivid, it was a no-brainer that it would connect with the people like it did. I mean, "Protect Ya Neck" and "Method Man" had both connected with a fairly large audience, but not like "C.R.E.A.M." did. If the world wasn't watching before, they were definitely watching us now.

We hustled up our shit to get our little first promo records pressed up, but when RCA gave us that deal, that was it. There was no going back. Their money was ten times larger than our shit. They put corporate money behind us. They gave us T-shirts, they got us bigger venues, they gave us the ability to spread our music farther and wider than we ever could have on our own.

Our budget was huge. They must have invested and marketed about thirty million into the Wu-Tang Clan, and in turn, we made sure to set it off. Once we started gaining buzz in the streets, we signed to Loud, and all they had to do was put gas on the fire, 'cause when we started creeping up and making those numbers, and they were sufficient and legit, they couldn't do nothing. They had to get behind us.

We may have been young, but we already had the structure of hard work ingrained into us, the work ethic of the streets ingrained into us. New York is a twenty-four-hour city, so you had to be hustling twenty-four hours a day. Your drug spot wouldn't be successful unless it was pumping every hour of every day, and if I wasn't out there, someone else was gonna be selling to my clients. That's the work ethic the dreads passed down to us, and we just took it and turned it into recording and the touring life. In other words, we weren't lazy motherfuckers.

We kept expanding, not just with live shows, but by diversifying our portfolios. For example, we were doing guest spots on other albums. I got on SWV's "Anything" with Method Man and ODB. We had the St. Ides commercial. We had Wu Wear about to take off. Everywhere you looked, we had different team members representing that W.

Dolla dolla bill y'all, indeed.

# 14.

## SABER-TOOTH TIGER IN THE BOOTH

While our efforts were finally paying off and we were busting through, I was rusty as hell at rapping. Mind you, I'd been locked up while the rest of the Clan was sharpening their swords over RZA's beats on *36 Chambers*. They were growing and getting iller while I was stuck inside, losing my mojo.

People think that when you come back out, you can go back to being the same person you were before you went in. That's not the case at all—it changes you, and anyone who says it doesn't is lying.

You need about the same amount of time back in the world as you served in jail. If you did three years inside, you're gonna need three years outside to get your head on straight. You have to catch up with the world that's kept moving on while you've been separated from it. You aren't just gonna walk out the gate and pick up your life right where you left off. You gotta readjust yourself, reestablish your routines, and above all, get used to the freedom of not being locked up, because that's one of the biggest things every convict has to overcome.

I knew some guys who came home and tried to hit the streets like they never left. Literally they ended up right back in jail within two weeks, with a brand-new sentence over their heads—right back to the plantation.

I didn't even write any rhymes while I was locked up, just my little contributions to *36 Chambers*. Because of that, I had to get back into the swing of things, which wasn't easy.

Would you believe I got booed at my first show? The first time I grabbed the mic at a show after coming home, I got booed. RZA had told me to kick a freestyle, and I wasn't really ready. I had the heart to try, though.

I got booed hard. I still remember Fat Joe there at the show, looking on when I got booed. It hurt, but I kept pushing. After shows, I would just go home and try and get my rhyme game right. It was tough trying to get them lyrics proper, especially since I'd been away so long, I didn't know what topics or even slang was hot on the outside anymore.

You have to understand, I got tossed into a professional recording situation right out of jail. My brothers were winning and eating well, and the only way I could eat was to do what they were doing. I had to make my shit pop, I had to do what I had to do to at least get nearer to their level of rhyming. I had no other option because I wasn't going back to the streets. There was no turning back for me.

All around me, everything was moving, my brothers were moving, but I was barely getting any burn. Raekwon got his solo deal. Then Method Man and ODB snatched their deals. RZA was doing the Gravediggaz album *6 Feet Deep*. I was still trying to find my style and my voice. I had to play catch-up with everybody else in the Clan.

But me flipping back and forth between the Island and jail meant I missed a lot of studio time. I literally got out and recorded my verse on "Chessboxin'," then got violated and went back inside a week later. By the time I finally came home for good, they were recording *Only Built 4 Cuban Linx . . .* , but I was all fucked up and off beat. I wasn't ready yet.

Keep in mind, we were touring at this time, but doing a live show is different than recording in the booth. A concert is all about output—I'm sending all my energy out to the crowd, and taking theirs in as well and using that in my performance. But being alone in the booth, it's all input—I'm taking everything I know and have done along the way, along with the beat and the vibe and everything else I have to keep up on, I take all that and swing it in my own unique style. Nowadays, it comes second nature, but at the time, I was having mad problems setting it off in the booth.

I've always been a team player, though, and even though I wasn't gettin' on tracks, I knew when others could—and should. Like when Raekwon and Ghost were trying to wrap up *Cuban Linx*. They were too stubborn, they had ego problems, and they got stuck while finishing it. I don't know why they didn't reach out to Cappa—I think they thought he wasn't a good fit for the album. But that was crazy. I remember thinkin', *Damn, you all are stupid. We on our way, just dropped a double-platinum album, and you not gonna go get this dude?!*

I put my own ego aside and jumped in my truck to go get Cappa, who was working as a security guard in 260 and selling belts as a side hustle. I found him and said, "Come on, man, jump in my truck, we goin' to record right now."

He said, "Word?"

I came back with, "I said *right now*, man!"

I dropped him off at Michelle Court, where he laid down "Ice Cream" right there. Then he came back later on and did "Winter Warz," for Ghostface's album *Ironman*. And after that, the dude was done—he didn't have to be a belt-selling security guard ever again. And that's why Cappa loves me to this day. One time he said, "Yo, man, you the only dude who came back for me. Rae and Ghost wouldn't have come back for me."

I went to get Cappa because I knew he had what we needed to complete that record. There's certain songs that you just can't get that rhythm to, no matter how much time you put in. Then you bring in the right someone else, and *bam*—that's exactly what it needed!

Plus, I know how to win. I've always been a team player; I can put my ego aside if it benefits the team. I can let someone else jump ahead of me if he's got skills that I don't have. Cappa was ready. I wasn't. That's why he was on *Cuban Linx* and *Ironman*. That all led to him getting a lot more verses on Wu projects, and he got on *8 Diagrams* as our official tenth member. And all of it furthered our cause. If he won, then the whole team won.

Plus, I think it added to the mystery of Wu-Tang that there were dudes like Masta Killa and Cappadonna and me still popping up on the fans here and there. It's hard to hear that, though, when you wanna get your rhymes off, too. But the most successful crews know when it's time to let your man rock instead of you. Let the stronger teammate go to bat and hit a home run. So long as the whole team wins. Having all those different styles within the Wu to inspire us, and the willingness to compete hard with one another, made us better.

Matter of fact, it made us invincible at the time.


The recording booth and I were just not getting along. It was a nightmare—I actually had nightmares about trying to get a verse off and not being able to. I'd try to get on songs with the other members, but I got laughed at and kicked out of the booth over and over. It happened at least fifteen times—literally, they would laugh at me until I left the booth. I sounded off beat.

Of course, RZA put me on a song called "Knuckleheadz," on *Cuban Linx*. Like he was making a quiet statement that Rae, Ghost, and me were fucking knuckleheads. Before I could even really get started, he's already labeling me a knucklehead.

Plus, he only gave me one take—I didn't even get a chance to get familiar with the verse and get a couple takes down. What you're hearing on "Knuckleheadz" is my first and only take, and it really pissed me off. It made me feel like I really was a fucking knucklehead, already fucking my shit up. Anyway, I got the lyric off.

Nas was there that day, too, recording his verse for "Verbal Intercourse." We were in the booth together. He came in by himself, too. At the time he was a little G. I give that to him. To come into the studio and be around dudes you don't know and be comfortable like that, he was a real laid-back dude. He had heart.

After "Knuckleheadz," I got on the hook for "Investigative Reports," on *Liquid Swords,* and went back to trying to find my bounce again. I might not have found it for a while longer if it hadn't been for Cappadonna. That's why it turned out to be even more of a blessing that I'd gone back to Park Hill to get Cap. He was a necessary force on the team. And with a few simple words of advice, he paid me back for pulling him into the Wu.

But I felt like everyone in the Clan was still looking at me like I was a fluke-ass dude. "The Four-Bar Killa," they called me. I hated that fucking nickname. I didn't want to get labeled like that during my awkward growth phase. I didn't complain, though, I just kept studying.

In 1995, I did a track with Cypress Hill called "Killa Hill Niggas" with RZA that gave me a little bit of hope that I was getting better. I knew it still wasn't right just yet, but I was hearing the progress in my bounce. So I kept writing. Every day I would go through a few pages of my notebook.

One day, while I was struggling with writing this particular rhyme, I looked over my shoulder to find Cappa reading it, nodding his head to the beat. "Yo, that dart is crazy sharp, Uey. That's gonna be fire. You just forgot to put a word right there."

He points to a space between two words on the page I was scribbling on. I read my rhyme over and over again 'til I saw what he meant. It just hit me like enlightenment, or something instant like that. It all fell into place after that one little bit of advice. Another brain jump.

But I still kept getting kicked out of the booth. The only thing I knew was that I had to keep going. I had no other choice to get it right. No was not an option for me. That's when I learned about the difference between being a warrior—a champion, really—and a regular person. It was the difference between giving up and get-ting back up and trying again. Some people take a loss and it breaks them spiritually. A true champion is a motherfucker who can take a loss and rise back up with a full heart and keep going until he wins. I got kicked out of the booth over and over, but every time I picked myself back up and got back in there. I never, ever stopped trying.

And on my fifteenth try, I recorded my verse on "Winter Warz" for *Ironman*, with Cappa coming in on the back with his long-ass verse. That's when I started getting my momentum back. It was a banger. It wound up being a gold record.

At the time, there were rumors swirling around about how I should be kicked out of the group. Then I came with "Winter Warz." I came with this other shit, getting a verse off on "Black Jesus," another one for *Ironman*. Now I'm getting on a track here and a track there. I just started dropping them. Bong. Bong. Bong. I started doing soundtracks (*The Great White Hype* and *High School High*). I found my speed. I found my rhythm. I was getting my balance. I was getting oily. My practice was starting to pay off.

I was getting better at laying vocals and writing rhymes, but now I was torn about what my subject matter should be. Should I talk about the streets? How would I distinguish my style from the eight other guys in Wu-Tang Clan?

Raekwon was claiming that crime rhyme shit for himself. He was repping that Gambino/Scarface shit hard, so that threw me off as far as where my lane was. Rae was always rhyming about crime since the days in front of 160, when he was a Kool G Rap disciple, so I couldn't get mad. Plus, he'd been pumping out the gate, so he had his street stories to tell.

Ghostface was always a big thug, so he was claiming that chamber, which was cool because that's how he always was. He changed up a bit after his verse on "Protect Ya Neck," to incorporate that "silk shirt, suede Wallabees fly shit" for Raekwon's album, but it was still Ghostface. He wasn't perpetrating the fraud at all.

Method Man was just that dude. He was always entertaining and popping, and just had that magnetism that would carry him far.

Deck was a quieter type; his style was efficient, no wasted words or bars. He wouldn't open up his mouth until he had that rhyme polished and ready. Then when he would spit, everybody would be in awe. Just incredible the way he was so descriptive. Deck was always on point.

GZA and RZA were like scientists with their rhymes. They read a lot and studied science and philosophy, and were just very learned individuals. Masta Killa was a disciple of that chamber, too.

ODB was his own unique entity as far as style; no one could do his chamber like he could. Cappadonna was more abstract with it but dead nice, and all his unorthodox styles were really original.

My style is the project kid who was the real, actual street dude who fought against all odds to make it. When I rhyme, I rhyme like a superhero based on the fact that I had to overcome all these obstacles, everything I had to do to survive in the hood. Dudes are always tellin' me that when I rhyme, it sounds like I'm a warrior, like I'm going to war, in the biblical sense. In fact, *War-rior Spirit* was one of the possible titles for my next album, the one that ended up being called *Venom*.

I was also the one who'd been in jail for that street shit, so I felt a bit entitled to that subject matter. I didn't have a beat to write to, though. Even though jail is where all the slang is from, I couldn't put it together. One thing I did get while in there was I was writing mad notes. I was just writing, writing, writing. I had mad lines, mad concepts by the time I came home.

Even when Meth wrote "All I Need," *I* said that shit to him first. When I was upstate in shock, which is a kind of military-style program, that's when I gave him the inspiration over the phone to write a song about his girl.

Here's how it went: I was getting to come home early to go on work release. They would let drug offenders come in real fast, do your time, come home. Except I got kicked out because my crime was too violent, so I got disqualified.

I was talking to Meth—at the time, the only people I was really talking to in the outside world was my main seller, my mom, Meth, and a couple of women. I'm on the jack like, "Yo, son," because he was passionately in love with my baby mother's sister. He was in love with Tameka, he loved her so fucking much. Actually, he went on about her so damn much, I kinda got tired of hearing about it.

I told him, "Man, you gettin' on my nerves with all that. Why don't you just write a song about her? Tell her how you feel." Next thing you know:

*"Shorty, I be there for you anytime you need it . . ."*

He was like, "Yeah, man. You know. Once you come home, we gon' get it on." Funny thing is, RZA's version of that song didn't win Meth his Grammy, it was Puff Daddy's remix that won. After

Meth won his Grammy, RZA separated us—he made sure we didn't work together anymore.

Back in the day, me and Meth were *the* writing team, we used to come up with routines together. We used to be together every day. We had songs together. We had routines together. That's what happens. That's the reason why the dudes he's with right now, they get more worried about writing rhymes. The dude sucks because he doesn't have his fucking writing partner around now. I'm gonna fucking let him know to his face, "Man, you're gonna hear when my record come. You gonna hear my new record come from my old shit."

Because I'm writing now, I'm oily now. I'm right here. I've been in the studio. I ain't going to jail, you ain't gettin' rid of me like that. I ain't going no fucking goddamn where. I'm in the studio. I got my lines right. I got my hooks. I got my concepts going. Why? Because that's what me and Meth used to do—we used to share ideas every day.

Even now, I put Meth on one of my songs on *The Keynote Speaker,* and he fit like a fucking glove. And when he got on that, I know he started to think like, *Wait a minute.* 'Cause the last record he did was with a bunch of hood guys. His label wanted him and me to do an album together, but instead he did one on his own, and that shit fucked him up. I know what he was thinking—he's a street dude at heart, and he wanted that street cred, but the album ended up flopping because nobody knew these motherfuckers. I know he was tryin' to do these brothers a favor, trying to take them up out of the hood like we did all those years ago, but for some folks it just ain't gonna happen like that. You can't save everybody.

Not only did that project tank, it shot down our collaboration with that label as well, because we never made money on it. When I heard about it, I was like, "Dawg, that shit's like where I was ten years ago. You're where I was at a decade ago." That shit fucked his value up. I wanna know who the fuck told him to do that? And now I gotta get him back up again.

See, I have a lotta love for Meth, but the dude doesn't know how to value himself. He's a Grammy-winning artist, but instead of taking himself higher, he tanked his stock by trying to do this straight-outta-the-hood album, which wasn't him at that time.

So the one I put him on, everyone who hears it is like, "Wow, this shit is hot! You two are back together again!" And I'm like, "See?"

'Cause at the end of the day, it's not just about writing rhymes. It's about your songs. It's about your concept. It's about what you're talking about. What's the song topic? What's the song about? What's the theme of the album, and how does that fit who you, the artist, are at that time?

Since we had gone on our second promo tour for *36 Chambers,* we started getting paid better for shows. Checks also started coming in from the soundtracks we were doing, like *High School High* and *Fresh.* We had been on the road for sixty days at a time, so I had just kept my things at my mother's house and traveled the world, living out of hotels and vans. Once we got some of that soundtrack money, me and Method Man got an apartment together.

But as soon as Meth got his Def Jam deal in '93, he moved out of our crib. He bounced, and it was crazy that the dude I'd been looking out for on the street was taking off now. It was humbling.

Even worse, he left me with GC, a slob who'd leave his used condoms on the floor, cigarette butts everywhere . . . just a total mess. So I told GC he was out, and I changed the locks.

For the first time in a while, I was by myself in the crib, working on my rhymes and trying to stay off the streets. I just sat in the crib and bought some notebooks and just tore through them with ink. I would spend hours writing. It didn't even have to make sense. Sometimes it did and sometimes it didn't, but at that point in time it was more about putting the words together so it flowed. Just practicing my flow, my cadence all day. So the more I hit the mic, the easier it got, and the more my anxiety went away.

That was about the time that things really started getting better, not only for me, but for us. Between the touring and the solo projects, the Wu-Tang was moving forward as one, our minds and bodies together, forming that sum that was greater than any of its individual parts. It was too soon to know whether we were gonna to be able to feed our seeds of music forever, but in the back of our minds, we knew we were on our way.

We went back on the road to promote the latest Wu-Tang albums (Raekwon's *Cuban Linx*, GZA's *Liquid Swords,* and ODB's *Return to the 36 Chambers*). We were going into the studio more, and I was really starting to feel comfortable in the booth.

But just as I was getting into the groove of things and coming into my own, I got some heartbreaking news that threw my whole world into upheaval—my baby boy had been shot in Stapleton.

# 15

## THE NIGHT THE EARTH CRIED

I was nineteen when I first became a father. The girl who became my baby's mother grew up in the projects with me. She lived at the top of the hill. Her mother was real loose with having neighborhood boys come over, it was never an issue. I remember they had bunk beds, and the middle of her bed had a depression, like a sinkhole. And I'd come up there sometimes in the middle of the night.

I was just a horny little motherfucker, and that girl was a little cutie-pie from the hood. I wasn't loyal to any of the Park Hill girls I got with; after my first girlfriend broke my heart, the concept of loyalty went right out the window. I was just trying to fuck anything that moved.

And then she accidentally got pregnant within three months of knowing me. Like a lot of things in the ghetto, it was an accident. It was rough, because I was still too young to understand how my world had just changed. I was running around in the streets. I was still dealing. I was scared, too. I didn't know what the fuck to do. I was also kind of upset at the whole situation, because again, it was nothing we were planning for, but here it was.

Teenagers in the hood need to understand something: Children are for married couples. People shouldn't be having babies unless they're married. They're not taught that in the hood. Motherfuckers are having babies at the drop of a hat. "Oh, I'm having your baby." "Baby, I'm not even with you like that. We're not even married. I was with you for a week. I was only with you for two months. Or maybe not half a year. You're not even supposed to have that." But it doesn't happen like that in the hood. If a woman gets pregnant in the hood, she's on that shit. And back in the day, abortion wasn't even an option. They don't believe in that shit.

With my son's mother, I gave it two or three months to see if we could make it work, but we weren't really connecting, so I left. I let her live her life, instead of being stuck with me through our child for the rest of her days. But I wasn't about to just up and leave them, either; I'm no runner—I'm not abandoning anybody. That's a big reason why I'm still in New York City today—because of family.

A lot of raising Dontae happened through trial and error. It wasn't the thought of caring for a baby that was the issue. Since I had taken care of my younger brother growing up, the idea of raising a child didn't really faze me. I just didn't have a lot of stable families as role models. My mother was never married and was always working, so I didn't have a lot of structure growing up. A lot of the time, I didn't know what was going on.

Truth be told, I was mostly upset about having to spend more money. But don't get it twisted—I love my children and would do anything for any of them. When I was home, I was always around. All my babies know who their father is.

And Dontae was another reason for me to get out of the street life. He's a big reason why I went to college. But at the time, I still couldn't earn enough to feed myself and care for him and stay out of jail. The kinds of jobs available to me at the time didn't pay enough to feed a family. So I made the best of it, and then

Wu-Tang started taking off, which necessitated me being on tour a lot more. I would go out, tour around, then when I came back I'd make sure Tanya had what she and Dontae needed to get by. Back home, one of my female workers who used to babysit me when I was younger also babysat my son. My son's mother would give him to CeCe, who used to take him all around the neighborhoods. CeCe loved my son.

It just so happened that one day CeCe was in Stapleton, and some dudes started shooting, as they do in the hood. Guy—the dude I used to hang with back in the projects—was in the mix. He was trying to kill a dude named Shawn Berry, and they were shooting at each other. During the shootout, Shawn picked my son up and used him as a fucking human shield. Dontae got shot in the hand and the kidney.

He was two years old.

I was in San Francisco when I got the news. I flew back as soon as possible. My son died twice on the operating table, came back both times. They got him stitched up and pulled two bullets out of his kidney, which he lost. He dislocated two fingers, and some of the nerves in his spine were damaged. He's had many different kinds of therapy since then. A lot of it.

When I first saw Dontae in that ER, they had my baby boy cut wide open, operating on him. I was just fucked up mentally. And the crazy thing about it was that black people, we don't have any sort of therapy to help with something like this. I didn't know about none of that. Instead, I self-medicated; I got high and I got drunk.

RZA and the others didn't make it any better, 'cause they didn't give a fuck. In fact, they were just giving me shit. I didn't get no mental support, they didn't send me any money. You know, basically, RZA thought giving me a check for the work I did, that was good enough. I didn't get any support from these dudes who I thought were my brothers. Matter of fact, they rubbed their fame and their wealth in my face even more. They made my life even fuckin' rougher, much worse mentally.

So I was goin' through all that. You know, I got on records, I did all this, I did that, I got soundtracks. I didn't get any flowers from my brothers, they didn't send me any cards, none of that shit. The only person who was really there for me was Meth. Meth is family, we got blood together. Meth was in love with my son's baby mother's sister, so we related like that.

And I was in a fuckin' position, because when it happened, I wasn't with my son's mother, so I kinda blamed her, and she felt like it was her fault. And CeCe, my girl worker, the dudes in the hood pressed her so fuckin' hard, they forced her not to snitch. She didn't ever really tell me what went on. She slipped off her rocker; she went crazy, literally nuts, and she was never the same.

I told her, "You gotta make a fuckin' choice, you gotta tell me what happened." And she didn't wanna tell me. To this day, she still don't wanna tell me. So I had to hear little bits and pieces from outside sources and all this stuff and I'm like, "Yo, how you gonna sit here and not tell me what's goin' on, but you in my house, you in my son's mother's house like this?" Finally we had to disown her.

And ever since then, Guy, the dude that accidentally shot him—I knew it wasn't meant for my boy—thought I was gonna come and kill him. So they called the police on me, they thought I was going to set up some retribution, had me under surveillance, do all types of shit to make sure they knew where I was—they were scared for their lives. They're still scared for their lives. Of the people who had anything to do with that shit—there's like five motherfuckers associated with it—three of 'em are dead as of today. Now, I had nothing to do with any of that—sometimes the streets serve up the best kind of karma.

Dontae had a hard recovery, there was a lot of rehabilitation and such. It deprived him of his youth. He spent his whole childhood—from three years old to almost sixteen—in and out of fuckin' hospitals. He had asthma, and had to go through the ordeal of losing a kidney from the bullet and being forced to use a shit bag for many years. He had to wear diapers for years. My boy's left leg is still messed up. He walks with a limp to this day. It was fucked up.

Between his asthma and other things—he got hit by a car, broke his arm, and right after graduation, he broke his leg in three places while playing football—my son went through so much fuckin' pain, but the pain made his mind jump. He was also strong, and he never let any of it whip him.

My son just graduated from college. He went and got a bad bitch and he's living on Staten Island, so he's good now. Well, mostly. He went to school to get a degree in film. I told him, "You don't need a degree for film, you can just pick it up and learn it." But now he gotta pay back those student loans on some shit that he really can't get any money from. You can't get no money from being in film unless you know how to do the damn thing. So I told him he needed to go back to school and learn certain things. But he's kind of resistant—he wants to do film, and nothing but film.

And as I see him struggle with his career, I realize something that parents, especially black parents, are doing when they raise their kids. It's not really our fault, because of how we were raised. Looking back, I spoiled my son a lot, and I don't regret that at all. But I would have been sterner about him picking a career that was more secure and made surer, more consistent paper. That's how a lot of immigrant groups get ahead in a couple of generations. They're not letting their kids pick something fun like film—

not to say film isn't a profession, it's just not secure. Parents should guide their children to make money first. Young people often want to pursue something a little bit impractical rather than securing their future.

Like my son. He's got a degree, but he's still struggling because his field is competitive, and budgets are low even if he does get work. It's a start, though. At least he's not in the projects pumping crack and ducking the cops. He's never done a bid, or even been arrested. He's got a smart girlfriend, and he's making his way in the world without resorting to crime. His kids won't be doing that, either.

I remember this one time, right after my son got shot, I was walking with him down the street. He was limping along, and I was guiding him by holding his hand. It was frustrating for him— he wanted to walk by himself, but he was hurt and was gonna need some time.

I will always remember the way my man Tinker rolled up in his whip and hopped out. He'd heard about what happened to my little seed, showed him a lot of love, and even got him to smile. He even gave my little man a hundred dollars before he hopped back in the car and drove off.

A few weeks later, Tinker got killed. He got shot in the head, but was able to draw his gun and get off one shot. He killed his killer; they canceled one another out. I cried when I heard about it.

Shit like that killed me a bit; it was like a constant influx of bad news. Whether it was my boy almost getting killed, or a friend like Tinker getting killed, all that made everyday life hard to deal with sometimes. But if I was truly gonna give my son a better life, I had to get back to my music career. It needed to be solidified so we could take care of our peoples and our seeds, and break this constant cycle of violence.

## 16.

REDEMPTION

While dealing with the aftermath of Dontae getting shot and his recovery and everything that went along with that, I lost myself. I forgot who U-God—Lamont Jody Hawkins—was.

So I went back to the hood. I went back to Park Hill, which was still just as shitty and drug- and gangster-filled as when I left. But even amid all that, in the midst of the projects, I managed to find myself again.

I was there with my DJ at the time, his name was Homicide. One day, I'm on the phone while we're just fooling around, listening to music—I still was into music, of course, would think nothing of dropping two grand on records at a time—and smoking and drinking, when all of a sudden we hear gunshots go off. *BOOM BOOM BOOM BOOM.* We were like, "What the fuck was that?" but then we went right back to what we were doing, cause that's how it was, like Vietnam in the hood.

But two seconds later, I hear that one of my friend's friends, his name was Dutch, had been shot. We ran downstairs to find two motherfuckers laid out on the fucking street! Dutch was lyin' there with eight shots in his legs and lower body, and the second dude was sprawled in the corner with a bullet in his chest. Me and Homicide are just looking at this all cockeyed, like *what the fuck just happened?*

Dutch was in bad shape, going in and out of consciousness, so Homicide ran over and picked him up, and I could see the life come back into his eyes when he got that support. Before that, his eyes were rolling back in his head. Now, I was gonna help put him in the back of my truck and take him to the hospital, but we didn't know if moving him would make the bullets shift or whatever, it might leave him paralyzed. So we had to wait out there in the street for the ambulance.

Now, mind you, I had all this surveillance on me for years. Cops didn't show up for like twenty or thirty minutes. This dude's sitting there leaking, everybody's looking at him like he's a wounded Bambi in the middle of the street, no one even giving a fuck 'bout the other dude on the sidewalk, he's just sittin' there fucked up.

Finally the paramedics come, and we got Dutch to the hospital. Then, a couple days later, I had another epiphany! I had a brain jump, and I finally realized who I was. It came to me: *I'm fuckin' U-God from Park Hill. I'm that street motherfucker. This is where I'm from, this is where I'm at, this is what I'm gonna rhyme about from this day on.*

Along with that clarity hitting me, I was going through other stuff as well. That was when my daughter's mother got pregnant and told me she was having the baby, so there was all that drama going on, too. The end result was that I went a little crazy, enough so that I ended up spending fifteen days in an insane asylum.

To this day, I'm not sure exactly what happened, whether my vitamin D slipped, or maybe one of my girlfriends poisoned me, or what. All I know is one day I found myself in the middle of the street in my bathrobe, drawers, and Timberlands, running around like a goddamn maniac. And then I went crazy on my mother, so I checked myself in, 'cause I was off the charts.

Before I knew it, I was getting fluids and medicine, all kinds of shit. They gave me some medicine that I had to dissolve under my tongue, and the effect was whenever I tried to think, it would freeze my brain, so all I could see was little black and white dots. It was unreal; this shit stopped the thinking process cold, it shut it down. No daydreams, no imagination, you just—can't think. A side effect was that it shrank your dick up. Now, I don't know 'bout you, but I need two things working every day: my mind and my meat.

While I was in there, I saw some seriously crazy dudes. One guy, he couldn't say more than five sentences without barking. He'd be having a normal conversation with you, but in the middle of it he'd just start barking.

Another dude there had tried to kill his parents. He was afraid of the outside world. He appeared to be a cool dude who had it together, but when it came time for him to go home, this motherfucker went *crazy*. "What am I goin' home for? I don't wanna go home! I don't need to go home!" They had to give him an injection and put him on a gurney to get him out of there.

So I did a two-week stint in there, I was detoxed, I came home. I stopped smoking weed after that for two years. I also went to a therapist during that time. I didn't know shit about therapy, I didn't know anything about fuckin' mental barriers or any of that shit.

So I'm in there tellin' the therapist about what happened and all that, and he said, "Lamont, you never talked about what happened with Dontae to anyone?"

And I said, "Naw, I never had anyone to talk to like that." Again, the black community typically self-medicates when we're going through some shit; we don't talk about it, we don't express our horror, our fears, or our regrets; we just smoke weed or drink and just bottle all that up. There was no outlet for all that pent-up emotion; the only ones I had were fucking, running around, and rhyming, that was it. I didn't go to the gym, I didn't meditate or any of that kind of shit.

Then he said, "Lamont, you've been running and gunning ever since you were a kid." And that, combined with everything in my life—the drug game, jail time, stress over the rap game, my boy getting shot, and now I was gonna have a second child to look out for—just made me lose my mind for a bit.

And throughout all that, I never learned how to just live. I never learned about relaxation, taking a vacation. I never learned about downtime. What I did learn from this episode is that when your body and mind want to rest, when your mind has had enough, it's gonna lay down without you. You can sit there and act like you're tough and strong and all that shit, but if enough pressure accumulates, your mind is gonna shut down, and it will go one way, and your body will go another. And you're gonna split in half, and you'll wind up on the floor going, "What the fuck just happened?"

And that's what happened to me. So I took a break from intoxicants for two years—I didn't smoke, I didn't drink, I didn't do shit. I gained about thirty pounds, from about 175 to 210. I was just big ol' fat Uey. But during that time, I was taking my fish oil, my vitamins, I was just trying to get my mind right, get myself back together. And even though I had that meltdown, I'm blessed in that I heal pretty quick, that once I know what I gotta do for myself, I do it and come through that shit.

Before we knew it, it was 1996, and the time for a second Wu-Tang Clan album was upon us. We were all over the place, but we hadn't been back fully together in a good while.

A lot had changed since the release of *36 Chambers*. We were feeding our babies off this rap shit now. We had seen some of what the world had to offer. Wu Wear was popping (although of course that didn't turn out quite right, which I'll talk about later). The whole world was watching and waiting on our return. We had raised the art form of rap and changed a lot of its accompanying aesthetics when we busted through the door. Raekwon and Ghostface with their criminology talk. Deck with his concepts and flow. Method Man with the charisma and lyrics to match. ODB with his antics and sheer rawness. Just the whole moving with a mob of disciples, mad deep, became the standard set by our Clan.

Now the fans and our peers were waiting to see how we were going to come with it this time around. Could lightning strike twice? Could the Clan still give the fans that raw, blunt-in-the-staircase rap? The pressure was on.

It was also the perfect time for me to show and prove. The more you're in the booth, the better you get, so I was making it a point to stay writing and rapping.

Back then, when *36 Chambers* was still on the shelves and *Wu-Tang Forever* was on its way, shit was popping and everyone was down to work because the only alternative to music was the street. Nobody wanted to go back to that shit, so we went hard on the road and in the studio. Plus, we were having so much fun touching and seeing shit we'd never experienced before. It was all new to us, and we were hell-bent on enjoying ourselves back then.

The budget for *Wu-Tang Forever* from Loud/BMG was much bigger than what we had for *36 Chambers,* so RZA set us up in a mansion in the Hollywood Hills for about six months. The whole place was ill. It had been used as a porn set before we got there, and that crazy vibe continued for the remainder of our stay.

Now, I'm gonna tell you something: people think that the musician party lifestyle, with the women and the drugs and everything, is a given, but in reality, that's a choice. Because there's a lot of faithful guys out there who make music. At a certain point, it's like, how much pussy are you gonna get? How much Hennessy are you gonna drink? How much weed are you gonna smoke? How much is enough?

Nowadays, I've had enough. I've been all around the world. I've been to Hawaii five times. I've been to Paris fifteen times. I've done it all. I'm done with the excess. I'm a grown man, to the point where I'm not trying to fuck ten women. I've done it—at one time in my life, I was juggling twelve women at once. Twelve women at the same time. And it drained me—it was fuckin' hard work. Because they all wanted the same thing. Every night it was another woman; one would leave, another one would arrive. For two weeks straight, it was a different girl every night.

Then my doorman got jealous. Seems he was mad 'cause I didn't have to work his hours. I was coming downstairs in my robe at noon, smelling like weed. Well, that and the parade of women coming through my place every day. So he told one of the girls I'd had another one over. Then me and him got into it, and there was some more drama.

The bottom line is, your lifestyle is always a choice—you can turn it up sometimes or you can just sit back and chill. It's always your call to make, however.

But at the time, we couldn't resist. We were the hottest dudes in the game, and we were living in a mansion on top of a hill next to Kobe and Shaq. That was a fun time, and we lived it up to the fullest. All the celebrities coming through; Aaliyah and all that, Kidada and Rashida Jones (Quincy Jones's daughters), Ray J, Brandy, Kurupt, Snoop, Bokeem Woodbine, all of them. We had mad motherfuckers come through there. We were always throwing parties in the spot, and it was an amazing time.

And I ain't gonna front, I got my share, too. I was on fire in L.A. The first day we touched down, we had to stay in a hotel. I was in my room for maybe twenty minutes, then I went out in front of the hotel and bagged a bad-ass white woman in a drop-top BMW. Meth was in the backseat, goin', "U-God, you a fuckin' ill motherfucker." We out running through the city, homegirl driving us around and all that. We come back, eat, then I go to her crib, she got a house in the Hollywood Hills. Even I couldn't believe it, I was like, *How'd I bag her so fast?* It was an amazing night, let me tell you.

I came back to the hotel and the others were screwfacin' me— they knew where I'd been and what I was up to. They were just sour that I was able to get with a fine woman like that so quickly.

Another time, I was at the mansion when Raekwon brought this girl and a couple of her friends through. Now, Rae liked to front, he talked so fuckin' much it wasn't funny. Now, I'm not about botherin' with a girl someone else has designs on; I'm not one of those dudes who moves in on your girl or anything like that. There's plenty of women out there in the world for every-one, far as I'm concerned.

So Rae brings her and her friends through. Me and some other peoples are in the living room playing video games and whatever, I wasn't paying them any attention.

Eventually I leave and wind up going to another lounge with Kidada and the rest of the Quincy Jones crew. The girl Raekwon brought over, she came to the same fuckin' club. It's a small fuckin' world. I said, "Hey, how you doin'? You with Raekwon, right?"

She comes right out and says, "I'm not fuckin' with him. I ain't giving him none." Just like that.

Five minutes later, we're in the bathroom going at it. She had it going on, by the way. Afterward, she went her way, I went mine. I come outta the bathroom ten minutes later, I'm tired, my shirt's all mussed up. Kidada and the others are giving me a look like, "Uey, I know you didn't just fuck that bitch in the bathroom." I just sat back down at the table and didn't say a word.

I guess Raekwon found out, 'cause I went back to New York for a week, and when I came back, it was like he'd been fuckin' some girl in my room, there were condoms all over the bed and shit. I said, "Oh . . . this is supposed to be payback for homegirl." I went and told him, "Yo, man, she told me you and her weren't even fuckin'. She just jumped on me. Now why you runnin' around here lying on your dick, fat boy?"

And he just got this look on his face like, "Fuck you, U-God!" But it was all good, just some of the fun and games of being a rapper. There's plenty of girls out there. And in the end, it doesn't matter, he still can't fuck with me. I just go and do my thing.

Of course, there were plenty of other times my Wu brothers and me got our party on. Ghostface and me always had a good time when we'd go out to hit the clubs. Ghost was a bit of a trouble-maker, but we had lots of fun together. Sometimes, when we weren't working in the studio, we'd go hit the town. Hollywood was right on our doorstep, so there was always plenty of A-list par-ties to rock out in.

One night, we went to Brett Ratner's place for a party. Nobody else wanted to go. The only dudes in the house was me and Ghost. We said, "Fuck it. We goin' to the party."

So, we get to the party and shit. Big mansion, Brett Ratner has the Ferraris all in the front. Me and Ghost, we were fuuuuuuucked up. I mean, we were so fucked up. We threw a gallon of rum in us. I was smoking. Ghost didn't smoke, he just drank. We were pissy fucking drunk.

We came up in the spot, and there were tons of people there and all that. Leonardo DiCaprio was up in there. Q-Tip, Kidada, Metallica, Keenen Ivory Wayans, all of them was up in there, the list just went on and on. There were mad motherfuckers up in this house. Oh yeah, Heavy D, God bless the dead. Heavy D was out-side waiting when we came outside. It was off the fucking chain.

We were walking around Ratner's crib cuffing our bottles and just slamming that shit back. I got more shit-faced than I'd ever been before. Ghost was getting into his mischievous mode the more he drank.

That was the night I got into a fucking argument with Leonardo DiCaprio. Me and him had words. To this day, I don't know exactly what happened or how that came about, because he was with Q-Tip. Now, A Tribe Called Quest and Wu-Tang are like family, we all go way back. I hadn't seen Q-tip in a while, so I was giving him extra love and hugs and all that shit. Even so, he was acting real funny.

What happened was that Leonardo said something slick to me. I was like, "What? I don't give a fuck if you're a movie star. I will punch you in your fucking face." We almost had an altercation right then and there. Q-Tip was just like, "Nah, man, chill." So I calmed down, and we went on our merry motherfucking way.

On our way out, Ghost just ransacked Brett's crib. He tore the fuckin' house up, just did him dirty. Ghost pissed all on his floors. He pissed off his fucking balcony. At one point, when we decided to move on to the next party and we're outside waiting for the cars to pull up, Ghost starts tearing up the landscaping around Ratner's crib. Ripped up his goddamn flower bed outside. Why he did it, I don't fucking know—to this day I still don't know why he did it. He just had a total wild-out moment and just started laughing and trashing shit.

When Ghost was ripping up the plants outside, Heavy D was right there watching. He was just shaking his head. I'll never forget Heavy's face—he couldn't believe what the fuck we were doing, why Ghost was acting this way. Aaliyah, who was hanging out with us at the time along with Kidada Jones, was looking at us like we were crazy.

I was laughing, but toward the end, it started getting a little embarrassing. It had seemed like a good idea when we were inebriated to just wild out, but eventually we got ourselves back under control. We got back in our limo and left. I don't know if that's the reason why, but Brett Ratner was the one who filmed the "Triumph" video.

I think we hit one more party, but we were all so faded we just went back to the mansion and fell the fuck out. When we got home, we barely made it into the house before Ghost fell on the kitchen floor and passed out, pants sagging, drawers showing. Think he was even drooling and shit.

It was a great fucking night. Regardless of all the crazy drama and shit, I bet those dudes never forgot us when Wu-Tang hit the party. And I haven't seen Leo since. He came to the studio with Meth one other time, but I missed him.

That wasn't the only crazy mansion we went to, either. One time we went to Mike Tyson's house, but he wouldn't let us in, the motherfucker. 50 Cent ended up buying the place later on, and this place was so fuckin' big, I couldn't believe how huge it was. At least two blocks long, it was humongous—too big, if you ask me. I never want a house where I gotta get on a scooter to go to my bedroom. Even if I had a family, I want to be able to just walk down the hallway and see my son. I don't want to have to get on the intercom to go find him. Even if I made ten million a year, I wouldn't want a place that large.

There's some hotels that are like that as well. Like in Las Vegas. I've been there, it's an experience. I'm not fond of the city in general. One time I went to Caesars Palace. I will never stay at a Caesars again as long as I live—the shit is just too fucking big. Room service took an hour to get to me. I wanted to go to the pool—it took a half hour to get there from my room. And then I was at the wrong goddamn pool! I had to walk through the entire casino in my flip-flops, take another elevator. I was like, "Yo, man, this shit *sucks!*" And Lord forbid you forget something and have to go back for it. They need a shuttle to get you around there.

Then there was another time when we almost got into it with Biggie Smalls, two or three days before he died, God bless. At the time, Ghost and Rae and Biggie had a little gripe going on because Rae and Ghost are troublemaking asses, and they'd started some shit with Biggie.

It was at the Billboard Live, right on the Sunset Strip. We were going out that night, gonna have a good time.

But by the time we got there, they were closing the Billboard down. We got a chance to slide up in there like fifteen minutes before the place closed. When we did that, the vans were parked outside of the front of the joint. We were riding in a rented Suburban, the same kind of car that Biggie, God bless, got shot in. All the rappers had pretty much the same cars; he had a Suburban, we had a Suburban. He had his entourage, we had our crew.

So we were all parked outside and shit. We walked inside the club and saw Biggie and Lil' Cease. Now, Meth had been on the track "The What," on Biggie's album, but Ghost had thrown some shade, comparing the cover of Biggie's album with Nas's *Illmatic*.

When we came in, I told them to squash the beef; we New Yorkers needed to be making music together, not going at each other. We all came up and gave big hugs and all that fly shit. It was cool.

All of us came out the club together, Biggie, Cease, all of us. Gave 'em daps, told 'em where we were staying. We both pulled out at the same time. He was behind us. We was in front of them. We did the U-turn at the same time in the middle of the street. Little did we know, that was going to be the last time we'd ever see him. A few days later, he was dead, shot in the street.

When we heard the news, we were in shock. I mean, dudes got shot all the time and pulled through. Besides, Biggie was a big guy, so I would have thought that would have saved him. I've known big fat dudes who got shot, and their blubber saved them.

But not this time—those dudes fucked him up. That was heart-breaking, 'cause we all came up from the streets of New York together. It was Biggie, Nas, the Wu-Tang, and Mobb Deep representing the East Coast.

We were the only crew that stuck around the city afterward. Everyone else from New York took off when Biggie got shot, they all left L.A. We stayed—we were still recording. Matter of fact, we went out on the town a couple of times. We were at the House of Blues and there was a bunch of Crips up in there. Me and Meth were walking through the crowd, and the Crips said, "Yeah, man. These fucking Wu-Tang brothers. These motherfuckers are the realest. Y'all ain't running like little bitches. Them other NYC dudes ran like little bitches, man."

"Whatever's going on with them, we don't got nothin' to do with that shit," we told them.

They gave Meth a fucking gun inside the fucking House of Blues, both as a symbol of respect from the street and also as protection. They wanted him to put it in the van. Meth was like, "Nah, I'm good, man. I don't want that shit."

They said, "Nah, man. We love y'all out here, man. Y'all is real, man. The rest of them is just a buncha punk-ass motherfuckers." It wasn't the first time someone had tried to pass one of us a hammer, and it wouldn't be the last.

That night at the HOB was poppin'—we had a blast there. That was also the night I swear I could have gotten with Kim Kardashian. This was before she got famous and all that. This lil' girl with long black hair was in the back by the bar. I was sittin' there, I got her number and all that, but we couldn't get together that night. And fuckin' Deck ruined the whole thing.

See, Deck wasn't gettin' any at the time—he had no game. So when she called the spot we were stayin' at, he picked up the phone and was like, "No, U-God ain't here right now. Are you comin' over to fuck both of us?" And that was the end of that—I couldn't get her to return my calls or nothin'. I was so mad, 'cause she was so fine.

Years later, when Kim blew up everywhere, I remember thinking, "Was that the shorty at the House of Blues?" And our paths have never crossed again, so I've never gotten the chance to ask her. But if we ever do, I'm gonna find out. And if she says yes, I'm gonna go, "Motherfucker, I blame Deck, that son of a bitch."

After Biggie got shot, the world was all on fire. It was going crazy out there. Me and Deck were sharing a room at the time. We had the mansion, and we had a little hotel spot, too.

One night, we were out in the Suburban, just gliding. We ended up back at the Billboard Live again, back to the spot where we last saw Biggie alive. We were just sitting there, on the side over in the corner. We were just sitting real low, watching the traffic go by. We were just sitting there like, "Yo, I can't believe he's dead, man. I can't believe it. What the fuck is going on?" We were smoking a blunt in the car and shit. We were just mad low, observing traffic. You couldn't see us. Well, we thought we couldn't be seen.

We pull off, slide up out of there. Gone. We jetting. All of a sudden, I look in my rearview mirror, I see somebody doing the same moves I'm doing. It was a BMW. I'm like, "What the fuck? Yo, son, we being followed."

Deck said, "Word?" He's looking through the back. We can't see. When I move this way, the car moved this way, too.

I said, "What the fuck is this? Watch this." So I did a whoop-a-doop and made the right turn real quick. I call it the whoop-a-doop. They did the right turn real quick, too. I said, "Yo, son. It's on."

Deck said, "Word. Pull up in front of the hotel."

I said, "A'ight." We get to the hotel. I pull up. I stop. I get out the car. I got a beeper on me. I use an old hood tactic and hit the clip on it to sound like a gun being cocked. Make it sound like

I'm packing. A lotta guys been backed down just by that sound. I know a guy who backed down an entire posse with just his beeper.

Now, I ain't got no gun in fucking California. I'm looking at who's in the fucking car. Guess who the fuck it is?

Queen Latifah, along with three beautiful ladies.

I was like, "Latifah?"

She was like, "U-God! Yeah!" She gave me a kiss.

"What the fuck?"

"Nah, you know. This shit is going down here with Biggie and all this mad shit. We looking at you."

"No, we were doing the same shit you were, seeing what the fuck is going on!" Turned out we were all just looking around, trying to find some answers about what had just happened to the Notorious.

She looks at the hotel, was like, "This is where you staying?"

"Yeah yeah yeah," I said.

"Okay, I'm out," she said. And she peels off on me, taking her carful of lovely friends with her. I love Latifah, always have.

The purpose of the whole mansion arrangement was so we could bond. There was a pool and a pool table, and big TVs everywhere, saunas, music blaring, smoking, drinking, gambling, everything. We had a spectacular time. The way we figured it, you want to feel successful when you're recording, that way you're at your top-notch A game.

I took the room in the mansion that nobody wanted. My room was right by the front door, so it seemed too in the mix. I took the room to keep everybody from fighting, and God blessed me with a nice patio with the killer view of the surrounding hills. I could see the whole canyon, plus look down onto the pool.

Standing on that patio, looking out over all that, made Park

Hill and 160 and especially prison seem like a million years ago
and a million miles away. I was very grateful for the opportunity
that had been bestowed upon me. I couldn't complain about not
having been on the Wu-Tang albums as much as the others, but
it was time for me to really step up in this moment and ensure
my placement on this new project.

For me to get back into that mode I was hitting right before
my son got shot, I had to block all my doubts and fears about rapping in the booth and all the extra stress on my mind due to my
baby boy's injuries and having medical complications that might
last for the rest of his life. It wasn't easy to get that shit off my
mind. There were so many unanswered questions to the specifics
of what had transpired on that day. I had to push all that out of
my mind and get creative and have fun.

One day I was prepping for the studio with my usual ritual.
First I smoked a bean on the patio and then went and got a mas-
sage. I came downstairs to where RZA had one of the makeshift
studios set up. When I walked through the doors the beat to "Triumph" was playing. I still remember what it felt like hearing that
beat for the first time. It was rumping. I come into the room and
look around. That's when I heard Deck set it off:

*I bomb atomically, Socrates' philosophies*
*and hypothesis can't define how I be droppin' these*
*mockeries, lyrically perform armed robbery*
*Flee with the lottery, possibly they spotted me . . .*

Devastating. That shit was insane. He literally bombed that
track. After you hear a verse like that, what the fuck do you do?
How do you profess to get on after that? Who the fuck could follow that up? Deck went all in, and he nailed it.

I gathered my thoughts and got a copy of the beat. I put my

headphones on and went off into my corner of the studio and just
sank into the beat. Then it came to me:

*Olympic torch flaming, it burns so sweet*
*The thrill of victory, agony of defeat*
*We crush slow, flamin' deluxe slow for*
*Judgment Day cometh, conquer, it's war*
*Allow us to escape, Hell glow spinnin' bomb*
*Pocket full of shells out the sky, Golden Arms*
*Tunes spit the shitty Mortal Kombat sound*
*The fateful step make the blood stain the ground*

After you hear a verse like Deck spit on "Triumph," if you're a
true MC, you have to come better, or at least on that level he took
it to. If your shit ain't up to snuff, there's no way it's gonna stack
up next to a verse like that. That was the thing about being in
Wu-Tang when we were at our best. You'd hear a crazy verse, and
you either try to top it, or come damn close. Not exactly like crush
it, but at least try to come as hard as you can, or at least come with
your own style.

That's what makes our group so ill. You have nine or ten MCs
trying to outdo each other on every song. It's not in a bitter, competitive way, but in a way that raises everyone's level. That's some
ill competition right there, the kind that breeds champions. It
raises the bar every time somebody spits their verse.

But the thing about *Forever* that still pisses me off today is that
RZA came after me on a lot of fucking songs. Several times when
I'm on, RZA's right behind me, like a fucking rhyme stalker or
something.

Sometimes it would spiral out of control. Nine MCs going at
each other, battling for who gets on the song can lead to some
hard feelings, too. With the creative process, there's no way all

nine of us would be on the same page at the same time. But the moment you hear a heavy beat, you wanna get on it, and you gotta come with your shit harder and better than everybody else. It didn't work all the time, mind you. The same sword you swing can sometimes chop your own hand off. It was a fine line, and at least for most of *Forever,* we walked it.

Now that I'd regained my bounce, I was all for some competition among my brothers. I was in prime form. I think everyone was a little shocked at the way I took over *Forever.*

I set it off on the "Severe Punishment" beat so hard I went first. As the first performer, I set the tone of the entire song with my verse. The rhyme just came together. I was always working on my writing, so I already had a rhyme ready.

Same with "Bells of War." That was something that was already written. Sometimes I just write a bunch of sixteens and then when I hear the beat, I see which one fits the moment. I blacked out (completely lost myself in the music) on that joint too, so they let me set it off again.

I took over that album. I really took my time to perfect my flows. I would live with the beat I was gonna rap over. I'd ride around in the whip all day with it. I'd talk to it. I'd eat with it playing in the background. My whole day moving around, I'm listening to that beat.

Sometimes, though, that wasn't the case. Sometimes things were more orchestrated than that. For the song "A Better Tomorrow," me, Deck, and Masta Killa were alone in the studio together. RZA had already hooked up the beat, and it was playing over and over again. While it was playing, we just talked about different topics. We were always a diverse group, and sometimes you just don't wanna rhyme 'bout grimy shit all day. Sometimes you want to come with some conceptual shit that has some jewels for the listeners going through hard times. As the 5 Percent, it was our duty, after all, to try to always guide people in the right direction. So we came up with the concept for the song to be about hardships and the state of the world and how the babies were being led astray.

I try to talk about all the things I've gone through in my music. My pains, my weaknesses, all that. I want to try and put all that out there for the listener to build on. I put those elements in my music because unfortunately, hardship is more relatable than success. So I poured my heartache, my betrayals, my incarcerations in the cage, out of the cage, the mistrust, the things I did, the things I still want to do . . . I just let my imagination run wild.

Cops must think I'm still on the block, 'cause my rhymes are so vivid it seems like I'm still seeing that chaos every day. I rhyme like my shit is a movie. I wanna give you the epic journey. Make you feel what I went through. Make you feel like you can go through all I went through and still make it out of a fucked-up situation.

I don't just listen to rap when I write; I'm trying to get in that Bob Dylan, Johnny Cash mode. I want to kick some relatable shit that will make people aware of the similarities in all of us, as opposed to the differences.

With "A Better Tomorrow," I decided I'd address my baby boy getting hit with a stray shot. I'd been through a lot, but that was a very traumatic part of my life. So I sat down and penned my thoughts and emotions and got it all on the page. Sometimes music is like therapy, but not in this case.

I didn't feel better. It wasn't therapeutic whatsoever. Shit, I wish it had been more therapeutic, but that was just me expressing some pain I was living with.

On *Wu-Tang Forever* I had something to prove, whether motherfuckers wanted to acknowledge it or not. I had a score to settle, a personal vendetta, so I didn't care for acknowledgment. You could be crazy nice, and no one is gonna acknowledge you. You need marketing for that recognition, for the most part. I'm being a bit facetious, but it's true.

Making *Forever* was a great experience. Aside from me coming into my own, we had a steady parade of well-wishers coming through the mansion. Aaliyah, Heather Hunter, Ray J, Brandy, Kurupt, Daz, Snoop, Brett Ratner, Busta Rhymes—we had a good old fuckin' time. It was inspiring to be around all of that on a daily basis. It was another one of those moments that I had to stop and just inhale to get the full effect of, like the last time I left prison. Almost every morning on the patio before going into the studio, I would remind myself to really be present and be in the moment so I can really appreciate everything. As a result, all kinds of shit was inspiring me.

One day as I was sitting in the tub with some girls, I started reading the ingredients on the back of the body scrub they were using to soap me up. It got me thinking. There's also a blaxploitation film called *Black Shampoo*. We were always watching blaxploitation films back then. So I mixed all those components together, and when I went into the studio later that night, I went in the booth with "Black Shampoo" in mind. I'd already been sitting with the beat for a good while, as per my usual ritual, so once I had the rhyme together and stepped in the booth, I told RZA to cue up that beat. Inspiration comes from everywhere when you open your mind.

Like my verse for "Impossible," for instance. That was inspired by Silk, my girl at the time. She was very rebellious, a revolutionary type. We were reading a lot of books. She would pass me things that she felt would add to my perspective on the world. *The Art of War*, the *I Ching*, *Strategies of Leadership*. She taught me about chi and spirituality, how to take my mind to a different place. She taught me the power to get into that creative zone. That brought a different style out in my writing, and it's evident on "Impossible." That verse was a reflection of that creative zone, and wanting more mature things for myself, like eating better and getting my shit all the way together. I didn't know anything about that before. I was coming straight out of the staircase. Before that album, it was all just beer and weed, and the outcome was drunken word architecture.

All kinds of things were opening my mind up. Like shrooms. I did mushrooms for the first time while we were recording *Wu-Tang Forever*. RZA and I were in the studio one night, and one of the disciples comes through with a big bag of shrooms. RZA had done them before, so he suggested we boil it and make a tea from it.

Like I said, we were straight out them project staircases, so after boiling the shrooms in a pot, we strained 'em through a stocking cap to keep it hood. We drank the tea, lit some weed up, and waited for it to take effect.

I don't remember exactly when it hit. I just remember smoking a blunt while freestyling shirtless in my socks. We were freestyling for hours and hours and hours and hours. Looking back, I was still trying to get over my shyness of rapping, so I was just flowing.

At one point, I remember RZA trying to snap on me, I think, and coming up with the hook for "Domestic Violence."

*You ain't shit.*
*Yo momma ain't shit.*
*Yo daddy ain't shit.*
*Yo money ain't shit . . .*

We just kept rhyming. That was the best time for us, I think. We were all still close then, before each of us started developing our own individual visions about what we thought our careers— and Wu-Tang as a whole—should be.

We were able to work through it all on *Wu-Tang Forever* because we still weren't that far removed from each other. We had all grown up, but not apart yet.

I couldn't wait to showcase what I'd been honing for the past few months. The other guys couldn't believe I came with it like that. That's what I mean about learning about yourself. Dudes told me "no" fifteen times in a row. And on the sixteenth time you shut motherfuckers up because your bars are finally up to par. Their eyes said it all when I stepped out the booth.

That was the best feeling ever. Now the same dudes who had laughed me out of the booth months ago were talking about me having the hardest verses on *Forever*. I just never gave up, though. It all has to do with your resolve. It's bigger than talent. It's bigger than ego.

I remember Scotty Wotty, the illest rapper in our hood back in the day, who we all were influenced by when we were growing up, and who was sort of my mentor, came around for a few sessions. This is why I knew I was a tough motherfucker for coming back all those times after I got laughed at and shot down and kicked out of the booth.

He came in to record and possibly get on the album with us, but he got kicked off the mic because he wasn't fitting right on the song. But instead of reworking his rhyme to better suit the track RZA made, he copped an attitude with RZA. I tried to talk to him about it, but his ego was bruised. "RZA ain't respecting me, he ain't respecting the art and my seniority . . ."

"Yo, dog, you have to come back, though, until you get it right," I told him. "You have to try it a few times to find what works."

But he never came back. His ego couldn't take it. Mentally, he wasn't strong enough to put aside the doubt and pride and just get in the booth and do what RZA said. If he had come back again, RZA would have found something for him to get on eventually. He would've been on right now with us, doing better for himself. Scotty has no idea where that one little verse might've taken him. It wasn't all his fault, though. It's hard to let someone coach you when it comes to your art, especially when you've been doing it your way for so long; it can be difficult to follow someone else's lead.

Scotty Wotty is the last of the street rhymers. After him (I put him on "Heads Up" on *Keynote Speaker*), I didn't deal with any more street dudes. They're just too rough around the edges. They don't have common sense, they just ignorant. They don't really know about the business and how things run. You have to constantly remind them. They blow up, they get mad, they get frustrated real easy off some stupid shit that doesn't even matter. You can't be uncoachable if you want to work with real producers, not just beat makers.

The main thing I learned while going through my hardships was that you're always supposed to keep working. Some dudes experience some hardship and get back in the zone. Others fall off, and let the tribulations and troubles take them off their square. You have to work through that shit until you find that gem again. You have to find yourself, or find the new you. That's how it goes. That's the pain of an artist especially—always trying to find a new self. How do you stay new?

When you create, you have to be in that mode. It's weird how inspiration comes to motherfuckers. You have to be in your zone. It could be a talking-shit zone, it could be a deep-concentration zone, or it could be a bouncy, happy zone. There's several types of modes you could be in. It's about just quieting all the extra shit in your head and listening to that creative voice—that's what that zone is.

And when you're a professional musician, there's so many other factors that have to be calculated that take away from the creativity—mainly the money and the politics of the music industry. I had to see past all of that though to get fully back in my mode.

I realized something else when I was writing and working on my craft that helped me as well. Though I drew inspiration from Rakim and other great MCs, I wasn't trying to be in the Top Five of any list. That's a dangerous place to be, 'cause once you fall from there, it's a long, long way down.

That's why I'm just happy being in the arena and competing. I don't need to rush for hundreds of yards every game. I'm good just getting a few first downs, rushing for some yards, putting my little stats on the board consistently and *boom*, I'm good.

# 17

# TOUR LIFE

Now that I was getting ill in the booth and the album was dropping, we had to hit the road again. With the release of *Wu-Tang Forever* in '97, we were practically a household name. This round of promotions and touring was gonna be a much bigger deal. Before, when we were doing shows promoting the first album, the venues were up close and personal—which sometime made things crazier. Things were haphazard, security was shaky, and promoters were shady.

Regardless of the unprofessionalism that went on in those early days when we were learning the industry, the tours were still a lot of fun. Even when shit got thick, we had each other to hold it down. Sometimes we fought to protect ourselves against a mob at a venue with inadequate security. Sometimes we were the aggressors. We stomped a few dudes out on some rah-rah shit, for no real reason other than angst. That was just the era. Rolling deep with a crew in fatigues, skullies, and hoodies was just the aesthetic, but we had a head start on everybody. Why do you think people always make metaphors and similes about being deep like the Wu?

We had so many other soldiers and cousins and producers and offshoots of the Clan and MCs in training on the road with us at times that we'd wind up sixty deep on a regular day, omnipresent forties and blunts getting passed around, etc. It was like we brought the hood with us everywhere we went. Rolling with a mob might get you sweated by the punkass cops, but it could save your life, too. These were the days when hip-hop clubs were still grimy. A shootout with a few fights sprinkled throughout the night was almost a given.

You had to have some dudes that were experienced in throwdowns and were gonna hold it down if shit got hairy. Every man in the Clan was already just that on his own, so together? We were definitely a problem when we wanted to be. Dudes were always testing back then, out of boredom maybe, or looking for a rep. Maybe some of 'em had that crab-in-the-barrel mentality, just didn't like seeing other brothers getting successful. Whatever the reasoning, we were gonna get tested at some point.

If I saw a problem comin' at us, I didn't let it fester and always addressed it right away. As I got older, though, I learned how everything was a test. When you're young, the answer is violence, or at least being abrasive—either you pop off or you knuckle up. Over time, you learn how to handle those tests differently. Then maybe, as a last resort, if you absolutely have to wash somebody up in the streets, you do it. Took my whole life to get to that level of maturity. We were wildin' for years before I outgrew that nonsense.

Sometimes dudes would try to rush the back door so they wouldn't have to pay and try to fuck some people up in the process. Some dude and his crew tried to come through the back door at one show. I knocked him down with a two-piece (two punches), and Masta Killa stomped his face. The rest of the Clan was right behind us, so his boys backed down real quick.

It's awesome when you have your mob behind you; it's like having a weapon you can't get frisked for. But sometimes that Clan mentality gets out of hand, too. Like one night after a show in Europe, we thought someone had stolen Ghostface's jacket. At the time, there was a dude on the bus with us. I don't know if he was a fan or something, but he was the only outside dude that wasn't down with us. We were conducting our own little investigation, and we were like, "Yo, dawg." We brought him up into a fucking hotel room and started beating his motherfucking ass, trying to find out if he'd stolen the fucking jacket. I mean, I'm jumping off the bed onto his head, smashing him with chairs, all this shit. We were tearing this motherfucker up. We whupped his ass so fucking bad, I thought we was gonna kill this guy.

Then it turns out we did all that fucking sucker shit for nothing. Popa Wu had taken Ghost's jacket and hidden it downstairs behind a goddamn vending machine. So we just let the poor, fucked-up guy go. Live and learn, I guess. It was unfortunate, but the violence we inflicted was born from a place of loyalty. That's not an excuse, it's just the way things went down.

And sometimes shit goes down and you don't even know what the fuck's goin' on. We got shot at in Chicago once. That was a crazy night. Some dudes shot at us over there. We were just coming out of the venue when somebody started shooting. Fucking bullets flyin', so we hit the floor and shit. To this day, I don't even know what the fuck it was about. It was just more drama.

Another time, we were touring in Florida. Me and Meth are sitting in a room, smoking, drinking, playing video games, whatever. We were invited to go to this little gathering Luke Skyywalker from 2 Live Crew was having. But Me and Meth were like, "Man, we ain't gonna do that shit." We're just keeping to ourselves.

Then one of my peoples, General Wah, calls up. "Yo, son, you gotta get down here. There's fucking mad bitches everywhere. This dude Luke is off the chain."

At first, we were like, "Ah, fuck this, man." But he called so many times, we finally said, "Fuck it. Let's go."

So me and Meth skate off to the motherfucking party with our crew. We get to the spot, and there's a long corridor. This dude named Born was also with us at the time. Raekwon and his cousin

Rico were there. We had these dudes who had just came out of prison, you know? Part of the entourage. All these motherfucking gangstas was already there.

We get there, Wah's already coming out of the party like, "Yo, son. You ain't gonna believe. Your man's in there bugging the fuck out."

We were like, "Who you talking about?" This dude Born was Busta Rhymes's man. He just came home from doing eight or nine years. He was having a fucking good time. But I didn't know the extent of the good time he was having yet.

We walk up in the door. And General Wah was like, "Yo." He was on his way out.

I said, "Hey, man, how you gonna tell us to come to the spot and you leavin' when we come here, motherfucker? Fuck is wrong with you?"

"Yo, son, you gotta go inside," he said.

We get inside. Mad commotion goin' on. Women are doing their little strip-dancing shit. As we got closer, the shit started opening up. In the middle of this fucking parted sea of people, this dude Born's in there eating this girl out right in front of everybody.

Luke is looking at us like, "You! You with this dude? Is he with you?" I don't know this motherfucker from a hole in the ground. I just met him that night, so I didn't really know him all that well. He's a 5 Percenter and had just come home after doing eight years, that was about all I knew. But we felt his pain, so we accepted him into our crew that night.

Now, one of our entourage was Reef, a straight-up gangsta who'd been with me since Sacramento, just a motherfuckin' magnet for trouble who'd spent more than half his life behind bars. And this dude was still prone to violence. Every time I was around him, I had to wear my vest, 'cause we'd either end up in fistfights or shootouts. The really crazy thing is that nothing would ever happen to him directly—other dudes would get fucked up, but somehow he'd always manage to skate through.

He walked past me. "Yo, we gonna fuck your man up," he whispers in my ear.

Now, everybody in the hood would say, "That's your man." That's project slang. Like, if I introduce you to someone and I say, "Yo, that's my man over there. Domingo's my man." If I didn't know someone, maybe I'd just met them once before, I'd just say, "Yo, that's your man." To clarify that he wasn't one of my peoples. They'd also say, "Your man Domingo." Saying "your man" indicates that you're connected with the person they're referring to. And if I'm saying that, I gotta really know you down deep. Saying someone is one of "my peoples" isn't done casually.

Reef came past me and said, "Yo, your man Born's up in there. Look what he doing." He was having a grand old time. I turn to my left, I see Kid from Kid 'n Play there. I'm like, "What the fuck?" He in the back room over there. I turn around the other way and I see Father MC. I'm like, "What the fuck? This whole shit is crazy right now." But this dude is still going down on this girl. I was like, "What the fuck is going on?"

We were just sittin' there in astonishment. Reef and all the rest of these gangstas were all staring at this dude like he's a piece of meat they're about to tear apart. Because he's embarrassing the entire crew. We're sitting there in the establishment, and Reef and all the rest of the gangstas are like, "Oh, shit. He's embarrassing us all right now in front of Luke." 'Cause he came in with us. Now Luke's already thinking we little gangsta motherfuckers, so this is out of pocket for us.

All of a sudden, it gets weirder. Motherfuckers start cheering him on, "Go! Go! Go! Go!" He was tearing it up, eating her out faster, faster, and faster, and she was coming everywhere. Squirting all in his face. He got to the point where he pulled his fucking drawers down. He's about to fuck her right in front of all these dudes.

Anyway, underneath his pants, he's wearing a G-string with palm trees on it. We done lost our goddamn minds. We couldn't believe this shit. I came from the streets, I ain't never seen this shit before. I mean, I came from the can; we had dudes in their boxers and briefs and everything runnin' around there, but I ain't never seen some dude wearing a palm tree G-string before in my life, especially this up close and personal.

Reef's ready now; all swoll up, getting hyped. He was getting ready to throw down. He walks past me again, sayin', "I'm gonna fuck this dude *up.*"

I was like, "Aw, shit!" We were gettin' ready to leave. This guy's whole collar was wet. He didn't fuck her, but the shit definitely got out of hand.

We finally pulled him off the girl, and we leave the party. He gets in the other car with all the fucking gangsta criminals. Now there's levels of criminals. Me, I'm an ex-con, I did my little three years, don't get it twisted. But these guys were hard-core *criminal* criminals—they've done a dime, twelve, thirteen years. Serious dudes.

Me and Meth and our dudes get in the other car, the light car. We were jetting around in little minivans with the sliding doors. We're on the highway moving; Meth and me are in the first van, with the other dudes following us. We must be doing eighty going back to the hotel. On the way, I turn around to see the other van swerving all over the road. Then I see the sliding door open, and shit is rumbling in the back. I said, "Yo, they fuckin' that dude up in the back of the van."

We're still doing eighty miles an hour. Then I see Born hanging out of the fucking sliding door for dear life. Reef is trying to kick him out of the door at eighty fucking miles an hour. Finally,

Born loses his grip and falls out of the van. He rolls into the fucking grass. I thought the dude was dead for sure. I was like, "What the *fuck!*"

The other van stopped. We kept going. "Man, keep going. Keep going. Fuck them dudes," Meth said. So we kept going back to our hotel.

Everyone went upstairs, but I hung around in the lobby, waiting for the others to show up. The van finally pulls up, and Born's back inside—somehow he survived being kicked out of a moving van without getting too busted up. However, Reef's in there *still* fucking him up, still punching this dude in the face.

I get out there and said, "Yo, man, chill, G. That's enough, man. Just chill before you kill this dude." The other guys leave. I hail a cab down in front of the hotel and say, "Yo, Born. Bounce, man, or they're gonna hurt you for real."

While he's sitting in the cab, Reef comes back out of nowhere like a fuckin' ninja. He grabs the luggage rack on the roof and swings his entire body through the open window to kick Born in the fuckin' face. One last time for the road. I was like, "This fucking guy." It's incredible. He survived that shit and made it back. He did it all on pure adrenaline. What a fucking night. The funniest part is that General Wah, the guy who called us out in the first place, he split when we got there and didn't even stick around for all the drama.

Wherever Reef went, drama was sure to follow. He was a good man to have with you, because he always carried his weight, and you could count on him to watch your back. On the other hand, if he was in the mix, sooner or later something was gonna go down, and nine times outta ten he'd be at the center of it.

One time he got mixed up in some trouble with RZA's brother Divine, and they ended up in a genuine shootout on the highway. I don't know exactly how it went down, but Reef and Divine were at a club in Atlanta and got into it with some dudes. Long story short, they ended up with Reef driving their Land Cruiser like a madman at a hundred miles an hour down the highway, with these dudes chasing and shooting at them.

Divine was in the passenger seat, he couldn't believe the shit he's in now. Finally, he had had enough of these dudes. Reef had a pistol on him, and Divine took it, then Reef slowed down enough so the guys pulled up close, and that's when Divine pulled some real *Die Hard* shit and returned fire. I mean he just let off on them, backed those dudes right off.

Reef and he come back to the hotel in their bullet-riddled car, and I just went, "See? This is what happens when you hang with Reef." The whole scene was absolutely crazy.

And no one was immune, either. One time, RZA told me he was going to Vegas with Reef for a couple days. Now, I warned RZA, told him to wear his vest and be on point and careful, or he was gonna get popped.

He was like, "Nah, I got this." Now, RZA may look kinda nerdy, but don't let that fool you—Bobby Digital ain't no fuckin' punk. Regardless, two days later, he shows back up with a busted lip.

So I asked him, "What the fuck happened?"

He says Reef and him were at a party. Sure enough, when Reef got into an argument with a guy who had a bunch of dudes with him who were part of Tupac's entourage, RZA ended up getting hit from behind, then got popped in the mouth and got his chain snatched.

When Tupac found out RZA had been the victim of the altercation, he ended up getting the chain back for him. He knew the guys who had rolled up on RZA, and in a matter of minutes Tupac got it back. He even arranged for RZA to see the dude who took the chain for a one-on-one if RZA felt like getting some getback. Nowadays that might be a big deal, but back then that was how the generals of movements could move.

When RZA came back, I just looked at him and asked, "Didn't I tell you to watch yourself with that dude?"

This sort of shit happened all the time with Reef. Just another day in his life. Eventually he got busted for slinging drugs, but he did his time, got back out, and is turning his life around today.

As usual, on the road or at home, the main concern was usually the cops rolling up on us. It's amazing that we didn't catch all kinds of cases. I remember once early during our tour days, we were somewhere in North Carolina. We got to our hotel late at night and rolled up some weed. We smoked everything we had—I mean the whole hotel was full of smoke—and fell asleep.

Me and Masta Killa were sharing a room at the time, and woke up the next morning with someone knocking on our room door. I remember hearing walkie-talkies in the hallway. I was like, "What the fuck is going on?"

Half asleep, we open the door to reveal an angry female sergeant. Someone had called the cops. The trees we'd been burning had stunk up the whole place, and the cops were there, and they were out to get us.

The sergeant had the entire floor locked down. The police were shaking down everybody on the goddamn floor. They were opening each door trying to find where all the weed was at. We didn't have no fucking weed; me and Masta Killa had already smoked all our shit. We tried to explain we were just artists passing through their fine town on our way to the next. They were out for blood, though. Police—fucking vampires.

When she came to our room, we said, "Ma'am, we don't have anything in here." After searching our entire room, she couldn't find any weed anywhere. We thought we were in the clear. She's getting more frustrated as her search keeps turning up jack shit. She really wanted to bag us.

Suddenly she stops by the desk she had passed several times while tossing our room. Right there in plain view are two seeds and a stem. That's all that's left from our smoke session the previous night. It's enough for her to lose her fucking mind, though.

"Aha. I knew something was up!" she said. "Y'all two going to jail. Don't go nowhere."

We're sitting there just staring at this lady. We said, "Lady, are you serious?"

She said, "Yeah, I'm very serious. Y'all don't go nowhere." All for two seeds and a stem.

She left us in our socks and drawers and went down the hall to get some of her goons. Soon as the door slammed, Me and Masta Killa looked at each other and without a word we threw on our clothes and grabbed our shit. I stuck my head out the door into the hallway. Some cops were up the hallway but they had their backs to us. We ran out of the room and into the fire exit. Tripping on the clothes we're carrying, we ran all the way downstairs, out into the parking lot behind the hotel, and jumped in the Wu van. We locked all the doors, hid under all the luggage, and stayed there, barely breathing.

The whole place was just crawling with these dudes. All around us, we could hear walkie-talkies and cops talking to each other while they searched for us. For two or three hours we had to stay hidden. All this bullshit persecution over two seeds and a stem with not a single hair of marijuana on it. Luckily, they eventually gave up on the search and we broke out to the next town.

Another time, Me and Ol' Dirty didn't have passports. The Clan was going to Canada, and we didn't want to get left behind. So we hid in the luggage compartment underneath the bus and snuck across the border. They didn't even look inside. This was before 9/11. It was a lot more loosey-goosey with security at that time.

Considering how many of us there were, and how wild and

straight out the hood our dispositions were, we could've very easily gotten locked up in every town we hit. But we were used to stashing shit on cops and knowing how to get out of situations.

For instance, punk-ass cops would shake down our tour bus all the time. They'd pull us over and make us stand on the side of the road while they tossed our belongings. But we were ex-drug dealers, so we know how to stash on those simple out-of-town cops.

I don't think any of us ever got bagged on tour. Isn't that kind of crazy? Other musicians are out here catching charges, but with the exception of ODB and Ghost, none of us really got too wrapped up with the law once we got famous. Ghost ended up doing six months on a gun possession charge, but he did his time and has been clean ever since.

To be honest, I think it's because crime is at record lows nowadays around the USA that cops are going around snatching up dudes. They have to still go hard, even though criminal activity is down. Ain't no big kingpin, high-profile collars in the street anymore, so they target singers and rappers. Rappers weren't really targeted back then, not until Tupac and Biggie and that whole thing. When we were making our promo tour rounds, gang violence was through the roof. Now that things have drastically quieted down on the streets, we rappers are the "big fish" cops are following and keeping tabs on.

In 2012, under the Freedom of Information Act, the dossier the feds had compiled on the Wu-Tang Clan for years was released, detailing how we were "heavily involved in the sale of drugs, illegal guns, weapons possession, murder, carjacking, and other types of violent crimes." I read it myself and was surprised at some of the things they tried to pin on us. I mean, I was a drug dealer once upon a time. I have carried illegal guns, which by default is weapons possession. But carjacking? Murder? I have no idea how they tried to tie us up in all that. Oh, and the "other types of violent crimes"—well, you've read the stories about Reef and those guys, so one might say that some members of the Wu knew people who would commit those types of crimes, yes we did.

Anyway, for years they kept tabs on us, hoping to gather enough "evidence" to charge us under the RICO act. That also wasn't happening; once we started making the legal money, it was easier than ever to leave anything illegal behind. Needless to say, nothing ever came of all these investigations. And I've kept my nose clean for the past twenty-five years, too. I value my freedom, because I know what it's like to lose it.

Overly suspicious cops and troublemaking roughnecks were only the tip of the iceberg of trouble on tour. Fucking with promoters was a whole other element. That one promoter trying to catch us with the fake hundred-dollar bill was light.

One particular shady-ass promoter comes to mind. This was when we were first starting out. We had already learned that you get up-front money before making a move. Then you get the back-end money upon your arrival at the venue. We made the mistake of performing once without securing the back-end money. The promoter started crying broke to get over on us. Not a smart move. You don't tell a bunch of hungry former drug dealers and gun busters that you don't have their paper. Especially when you're standing in front of us with a ten-thousand-dollar Rolex and mad gold chains on. Are you stupid?

Midway through one of his pleas, one of our crew just grabbed him and literally flipped him on his head. We all reached in his pockets and took his jewelry. Then our people just dropped him on the ground, and we was out the spot. He learned a lesson that night. WU-TANG CLAN AIN'T NOTHIN' TA FUCK WIT'!!

Unfortunately, we had to teach that lesson to promoters several times. There was an incident in Chicago that got pretty crazy. The infamous Chicago situation. We were on the *Wu-Tang Forever* tour at this point. After every show we would have after-parties. Sometimes different Wu dudes had different after-party situations set up.

This one promoter tried to be slick and put our name on his flyer. He figured with so many Wu after-parties going on, we wouldn't notice one more. Unluckily for him, though, we did hear about it.

He came to the show, unaware that we already knew about the sucker shit he was pulling. Some of our crew took him to one of the hotel rooms to sort matters out. He admitted to using Clan members' names to boost his party. An example was made of him that night. Dudes beat the shit out of him. He got a black eye, broken nose, we just did him dirty. He ended up with broken ribs that punctured his lungs. He sued us, too. Actually, that was one of our first lawsuits, but definitely not the last. Again, WU-TANG CLAN AIN'T NOTHIN' TA FUCK WIT"!!

Sometimes, we had disagreements with radio stations over promotion or sponsored appearances. One time, we got banned from Hot 97, the legendary NYC radio station. We loved those motherfuckers, man, we thought they were family. And we thought these motherfuckers loved us.

We'd dropped *Wu-Tang Forever* and were on the road hard. They also had dropped Biggie's shit (*Life After Death*). Both sellin' through the fuckin' roof. We debuted at number 1 on the Billboard chart and sold 612,000 copies in the first week of release. Crazy shit.

Hot 97 said they wanted us for the Summer Jam. We said we couldn't do it that year because we were touring Europe. They said, "If you don't come back and do Summer Jam, we're not playing your fucking record no more."

We were like, "Yo!" There's nine of us, so we voted. Some of us said, "Let's go back and do it." Some said, "Nah, man. Let's keep moving. Let's keep doing what we do. We'll fix that shit later." The dudes voting to return won.

We wound up going back to New York and doing Summer Jam. Little did we know it was a fucking setup. They had us headlining only a few months after Biggie Smalls died. Ain't no way in the world you can headline a show like that after the passing of a dude who was so iconic in the hip-hop game and so beloved by the entire city of New York. They shouldn't have expected us to be the headliners—it should have been a tribute show to the Notorious B.I.G. It shouldn't have gone down like that.

Twenty-five thousand motherfuckers in the arena. Lil' Cease and Junior M.A.F.I.A. was going on before us. We sit back watching their shit. Them dudes got all the New York shit on. They got all their shit together. We all fucked up because we're off balance. Mind you, we didn't get a sound check, because we just jumped off the plane and headed straight to the venue. I used to have nightmares about this shit every so often. They're gone now, but every now and again it would come back on me.

So, it's our turn. They put us on an elevator lift. They lift DJ Mathematics up. On the way up, you've got the turntables. Back then there was no Serato. None of that shit. It was turntables and mixer—good old-fashioned hip-hop. The lift was shaking. The needle kept skipping while he was being lifted. I mean it was making big, fucked-up noises.

I'm standing behind Math. Math is turning around and looking at me. I'm looking at him. He finally gets to the top. I shit you not, he starts trying to rock, the turntables are spinning, and he's trying to get us back on course. He starts trying to get the vibe going again. Half the fucking stadium starts getting mad. It was obvious Biggie had his fans, and we had ours.

The shit was so fucked up, Ghost gets on the speaker and says, "Fuck Hot 97. They sabotaged us. Ain't no way in the world we could come behind Biggie Smalls after he fuckin' just died, motherfucker. Fuck that."

Then, all of a sudden, all of Biggie's fans start leaving. He had about twelve thousand fans. We had about twelve thousand fans. Ours stayed. Biggie's left. We rocked on. We did what we had to do. After that, Hot 97 calls up and said, "Y'all is blackballed." They never played a Wu-Tang record again. I'm still pissed off over the whole thing. We've gone back in later years—performed there in '06 and '13—but the vibe was never the same.

That was a fucked-up situation. The whole situation was a sucker punch. But at the end of it, I guess it was all fair in love and war. We didn't care, we were just trying to rock, but I guess some people took it more seriously than that.

On rare occasions, it wasn't just the hooligans at the shows or the cops outside the shows. Sometimes we'd get into it with other rappers. Jack the Rapper was this huge rap festival during the early nineties. Every year, rappers from all over would flock to Atlanta to "network" with both established and aspiring artists and label executives.

One of the times we were down there, maybe our first time, Luke from 2 Live Crew would not give up the mic. He wouldn't let us on. 2 Live Crew was mad deep down there, and supposedly had been getting rowdy during the whole convention. Maybe Luke was trying to protect his market because we were down south. Whatever his reasoning, we were up next and he was keeping us from going onstage. We tried to be patient for a few moments, but you know how that goes when you're hungry for recognition. So after a few moments, the Clan had to rush the stage to ensure we did what we came to do. In the fracas that ensued, Luke's DJ got knocked out.

We didn't care, though. We had to get up there 'cause that's what we were there for. Unfortunately, after rushing the stage and finally getting it rocking, we only had time to do two songs. Just as well. Rushing the stage did as much for us as performing would have in terms of recognition.

We had a few other little skirmishes here and there with other rap groups, but the funniest rap rivalry to me was one that a lot of people might not even be privy to.

Akinyele and ODB were like Batman and the Joker. Usually Dirt was the one setting it off, so I guess he'd be the Joker. He'd run down on Akinyele at the drop of a hat.

I still don't know what their beef originally stemmed from. All I know is no matter the place or time, if ODB saw Akinyele, it was like Uma Thurman in *Kill Bill*—an alarm would go off in Dirty's head. We'd walk up in the club or whatever, and Dirt would spot him: "I can't stand this dude." Even if Akinyele was up onstage performing, Dirt would run right up on him and swing. Akinyele would swing back, and the next thing you know they'd be wrestling on the stage and rolling around on the floor.

It went down between them in ATL once when ODB rushed the stage. They fought over the mic for about five minutes before they were separated. And that wasn't even the best throwdown between them.

The wildest fight between Dirt and Akinyele was somewhere in Brooklyn. No lie, I think this was the wildest night in history, period. I have a lot of stories of wild nights, but this one particular time in Brooklyn was the epitome of wild. Of course, it starts with ODB spotting Akinyele onstage rhyming. "Oh, this bitch ass is here? Fuck this guy. This cornball-ass motherfucker, what's he doin' here? I *hate* this asshole."

Before anyone can say shit, Dirt's onstage fighting with Akinyele. The two of them are rolling around, cursing and fighting for the mic. As usual, Dirt emerges the victor, complete with mic in tow. So Dirty goes to the front of the stage and gets ready to talk his shit. Someone in the crowd lets off a shot—*POW!*

Right after that gun went off, "Shimmy Shimmy Ya" dropped right on cue. The entire crowd, everyone in that building, lost their goddamn minds. That energy, though it was teetering on a really negative vibe the whole night, still felt positive. In the crowd, dudes was smokin' dust in the spot, mad trees is burning. People pushing and jumping around. A few people got punched in the face and beat down in the fracas, but ODB was still rocking. Toward the end of his second song, though, shit turned into a royal rumble. Everybody started fighting.

There was mad commotion everywhere, so we all congregated in the back to keep from getting swept up in the shit. Slick Rick the Ruler was there, watching the whole thing go down in the back with us. He's in there in all his big-ass gold truck jewelry. There were bar stools getting thrown, glass breaking, someone got shot in the ass outside the club, people were getting stomped. All around us was chaos and bedlam, but no one touched Slick Rick. He was like the Statue of Liberty, motherfuckers just had respect for him like that. We made sure he was just shining with a sea of us goons separating him from the melee. The brawlers ended up taking their shit outside into the street.

With most of the fight outside, we took advantage of the little lull in action to gather up the soldiers and head out. As we're getting everybody together, one dude walks up to us. He had obviously been fighting, judging from his head leaking all kinds of blood down his face. He didn't seem fazed at all, though. In fact, he was hyped. He recognized some of the Clan and saluted us.

"Yo!" he shouted. "This the illest party I ever been to in my entire life! I fuck with y'all!" That's all he said. Didn't wipe the blood off his head or anything. Just said his piece and walked off.

We had a lot of characters on the road with us who would always keep things interesting. Popa Wu was a perfect example of one such character. He was the OG, the older god, who reaffirmed a lot of the 5 Percent lessons and was somewhat of a spiritual guide for a lot of the core members of the Clan.

Popa Wu was always very clean-cut. He always stayed on some dapper, gentlemanly type shit, rocking a fez and always in some slacks and fly silk shirts or a suit and some hard-bottoms with a fresh hat. He was real slick with the Supreme Mathematics too. He knows 120 backward and forward, and runs them off to you so fast you'd think Twista was rapping.

He'd seen a lot growing up in Brooklyn during his day, so he knew how to always keep his wits about him. Being so cool, calm, and collected got us out of trouble plenty of times.

He talked Method Man's arresting officers into letting Meth go on several occasions. Meth was always getting into some kind of trouble. One time while we were on the road, he was already cuffed and in the backseat of the police cruiser. Popa Wu approached the arresting officer and had a few quiet words with him. To this day no one knows what Popa Wu said to the cops. He talks like he's the president or some shit. All we knew was that every time Method Man got arrested for smoking weed in public or possession of marijuana or disorderly conduct or whatever—at least nine or ten times—within minutes he was out of the back of the cop car, uncuffed and back on the tour bus. Popa Wu was a motherfucking smooth talker, and he always got Meth and the crew out of some fucked-up situations.

That didn't mean he always kept it together, though. Once while on the road in Virginia, one of our crew, Daddy O, had a dirt bike and was riding it up and down in the hotel parking lot. It looked like fun—I can't front—but I wasn't getting on that shit.

Popa Wu, however, felt differently. "Yo, Daddy O! Lemme get a ride on that bike!"

Mind you, Popa Wu was dap (well-dressed) always. He had on

some loafers and slacks and a fresh silk shirt. Daddy O tried to warn him. "Man, you too fly to be riding on a dirt bike."

"Listen, man. I was down with Tomahawks [a well-known gang back in the day] in Brooklyn. I can handle this little toy you got," he says.

I had a girl waiting in the lobby, so I went to meet her and take her upstairs to my room. As I walk off to the lobby, I see Popa Wu drive off. I meet my shorty, go upstairs, and I'm back downstairs in less than a half hour.

When I get back to the lot, I see Lil' Free, aka General Wah, Daddy O, and everybody else out there laughing their fucking asses off. I ask Free, who was crying he was laughing so hard, what happened.

"Yo, you missed it. Popa Wu totaled the bike and fucked himself up. We told him not to ride that fuckin' bike."

Sure enough, in the back of the parking lot, the bike was lying on the ground, completely totaled. The slip-ons Wu had been sporting were scattered on the ground as well. I looked in the tour van and saw two feet as big as meat loaves sticking out of the backseat. I went back to find Popa Wu lying there. When I'd left him, he was all crispy and shiny with his immaculate silk shirt, looking like an icon for flyness. Now he was all fucked up, his clothes ripped and bloody, and his feet were all swollen up like the Elephant Man. Turns out he broke one foot and one ankle on the motorbike.

Even so, he tried to tough it out by driving to the next town with us, he rode for eight hours with two fucked-up feet. By the time we rolled into town, he had to go to the hospital.

You'd think Popa Wu would have learned his lesson after that, but nope! Once, we were in Hawaii at this really dope outdoor spot, with food and drinks and ATVs whipping around. Popa Wu must've gotten tired of seeing us have all the fun on the ATVs, because he decided to hop on one, too. Again, we warned him not to, and then warned him a couple of more times for good measure.

"Take it easy on them shits, Popa. They move faster than you think."

His response was typical. "Man, I was in the Tomahawks in their heyday when we used to ride all over . . ."

Before anyone can teach him the ins and outs of riding the ATV, he squeezes the throttle with mad force. The ATV peels out, and he almost catches whiplash the way it takes off. He tries to straighten out the handlebars. We're all yelling instructions and telling him to slow down, but he doesn't listen, or maybe he can't do what we're telling him to do because he doesn't know how. He goes flying right into some bushes. The brush was so thick it caught the bike and him and just stopped it dead in its tracks. It stopped so suddenly, he flipped over the handlebars and goes flying.

We're all laughing, but we're hoping he's okay. When we go into the bushes to drag him out, we realize we're on the edge of a cliff. We had no idea. Don't you know if those bushes hadn't caught the ATV and stopped it, Popa Wu would've flown straight off the damn cliff for sure.

After that, we didn't have to tell him to stay off the bikes anymore. It took a couple times and a near-death experience, but he finally learned his lesson. At least he didn't end up in a wheelchair.


Going all around the world, we had to get over our share of culture shock. This was nine dudes from Staten Island crossing oceans and ending up on the other side of the planet.

Like getting on a plane for the first time to go to Japan in 1994. We were a little reluctant, but it was for the fans. Japan was a different monster. You had to get on that plane for fifteen hours. But when we got off, I was so glad I had come. That was also when we were filming a documentary of the tour. I love Japan. The culture was more exotic than anything I had ever experienced. We were the only black people for miles. While I was there, I felt like me and my Wu brothers were the only black people on the planet. We were so outnumbered, it really felt like we were aliens from another planet. When we'd go to restaurants, Japanese children would stop and stare at us because they'd never seen a black person before. They were in awe of us. I'd never felt like that before. It was really interesting. The first time getting my back walked on while wearing a silk robe and tasting sake was in Japan.

Also, at this time the yen was strong against the U.S. dollar. I had like a hundred T-shirts that I sold for fifty bucks a pop. I'd wanted to bring a lot more, but the main shipment got caught up in customs, so I couldn't make the really big bank over there. I wound up paying about a grand for the shirts I did bring, sold them all, and went home with about four grand. That was a good payday—when you're just starting out, to make a flip like that, it felt like I was back on the block hustlin' again, only this time it was all legal.

I'd have to say that of all the countries I've traveled to, Japan and Italy have the best food. The food in Japan is powerful, it's off the fuckin' chain. We had food prepared for us right in front of our eyes. It had a profound effect on me.

More important, you felt good after eating there. I wasn't even working out, and my muscles were just popping. Not like the shitty, sluggish feeling you get after eating a bunch of contaminated, processed American food. I was so glad I wasn't lazy about taking the long-ass flight out to Japan. They got so wild for Wu-Tang in those early years, it was crazy.

And we did some crazy things there as well. For example, Dirty loved to fuck groupies. The craziest ODB story I remember happened during our Japan tour. He came to my hotel room with this woman he was with at the time and asked me if I had any condoms. Now, I told him, "Yo, man, I don't have any condoms."

So he's looking around, but like I said, I didn't have any protection. Then he sees the food tray, which was wrapped in plastic, and says, "Yo, I'm gonna use Saran Wrap." He goes into my bathroom, locks the door, wraps his dick up in Saran Wrap, and fucks the girl right there in my hotel room bathroom. He comes back out with his little funny-ass grin on his face, and that was that.

The other thing we found out while in Japan was that they have very strict drug laws. We were coming through Japanese customs, and Masta Killa had three ounces of weed on him. Even so, somehow he gets through with the shit, so now we have weed in Japan—but we have no rolling papers. So we improvised, and rolled joints out of pages of the Bible from our hotel room.

When we told our local promoter about it, he said we were real lucky, 'cause getting caught with a joint could mean a five-year prison sentence. I couldn't believe my ears, but he was dead serious.

That's why I went crazy on another trip to Japan, when one of our entourage somehow got a huge bag of weed into the country. I damn near lost my mind when he pulled out this huge bag, at least two pounds, right there in my hotel room. I took a little piece—I'm not *that* stupid—then screamed at him about the rest, "Yo, get that shit the fuck away from me right now! You know how much jail time you could get around here for that? Don't you ever come around me with that again!" He apologized for bringing it. "Yo, Uey, I'm sorry, I didn't know."

But I wasn't about to take a chance—no amount of weed is worth a possible five years in the joint.


I enjoyed my time in Italy. It had cobblestone roads everywhere, and little alleys you could duck into and explore. We went by the

Roman Colosseum, the ancient gladiator spot, which was smaller than I expected. I thought it would be big like fuckin' Yankee Stadium, but that place was a Little League arena at best. The reality of it broke my heart. I remember thinking Hollywood had fed me some bullshit with the *Gladiator* movie and all that about its size.

Late at night, you'd go down into this little speakeasy-looking place, this little back-room bar that looked like nothing. But then when you get inside the spot—bad fuckin' bitches everywhere! And they are dressed to the nines—I mean dresses, shoes, the whole outfit. Everybody in Italy is well dressed.

Sometimes it's the little things that have a big impact on a place. When I stayed in Switzerland, I noticed how amazingly healthy the people over there, especially the women, looked. Their skin was clear and glowing, and their hair was glossy and magnificent. I found out while I was there that Switzerland has some of the very best tap water in the world. When I said I wanted to get some water, someone told me to drink the tap water. I replied, "I don't drink tap water!" but they said here in Switzerland, you can. They claimed it was the healthiest water in the world, and from what I saw of the people, I could believe it.

We traveled all over Europe. My first time in Amsterdam was also a crazy moment. Of course, weed is legal there. And we were so used to getting locked up and shit that we had to adjust ourselves to the idea that it was perfectly legal to smoke in public. We'd be walking through the streets smoking, and the police couldn't do nothin' to us. It was a feeling of invincibility.

So me and Deck go for a walk, hit up the smoke shops. We ended up rolling up in a McDonald's. We were just sitting there, smoking a spliff, giggling and laughing the whole time. We ate there, too, and when we went to throw our garbage away, the wastebasket read "dank you" instead of "thank you." We were so high, we kept saying it all night, "Dank you, man, dank you. Dank you for this moment."

We also went to the red-light district. The hookers didn't want to get with us, because they said black men were too big! We tried to kid around with them, but they were serious, they wanted nothing to do with us, so we didn't get any. Still, we wandered around in awe at these women hanging around in the windows of brothels like ornaments on display at Macy's. Again, all perfectly legal.

My mind was blown at all this, so I checked out the history of Amsterdam and found out they legalized drugs and prostitution to stop crime. I mean, heroin is legal there, all that shit is legal. And the prostitutes are tested weekly for STDs. I found out that sex-related and drug-related crimes rarely happen there (burglaries and pickpocketing are another matter, however). I was like, wow, that's kinda awesome.

London was also nice—it often reminded me of New York City. Of course, in London, you had to be careful crossing the street, because you're used to looking one way in America, but in England, you gotta look both ways, because sometimes they have traffic coming from both directions in the same lane, so you had to watch out. That was the first time I'd ever seen a car with the steering wheel on the right side as well.

During that tour, we were dealing with English pounds; you had to transfer your money to pounds. I gave the woman at the desk one thousand dollars, and she gave me back four hundred pounds. I was like, "Motherfucker, where's the rest of my money?"

She said, "This is the currency exchange."

I said, "Oh, a'ight."

On top of that, we couldn't find anything good to eat in London. The food was different. It was bland, and when we did eat, it tasted different. One time we went to a restaurant that had the weirdest fucking menu I'd ever seen. I'm talking true Indiana Jones–style shit, like monkey brains and I don't even know what else. It was a real Andrew Zimmern moment. I wasn't even sure what I was looking at, but there was no way I was touching any of it.

We had good food in France, Paris especially. But what I didn't like about France was that a lot of the people there don't wear deodorant, so they kinda stank.

The fans over there, though, they were insane. As wild as my team was, sometimes the crowd would get wilder. The fans in Europe take their music festivals really seriously. They still do—to this day they are more insane, man. They're just a little rougher, a little wilder. Stage diving. Toilet paper rolls flying in the air. Crazy shit.

We did a festival with twenty thousand or thirty thousand people. We performed in a tent, and people were spilling out all over the place. Everyone is hyped and moshing, chanting, *"Tiger Style. Tiger Style."* As soon as the crowd heard the intro to "Wu-Tang Clan Ain't Nuthing ta Fuck Wit," they shifted into a higher gear of crazy. All you could see was thousands of heads jumping up and down, it was fucking insane. People in the crowd started climbing onstage and stage diving into the crowd. Most of them were successful and got to crowd surf for a few before the crowd would let them down.

I'll never forget, me and Deck were standing next to each other on the stage during our European tour, watching the crowd buck-wilding. Suddenly this one dude staggers onto the stage, takes a running start, and swan dives into the air over the crowd. He was suspended in the air for what seemed like a few seconds. As he was coming down, though, the crowd shifted, and suddenly there was no one there to catch him. Me and Deck burst out laughing when the dude landed on his head and neck, I mean, we were in tears.

Now don't get it twisted—that might seem kind of cold, but you gotta remember we weren't used to any of this—the rolls of toilet paper getting thrown around, the mosh pit, mud pits, stage diving—all that was new to us. So when this happened, we busted out laughing simply because we'd never seen that shit go down before. Fortunately, he popped back up off the floor and tried to act like nothing happened. The dude had to be hurt, though. Either physically or egotistically.

Me and Deck were on the mic shouting him out and laughing as soon as he popped back up. "We saw that, dude. God willing nothing's broke. Hope you a'ight." He looked around the crowd for an escape. Seeing the exit sign above the doors, he ran for it, holding his neck the whole time.

Another wild fan experience I had was in Aspen, Colorado. Our tour bus got caught in a blizzard and got stuck in the middle of nowhere. We had to spend the night in the bus, and thank God we had generators on the bus, otherwise it would have been one cold-ass night there.

We had to take vans into the mountains while they got our bus out. In Aspen, we stayed at this really nice lodge, where everything in the room was wood: the bed frame, the walls, the chairs, all of it. There was a bearskin rug on the floor. It was real nice but unexpected, 'cause I wasn't used to the skiing culture and all that.

So what happened was that the car company Scion threw a little event for Genius, Raekwon, and myself. Now, this was my very first time on the ski slopes. And the lady that was throwing the event tricked me out. She went out and bought me a complete skiing set, from the suit and boots to skis to a snowboard, I was all set up.

We get to the slopes, and I don't know about the ski lift, 'cause again, I've never been on one in my life. And this was what's called a T-bar lift, which is just a tiny little bar that you sit on, attached a slender pole running up to the overhead cable—and that's it. You're not sitting ina nice comfy double seat.

So I'm talking on the phone and not paying attention, all I know is that the lift chair is coming. But what I didn't realize is that we had to go up the entire side of the mountain on this thing. And once I was on it, I swear it looked like we were fifty thousand feet above the ground, supported by a cable that only looked about an inch thick. Even worse, it kept stopping and going as they let other people on, so we were swaying back and forth like crazy.

By the time I realized what the fuck I'd gotten myself involved in, we were halfway up the mountain. We'd go up for a bit, then stop for five minutes, leaving us stuck in midair swinging back and forth in the breeze. My feet were dangling in the air, and I was screaming at the top of my lungs at this woman the whole way. I seriously contemplated jumping off, but I could see there wasn't a lot of snow beneath me to break my fall. So I thought, *Fuck it, I'll take my chances.*

We finally make it to the top, with me cussin' her out the whole way. All I see are white people everywhere. There was a snowboard run up there, and there were dudes doing tricks on the pipe and all that. Cute lil' snow bunnies riding by on snowboards, that made me sit up and take notice, like *Yo, where the fuck am I at?*

Now, they did know how to take care of their peoples there; there was a full bar, and a bunch of tents along one side of the slope. I head over there, order me a drink. What I didn't remember was that I was eight thousand feet above sea level. Of course, the alcohol had a supercharged effect on my brain, and I had no idea it was coming. I had half a drink and smoked a spliff, and by the end of those I was so fucked up I couldn't believe it. I thought someone had spiked my drink, but the folks around me just told me I wasn't adjusted to the altitude yet. I asked how you do that, and they said I just had to keeping breathing in the air.

So I'm breathing in and out, and a Wu-Tang fan slides by on a snowboard, sees me, and asks, "Yo, you wanna come on the pipe?"

I stare back at him, and was like, "Are you fuckin' crazy? Look at my face." I'm totally shitfaced with a ski suit on, I know nothing about snowboarding, and this dude wants me to go in the pipe? That is a recipe for my demise. No, thank you.

I did, however, get on a snowmobile, and tore around on that. That's how I got down as well. That was a lot of fun—I was a little pissed off, like, why couldn't we have taken this up the mountain? I never did ski there—I'm not gonna try something like that without practicing it first.

We love all our fans, wherever they're from—they're the greatest in the whole world. And Wu-Tang's always had a special place in our hearts for disabled fans. One guy rolled up on me once outside of a concert and told me he got paralyzed at a Wu-Tang show. Don't know if it was true or not, but it still touched my heart. I felt bad, but he said it like he was proud. I felt we owed him something, though. So we had him escorted inside the venue. When it was time to rock we let him come onstage with us. Since then, anybody in a wheelchair is always welcome any time. A few times we would look out at the crowd and see someone in a wheelchair. We'd stop the show and go down into the crowd and actually get the person in the wheelchair. If there was no ramp to get onstage, we would just carry them up there and set them down on the stage. We'd let them chill with us the whole time we rocked. After the show, we'd take them back down into the crowd the same way.

Wheelchairs are always welcome. So much so, in fact, that people in wheelchairs can get into our shows for free. If they're outside when we're coming in, we give them passes with no hesitation. Those are our truest fans, because not even a physical disability will deter them from attending one of our shows. Those type of fans are the ones we do all this for, and we try our hardest to never disappoint.

Every Wu-Tang member has busted their ass onstage at one point or another. Except for maybe Rae, because he doesn't move around that much onstage.

RZA busted his ass a few times, but I remember this one time in particular, he was more hyped than usual, so he was sauntering around the stage like a wolf. The stage was a bit wet from us splashing water at the crowd and vice versa. Sure enough, when it's RZA's turn to set off a record, he runs to the front of the stage with mad energy.

*There's no place to hide*
*Once I step inside the room*
*Doctor Doom*
*Prepare for the—*

*Boom!* He slipped so hard his feet went right into the air and he came down, landing on his ass. Needless to say, we had a laugh or two about that. We always laughed at each other because we knew sooner or later it'd be someone else's turn to fall or crash a bike or whatever.

I took a bad spill myself at the Continental Airlines Arena in New Jersey, on the night Ol' Dirty Bastard died. The fall itself actually wasn't so bad, now that I think about it, although the crowd, about ten thousand strong, all went *"Ooooh"* when they saw it. What was bad about it was that I fell between two speakers and got stuck. Like, I could not move. The rest of the Clan was doing their set, so no one would help me get out of the goddamn speakers. I'm practically lying there with the mic in my hand. So I yelled into the mic, "Somebody help me! I'm stuck between these speakers!"

Security came and helped me get out, and I rocked the mike, and the show went on. The others joked about it for hours, of course. The very next day, we heard Dirty had died. I think that's why that Continental Arena show will always resonate with me. It was the last Wu-Tang show that Dirty was alive for, even though he didn't attend.

Now I'd known years earlier that ODB was gonna die before his time. I got one of my crazy brain jumps about him, a flash of what was gonna happen. Before Dirty passed away, I told Masta Killa that he was gonna die young. I knew his character, and when he went to jail and he was a drug addict, I understood where he was coming from, that he wanted to be the man again. And he came home and wanted to pick up right where he left off. Like I said earlier, you go to jail for three years, you need three years back on the streets to get your head straight, get your bearings. But when you want to rush back into being a star, that takes a little time. You're rusty—you don't know how rusty you are, but you are rusty.

He needed to take his time to ease back into things, but Dirty didn't have that kind of patience. Before he went to jail, he was on drugs, coke and all that crazy shit. And then he was in the crazy house, and who knows what they shot him up with when he was in there. At the time, I said if he's not careful, Dirty's gonna fuck around and die of an overdose. And unfortunately, that's exactly what happened—he came home and tried to get into that lifestyle again right away, without realizing that he had to ease back into it.

When Dirty passed away, that was a more emotional switch, 'cause that was our brother, and he and I were kind of close. We all came out of the streets together and became a successful rap group, and there's this bond that joins us together. It's fucked up when you see somebody that you love every day, and then they're just gone. I cried so fucking hard when I heard he died.

It was hard at the beginning, when we were getting our feet wet on the road, but fun, because we were embarking on something new. But overall, touring is a lot of work, and you need a crazy amount of tenacity to withstand the wear and tear of life on the road.

And now, after decades on the road, it's still rough because you still have to put that work in every time. Traveling, on the plane, off the plane, go to hotel, unpack, go to the show, do the show, come back, pack up, get on the plane, off to the next venue, and it starts all over again. That's why I got especially mad at my Wu brothers this last go-round with the work surrounding *A Better Tomorrow*. They didn't want to do the work this time around, and the album promo suffered as a result.

'Course, we still found time to get our party on.

One night, after the American Music Awards, Ghost and I went out hunting for some parties to hit up in Las Vegas. We had the limo, so we were going over there and then over here and then back around the Strip hitting up different parties. All the parties we were hitting at first were wack at best.

"Yo, Ghost, let's hit Puff's party. I bet it's popping off!"

We made a few more rounds before heading over to Puff's. We finally get to his shindig, and the party was popping. The first telltale sign that it was gonna be a hell of a night was that Mary J. Blige was there. She was on her way out, but she still showed us love. Mary always showed us love since Method Man and she had that Grammy winner together. She was never too busy for a hug and quick chat. Once we saw her, we knew it was popping inside.

"I told you this was the party to be at, Ghost!"

It was all celebs when we walked in. Crazy champagne bottles and glasses everywhere. Puff throws the best parties. He's the king of that. With Puff, everyone feels comfortable. If me or some of my Wu brothers threw a party back in the day, people might not come because they thought it might be too rough for them, or they might get shot or stabbed. But with Puff, all types of people feel safe and comfy enough to just relax and drink some champagne. People going to a Puff party know they have to come correct. You gotta get right before you fall through one of those shindigs, ya dig? Put your hard-bottoms on, maybe a suit, get your chinchilla out the cleaners and put your diamonds on, because it's going to be a classy affair, at least in comparison to some of the functions I've been to. His parties were historic in their time. The late 1990s was just a really, really good time for hip-hop. Hip-hop was just becoming a billion-dollar industry, so money was getting thrown around. Dudes don't party like that anymore. There's rarely an occasion to get suited up or don a tux or even wear all white.

That night, I saw someone I'd had a crush on since I was a lil' snotnose in Park Hill watching *Good Times*. Every black kid in America had a crush on Janet Jackson back in the day. She was looking as fly as all outdoors. I noticed there were a lot of dudes kind of hovering around watching her out of the corner of their eyes, but they all seemed too shook to approach her because she was Janet (Miss Jackson if you're nasty) Jackson. You know me, I ain't scared of rejection. If you can master how not to be hurt or bothered by rejection, you'll conquer the world.

So I stepped to her with a swiftness, kissed her hand, told her I loved her. Right away I made her laugh. I knelt down next to her on a long couch—it was full up with Janet, Eve, Missy Elliott, Jermaine Dupri—and talked with her for a few minutes. She was wonderful, sweet and a little shy. I got a picture with her and a little kiss on my cheek.

I fucked up, though. I got up to make a few rounds around the club. I told her I'd be back. When I looked over my shoulder I shit you not, she looked kind of sad, like lonely. It's got to be tough being that pretty, man. I never made it back to chill with her because not long after that Eve came up to me asking me about the Ruff Ryders line in "Cherchez La Ghost." By the time I explained it wasn't a diss, Janet was gone. Damn.

I've shaken the hands of some of the most amazing people on earth. I've shaken Barry White's and Isaac Hayes's hand, God bless the dead. Little Richard. Cher. Garth Brooks. Britney Spears. Celine Dion. Bobby Brown. Whitney Houston, God bless the dead. Bono. B. B. King, God bless the dead. Lenny Kravitz. Macy Gray. Pamela Anderson. Tommy Lee. Deborah Harry. And dozens more.

I even shook Donald Trump's hand. This was about fifteen years ago, at a mansion party in upstate New York. Me and my man Homicide came through, got pictures with Michael Strahan and Trump. I think Homi got that picture, though, 'cause I can't find it.

We really knew the Wu-Tang Clan was lit when we went on the tour with Rage Against the Machine in 1997. That was a great feeling. It was probably the biggest tour of the summer, and unlike some of our previous experiences on the road, this shit was completely professional. Everything was highly secured. Everything was new and nice and neat and clean and proper. This was not some hood shit, like when we'd just pile in the van and drive a thousand miles to Wisconsin. This was straight top-notch living. Everything and everyone catered to us.

The tour bus was official. We'd roll into town on that bitch and hit the venue for sound check. Then we'd have this Winnebago-type RV take us to the hotel. When it was showtime, the Winnebago would scoop us up and take us back to the venue. Then after the show and parties and after-parties, we'd pile back on the bus and skate out of town to the next one.

We were surrounded by super-professional people all the time, making sure we had everything we needed. Our hotels were immaculate. They'd literally roll out the red carpet sometimes when we arrived at certain destinations.

Wu-Tang was a worldwide phenomenon at the time, but still kind of a mystery to a lot of people. To satisfy their curiosity, a lot of music industry vets were coming out to our shows. We saw Aerosmith, Paul McCartney, Metallica, Pink, Black Eyed Peas, Soundgarden, Lenny Kravitz, all the rockers. The sad part was that for a lot of these, I don't have any picture of them, because this was before cell phones and all that, so if you didn't have a camera there, you didn't get the shot.

Also, a lot of times, at least in the beginning, I wasn't checking out who was performing with us—after our set, I would usually head back to the hotel. But I changed all that on this tour. That's how I got turned onto not only Rage, but Soundgarden, because I'd heard their music on a video game called Road Rash, and when I saw them on the schedule, I stuck around and checked out their set. Man, these dudes were total rock motherfuckers. That was the first time I really saw the electricity of really good rock music. I'm not saying that the other bands weren't rockin', but this motherfucker Chris Cornell onstage, his hair looked like electricity was going through it, his shirt was blowing, and he was out there on the stage tearing up these little young kids in the audience. And I was like, *Whoa, shit.*

That in turn had an influence on me trying to turn my music into that alternative style of hip-hop. That experience changed the way I looked at music. I was seeing how Rage and Soundgarden were doing it, and how there was a whole different audience out there compared to what we were used to. Now, mind you, the

Clan started out primarily in and for the black community, but as we grew more popular, our reach expanded to multiple races all around the world. That's another reason why we're so successful, because our music appeals to everybody in the world. As a musician, that's what you're trying to do, and that's one of the things I think is wrong with hip-hop today—it doesn't transition into other territories very well, not like it used to.

That tour was an eye-opener for me for several reasons. A big one was because it put us onto music festivals and shit like that. I love doing festivals. Those are the best shows. First of all, you're not rocking for a couple hundred people, or even a few thousand. No, sir. You're rockin' for fifty thousand hard-core Wu-Tang fans. It was some prestigious shit. There's no feeling like that. Since the Rage tour, we've rocked with Mos Def, Pink, the Roots, the Black Eyed Peas, you name it . . . shit, we'd run into everybody. We'd spend the night talking to some actors and directors, and then get back on that comfy bus on our way to the next luxury hotel. And of course, women were everywhere.

That Rage tour was so ill. I think the best show might have been the one in Hawaii. First of all, those islands are fucking paradise. You get there, the sun is on your back, everything is green and yellow and radiant, and the colors are popping out. It's phenomenal. The water, the Jet Skis, all that fly shit going on, it felt like we were kings there. The whole time I had the *Hawaii Five-0* theme song running through my head. I'm just a TV kid at heart.

At one point on the tour, Zack de la Rocha, the lead singer of Rage Against the Machine, sprained his ankle during a performance. We thought the tour was going to be fucked up. We thought it was going to be finished, but nah. Zack gets airlifted out by helicopter, goes to the hospital. The next day he comes back with a cast on his fucking leg and starts rocking again like a true champion rock star, still jumping in the air and around the stage.

Two weeks later, Mook comes and says, "Yo, the promoters, they're lowballing us. We could be getting way more money." Mind you, we done made crazy bread already. I'm thinking like, *Yo! We gotta finish this tour!*

Ghost and Rae, though, said, "Nah, man. We need to do this. We need to do that. We shouldn't be doing this." They talked us out of finishing the fucking tour, and we ended up cancelling the rest of the dates and fucking up our relationship with Rage Against the Machine. That broke my heart.

Pretty soon, with Wu appearances getting spotty, that fucked up our Mountain Dew endorsement. It fucked up a lot of shit— no, that's too harsh. It didn't fuck up everything, but things would've been better if we had just finished what we started. We had no reason not to. We were at our apex and rising, and I wanted to take it to the next level.

That's one of the main reasons why I was mad when our participation in the Rage Against the Machine tour started crumbling. We should've seen it all the way through, but things just got out of hand. When Ghost and Rae started complaining about the money, saying they were getting jerked around, things got fucked fast.

I never understood that. We were getting cake and expanding our fan base all over the world. At that time, we were at the top of our game, fifty thousand seats packed with Wu fans. My opinion is that sometimes, deep down, some people have a fear of success. I'll never really understand that, though—isn't that what we're here for?

I'm gonna tell the truth here. I really think that at the time, some of my brothers were scared to make that kind of money. People say they want to make millions of dollars, but if you had a million dollars in your bank account right now, I bet you'd be scared to death. I think the average person would be, at least. Now you're always looking over your shoulder, thinking everybody's trying to get at you. You don't know who you can trust. Those are the things motherfuckers with money are scared of.

And it is a problem. At first I didn't believe it, 'til it kept happening over and over again. Every time we started getting a lot of money, there was always a couple dudes in the Clan that would get real funny about it. They'd start acting weird, sayin', "No, we got to do this and this." They'd fuck it up for themselves and for all of us. And I was like, "Dude, what the fuck is wrong with y'all?" Then I realized what the problem was: *Wow . . . these dudes are scared to touch that type of bread.*

That has never been a problem with me. There's a certain way you gotta move when you have that kind of bankroll. You have to approach your life differently. You can't be around certain people, anyone who'll try to take advantage of you or get at your money. You have to take a more business-oriented view of your life with that kind of bread, that's just what it is.

But of course, you get nine guys, each one having a different view of what they should be getting out of the business, and feeling that they aren't getting what they need, that's when trouble starts to happen.

## 18.

## CRACKS IN THE FOUNDATION

If you really look at it, and my brothers understand this, too, we all pulled each other out of the fucked-up situation we were all born into. Without RZA and GZA laying that foundation—including taking losses with their first albums—we couldn't have done it. Then Method Man took us to another level with "Method Man." Raekwon and Deck kicked such real shit on "C.R.E.A.M." Power and ODB and myself all brought our individual skills and talents to the table to make something bigger than each one of us. Our verses on "Da Mystery of Chessboxin'" and the aesthetics of the video showed that the whole crew had skills. Then getting on SWV's joint made the R&B girls take notice, if they hadn't already. Each step took us further toward our goal, all of it took us as a group all the way to the top, and we couldn't have reached the next step without the previous one. And at the time, I was like, "Yeah, we got the illest crew in the whole fuckin' world."

That's why no matter what business or whatever gets a little messed up, I will always have love for RZA. He really put my head back on my shoulders when it needed to be and pointed me in the right direction. No matter what shit he may have pulled on me and other dudes, I will always have mad respect for him for moving me forward.

But things started getting more complicated as more money started coming in, and some of us got pulled into solo endeavors. Of course, there'd always been minor bickering between us. You can't have nine dudes on tour and in the studio together and not expect to disagree from time to time. But when we started out, we were all moving in the same direction. As we learned more about the ins and outs of the music business, however, rifts started forming over that side of things.

When Raekwon (*Immobilarity*, 1999), Method Man (*Blackout!*, with Redman, 1999), and Ghost (*Supreme Clientele*, 2000) ventured off on their own endeavors, I'll admit I felt a bit left out. I looked at it like Deck, Masta Killa, and me were on the sidelines while the rest of the group was doing their thing. Even when Deck and me each got solo album deals, we couldn't get the same support from the entire Clan the way earlier records had been supported.

When it was time to do my first solo album, *Golden Arms Redemption*, RZA only wrote and produced three tracks. I got beats from outside dudes instead. I got some darts here and there from my fellow Clansmen, but I didn't have that entire Wu-Tang chemistry that gave listeners that unified feeling. That all-for-one mindset wasn't there anymore, and *Redemption* didn't get the full support it should have. Regardless, my first album did good when I released it on Priority in '99.

My first single was "Bizarre," and was produced by Bink! That was my man. It was the first Wu-related single to chart in the top ten on *Billboard*'s hip-hop chart, debuting at number 7. I was out of the gate with a full head of steam, and my second single "Rumble" was on the first rap-related video game, Wu-Tang: Shaolin Style, so I was getting tons of shine.

At the time, Priority was home to N.W.A, Ice Cube, and Snoop Dogg. The owner, Bryan Turner, sold it to EMI in the middle of my record dropping, so tons of people were in and out the door at the label. I got no support from anyone, I was literally maintaining off the energy we had in the streets as a Wu-Tang member. Later, in 2001, Priority, bought for one hundred million dollars, went belly up and was dissolved into their catalog. To this day, I haven't seen one statement for all those record sales!

Hell, Masta Killa didn't even get to put out a solo album (*No Said Date*) until 2004. It was a great album, but it wasn't like the earlier ones. Those were all Wu-Tang albums, with certain artists featured more heavily than others, but everybody was present.

Deck had similar issues when it came time to release his album in '99. *Uncontrolled Substance* didn't get any support from the Clan at all. Deck should've been putting out a solo by that time, but a lot of his work got lost in a flood in RZA's basement. So much work was lost in that disaster. To make matters worse, RZA contributed less than a handful of beats, while Ghost, Method Man, and Raekwon weren't even present. Instead, some of the lesser-known Clan affiliates, like La the Darkman, Streetlife, Shadii, and Beretta 9, came through to get on tracks.


In 2000, as RZA had promised on *Wu-Tang Forever*, we dropped the next album, *The W.* Overall, I felt like it didn't have enough heat, like we didn't come hard enough with enough grit to satisfy our real fans. *The W* was the first album we weren't truly feeling.

*Iron Flag* followed a year later. Again, the sound was off to some of us. It wasn't what we wanted a Wu-Tang album to sound like. It wasn't the direction we all wanted to go.

Also, some of the members, like Deck and myself, felt like we weren't getting the full support of the Clan on our solo projects, and major signs of discord began to show. Dudes weren't happy with the current Wu-Tang Clan sound, and it all stemmed from what RZA was focusing on at that time.

RZA leveraged the group's success to make inroads into Hollywood, acting in and directing major motion pictures. Hanging out in Hollywood, altering his style and persona, he lost track of what made us hot along the way. The winning formula was lost, the focus on production of the music took a nosedive, the guys spent less and less time together recording, thus the music was flawed, and that edginess just wasn't there anymore.

This subsequently created a domino effect on the group. Our solo projects weren't riding the coattails or energy created by a platinum Wu album anymore. The music was still more or less solid, but fans missed that old, gritty sound they were used to hearing from the brothers.

This was also around the time when big budgets in music started drying up. GZA left Geffen, Meth and Ghost left Def Jam, Raekwon left Universal in 2003 after *The Lex Diamond Story,* and RZA had crashed and burned three or four distribution deals by then. I guess that's what happens when you put amateurs in charge of your business instead of people with actual business experience. Overall sales numbers started decreasing in general, both in the music business and for the group as well. This was also a sign of the times that the Golden Era was over.

In 2004, I took a flyer to put together my Hillside Scramblers project. I tried to set this up for two reasons: one, I was trying to expand my producing abilities, and two, I was trying to cultivate some new talent. I thought I had the perfect plan—I knew some dope, killer MCs from various projects in the city, and with me headlining the album as U-Godzilla, I'd introduce them to the world.

The only problem was that I wound up doing the same thing Meth did with his album *Tical 0;* I shot myself in the foot. The main problem was they were *too* gangsta! Every dude I brought on there was the hood of the hood. From the Bronx to Staten Island, nothing but grimy street motherfuckers. They were carrying guns, doing drugs, they just couldn't leave that gangsta shit alone.

In particular, my man Face—who was a *dope* MC—just couldn't shake that hood shit. I was trying to get him a job, trying to get him to put the drugs and guns down, to stop hustlin' and just focus on his rhymes, but he just couldn't leave it alone. Plus, I don't think he really believed in himself and his ability. If he had, and if he'd gone at it full throttle, *maybe* he could have done what he needed to do to get it poppin'.

In the end, I got into some drama with one of his peoples who tried to run up on me. I had to beat him up, put him in a coma in the hospital, and after that we had to call it quits. That whole project almost cost me my career—it definitely dealt a serious blow to my credibility in the industry.

After that whole thing crashed and burned, I was adrift again. And there was no one I could really turn to for help, either—RZA wasn't guiding me or providing advice or anything like that.

It was around this time that I found my current manager, Domingo. The Lord brought him to me during that time, and he came in and repaired all the shit I'd done, and we've been a team ever since.

Domingo actually saved me on a spiritual level; if he hadn't been around, I probably would have slipped up and headed back into Savagery and violence. But he humbled me and helped me find myself again. He's also helped with my temper, always telling me, "Uey, you gotta Gandhi that shit," when I wanna go off about something. He tells me to MLK it, to Malcolm X it and just turn the other cheek. And every time I'm about to go off, I just repeat to myself, "Gandhi, Gandhi, Gandhi." And damn if it doesn't defuse me and bring me back to a better place. And I got Domingo to thank for that, not to mention my repaired career.

Despite the growing troubles, Deck, Masta Killa, and me were just getting started, though, and our solo albums contained some of our best work. Masta finally got his solo album *No Said Date* released in 2004, Deck dropped *The Movement* in 2006, and I released *Dopium* in 2009. All of these were critically acclaimed, but didn't have the big budgets our brothers received via their major labels. I think one thing that hurt those releases is that we could never perform any new material at our Wu-Tang shows. That's something I never understood.

It's been a long time since we rocked new songs onstage. Shit, we didn't even support the last few albums with proper tours; I mean we went on tour, but stuck to performing the classics. That's backward to me. For us to ask the fans to support us, we had to support ourselves by performing new material—all for one and one for all—first.

Back in the day, when RZA put the Bat Signal up, the rest of us understood that we needed to stop what we were doing individually and come together, period. For there to be fruit hanging on the tree, the roots needed watering, so we would come together as Wu-Tang first, that was the priority. We were an unstoppable unit at that time, one for all and all for one—at least, that's what we told ourselves. We'd hit the road, and if one of us was in the middle of promoting a project, the rest would support that project, too. Like when *Cuban Linx* came out, no one knew that the record was supposed to be the next Wu album, but when Raekwon signed the deal, we all agreed to let him have it for his solo joint, no problem.

So years later, when revenue streams started drying up, members who were used to living crazy lifestyles started complaining about everyone's fees being equal. This led to some of the guys missing shows, holding the entire group for ransom before agreeing to go on tour. Bottom line, no solo member has ever played in front of sold-out arenas, the whole group is the foundation. There is no Earth without Wind and Fire!

Things started changing little by little, guys got fed up, and eventually we all got individual managers to negotiate and serve as a buffer from all the bullshit. It was no longer one for all and all for one. But now you had people in our brothers' ears, saying why you getting the same thing he getting? Now that the days of gold and platinum plaques had dried up, dudes started fighting over the W. The whole foundation that we were built on and that made us powerful fell apart. We weren't building anymore, we were destroying ourselves.

Right now, it just looks like the Wu brothers are not on the same page, going at each other's throats, missing shows, and all that. But, to me, it's really years of BS catching up to RZA. See, he put his family in charge of shit, and for years, we would go on the road but the money came up short. Whether it was because Divine overpromised or cut a deal he couldn't deliver, or he made bad management decisions, I don't know.

Don't get me wrong, at the end of the day, my brothers and I typically work things out and still come together as the Clan, but in twenty-five years of being in the business, RZA has never placed the group at an A-list agency. Instead, Divine has always placed us with these B- or C-list guys. I wonder why?

One time I asked him, "Vine, why aren't we with William Morris or The Agency?"

And he said, " 'Cause no one wants to deal with our bullshit."

I just looked back at him and said, "Our bullshit? Or your bullshit?"

Just talking about this shit frustrates me. I mean here we are, the Rolling Stones of hip-hop, and we ain't even got proper representation. Meanwhile, RZA's always had A-list agents repping him personally. What the fuck is that all about?

If you let him tell it, Divine would blame a lot of the shit that goes down on these low-level motherfuckers we're forced to deal with, subpar agents and the like. But if that's the case, why the fuck did you give your strongest asset, the Wu-Tang fucking Clan, to a shitty dude instead of a top-notch agent in the game?

I mean, my manager would tell me how some chick from Jersey was booking our European tours from *her house?* When I heard that, I was like, "Not *her* again! She owes me fifteen fuckin' stacks!" Whatever it was, it was always something, excuses, excuses, and more excuses as to why we were always coming up short.

Looking back, there's other things that I really question, too. For example, Wu Wear is coming back in time for our twenty-fifth anniversary, and that's all great, but what people don't know is that none of us—the original members who each invested a significant amount (around forty thousand dollars apiece) from our *36 Chambers* royalties and the Rage tour—ever saw a dime back from the first version of the line founded back in '97. And that's something that needs to be addressed and rectified.

There's also the use of our logo. Many people don't know this, but DJ Mathematics drew that logo on the back of a napkin back in the day. RZA quickly trademarked it, and to this very day his brother beefs when any of the original members attempt to use it. That to me is crazy—I mean, I understand if someone was using it without the group's permission, but the members of the group itself? Wow, that's just crazy.

Anyway, GZA uses a *G* that looks like a font similar to the *W,* Meth uses an upside-down *W* or an *M,* I have a *U* that looks like a *W* that's cut off—I guess you get creative when necessary, but we all stand behind that W in the end!

Divine always told us, "Y'all can't use that *W* without paying a brand fee, and if a promoter calls your manager direct to book a Wu-Tang show, best believe they're paying that brand fee!" Ain't that a motherfucker!

———

RZA also started becoming a bit of a control freak around this time. He wanted to control budget, publishing, writing hooks, everything. I kept quiet and kept working, but it didn't take a brain surgeon to see he was trying too hard to control the entire creative process.

Now, RZA's undeniably talented. He's also a good talker, smart, and a groundbreaking, genre-bending producer, but I wouldn't go so far as to call him a hit record maker. Remember, "All I Need" was Method Man's biggest single, but remember, RZA's version didn't win the Grammy—Puffy's remix with Mary J. Blige did.

A classic example of how he operates is "Gravel Pit" on *The W.* It was one of our biggest hits he wrote the hook for, but I hate that fuckin' hook. Me and Meth were supposed to write that one, but RZA came in and wouldn't let us do what we do best. He had to jump in the middle of the process to stop what we were building. It was like, "Yeah, you made the beat, now can we work on it?"

And RZA was like, "Nah, let's publish it." He just had to get his name on it however he could. It's like, just give the dudes the fuckin' music, let them go off by themselves and do their thing, come back with their idea—you know, how we used to do it. Collaboration, not domination.

Trying to exert too much control over grown-ass men leads to problems. RZA doesn't know how to let go and let motherfuckers be grown men anymore, like he used to back in the day, when it was four or five motherfuckers touring the country in an old Mitsubishi Scorpion. Somewhere along the way, he forgot to let his soldiers do what he initially recruited us to do and coached us to do. He forgot that you don't tear down your soldiers, you build your soldiers up. Because when they rise up, they bring you with them.

On the flip side, you need somebody calling the shots, or it becomes every man for himself. We still needed order, and he was the mastermind who had brought us up to this point. But it can't become a dictatorship, with everything coming from the top down. It takes a certain kind of personality to be able to run the ship but still be open to ideas and collaboration.

The other thing nowadays is working with RZA now, it's a race to get a spot on a good beat. In the old days, we'd all compete against each other, and the best man won. But today, it's like whoever gets there first gets on it, something RZA started. He pitted everyone against each other, so they were all thinking, "I gotta get on this beat, I gotta get on this record!"

It should be that you just give me the music I wanna rhyme to, let me go to my spot, listen to it, fuck with it, mess with it, fuck to it, drive to it, squeeze titties to it, drink to it, do everything I got to do to get my inspiration. And I'll come back in like a month or so, maybe two, maybe three, 'cause if it's that dope and I can't get a handle on it, I'm gonna wait on it, because sometimes creativity is a motherfucker. Sometimes the beat you wanna rhyme to gives you a blank. And you're listening and listening until *ping!* For whatever reason, the Lord comes outta nowhere and hits you with an idea. And you go, "Oh, shit! Yeah, I got it now, I got it." And then you're off and running.

But RZA won't let us develop our shit like we used to. Now we get into the studio and he's like, "We got two months to record." *Two months?!* Motherfucker, we can't do *anything* in two months! That's constipated! That kind of window makes you tight and stressed. You can't get loose with that deadline hanging over your head. When you're rushing to complete something, often you don't bring your A-game with you, and more often than not that'll be revealed on the final track.

And RZA doesn't want to relinquish control anymore, even though that would be best for everyone. To go back to the old way of doing shit, like me and Meth are doing right now, like I'm doing right now. Instead everyone's gonna notice the difference, they're gonna hear it, and they're gonna go, "What the *fuck?*"

I got into rapping because I just wanted to make a living free from looking over my shoulder, guns, and fucked-up people. I chose the wrong profession, because the music industry is the same fucking shit. You're dealing with people who want to rob you, who are getting mad at you because you're successful, who hate you. You can't show off too much, you can't show this, you can't do that. Now it's about contracts and all this other shit that people want to hold you to, that bind you for life, try to take the credit for the hard work you put in.

Let me tell you, you sign a contract with *anyone,* make sure you have a good fucking lawyer review every single line, 'cause people always saying a contract says one thing, but then you turn around and they're saying it says something else. Then they accuse you of not doing what the contract says you're supposed to do, or the other side isn't doing what they're supposed to do. It's just messed up.

During the early contracts, I was just playing the cut and watching. Raekwon, Method Man, and Dirty got solo deals damn near right out of the gate. See, that was a blessing to them, but it was also a blessing to me, Deck, and Masta Killa *not* to get signed for solo deals just yet. The first ones through the door always take the biggest hit because they're the pioneers touching new land. They're explorers who don't know the terrain yet. I didn't go through that. I learned by watching other people's mistakes.

First, I knew what I was getting into as far as how tricky the industry could be. As a result, I was extra careful about what I was signing and how I was moving. Like I said, I'm not nearly as well known as some of the other members, but I'm also not bound by contractual obligations like those same members.

And now, the game is very different than it was back then, when we were first starting out. For example, our contracts were executed way back in the day, before CDs, before MP3s, before any kind of streaming service even existed. Nowadays, all that shit's gotta be licensed as well. And if you own your work, those licensing fees come to you, and those fees can get heavy. That's where the cake is going to—anyone who controls those rights. This is just one example of how different the business is today and how you gotta keep up on that shit. If you don't, you will be left behind. And not only that, you'll leave money on the table for someone else to pick up.

Ultimately, I can't be bitter about not going in to get my shit correct and stay on top of my business. That's *my* fault now—there's no one else to lay the blame onto. It's my fuckin' fault for not going in and regulating my shit, for letting other dudes get over on me, thinking what was mine should be theirs. I let it happen, I let a lot of shit slide, and because I did that, it left me in a weaker position and made somebody else strong.

It's the same for the Clan as a whole—by letting other dudes be in charge, we let them come in and throw the rest of us off balance. If we had hung together as a solid unit from the beginning and had a lawyer represent the Wu-Tang as a whole, then we wouldn't be in this situation now. But no, they divided us and conquered us. And they're still trying to do it to this day.

Fortunately, in the end the Wu almost always looks out for its own. Like last year, when I filed my lawsuit against RZA, he tried to kick me off our live shows. Again, I've been in the Wu for more than twenty-five years, and I've never missed a show I've been scheduled for—until RZA tried to give me the boot. But after a week, my brothers found out what was going on, and they faced off with RZA and made him reinstate me. Throughout all of it, I didn't take it personally. I never let my emotions get in the way of business.

And though I will always have my brothers' backs, there comes a time when you have to look to taking care of yourself and yours first. So now I gotta get strong myself. I gotta go in and correct whatever I can before I take any other action. And that's exactly what I'm doing now.

There was more than just this rift over recording and solo versus group projects forming. There was a major rift over business with Wu-Tang Productions. RZA's brother Divine, Power, and RZA made up the executive hierarchy of the Clan, also known as Wu-Tang Productions. The three of them, along with Ghostface, executive produced *36 Chambers*.

Now, me and Divine have always been cool since our days at P.S. 57 in Stapleton. Not sure what it is, but we just always got along, never had any real problems. We argue, of course, but deep down we know it's never serious. We understand and respect each other. We were in public school together and gravitated toward one another way back then. We're both just some money-getting dudes. Long as money's coming in, all that bickering goes out the window. We realize what's important at the end of the day.

Other members in the Clan don't always have that understanding. They haven't been through what I've been through. It's just a different mentality. I can't talk business or economics with certain dudes. I can talk about investing and credit scores and equity with Divine. Other guys I just talk street shit to. Divine understands that it's a business. He and I went to court back in 2008 because I sued him over a small amount of money, and we settled that case. But we're still good friends—to a certain degree.

He knows and I know it's not personal. It's never personal, it's business.

But RZA, he knew more about the music industry—and also, it seems, about our cash flow—than the rest of us. From what I can tell, he got rich, but I still don't know what I'm due. And while I can't speak for everyone, I believe that's how a lot of my brothers see things, too. We thought we were all united, but at the end of the day, it turned out that it was all about Wu-Tang Productions, and we were just the workers.

Divine controlled all the ledger books and financial information, and RZA, at the expense of the rest of us, went along with it. He could have put a stop to it if he'd wanted, he could have gotten us all together and sat us down and worked it all out, but he didn't. He stood by and let it happen for years. Finally, I concluded I had no choice but to bring my lawsuit against RZA and the others in 2016, after all those years of not knowing what was happening financially and where I stood. All I'm really looking for is transparency: Where do I stand regarding each album I recorded? What am I owed, if anything, and who owes it to me?

And that's a fundamental difference between RZA and me. When I was in the drug business, at the height of my operation, I knew how to treat the people selling for me. I knew how to handle my crew fairly to maximize my business. I knew how to deal with people so they felt respected and would work hard for me. I respected them, so they were loyal to me, that's why they loved me so much.

But RZA never had a situation like that; he never had to work with employees on that level. Back in the day, when I gave him that package and he fucked it up, I should have known then what I know now, which is that he lacks business skills—the nerd in him won't allow him to put the right brothers in position to win.

Instead, he puts brothers he thinks he can control in positions of power.

And now that he's older, he doesn't have anyone he can really rely on, because he froze out the brothers who would have been the most loyal to him. He put achieving his own dream ahead of helping the rest of the group achieve theirs.

And yeah, he may have the trappings of a successful rapper and producer, he may have all the cars and houses, but he doesn't have anyone to share it with. He doesn't have a Kardashian or an actress or a model on his arm today. So what did he get all that fly shit for in the first place? Just to have it?

Because it wasn't just RZA or just Divine or just Power that got Wu-Tang into the music industry—it was all of us, a combined force. And as such, we all had to learn and go through certain things. That's the problem with my crew, especially when you have a small majority making most of the decisions. We were blind to certain aspects of the music industry, and other aspects we didn't even know existed. And as we grew, some of us learned that we'd been left out of certain parts of the business of Wu-Tang.

If the next person knows more than you, and gets a better deal, and gets over on you a bit, you can't be mad at them. You have to learn from that and correct what you did wrong for next time. It's not about getting mad when someone got over on you because you were still wet behind the ears. It's about working to fix the problem so you can make it better. That's the music industry. It's treacherous and shady. But if you wanna play, you have to realize you're gonna get dirty and a bit bumped and bruised until you learn all the rules.

Same goes for Wu-Tang Productions. Those deals might have reflected the lack of knowledge we had about the paperwork side of the business, but it still got us into the game. Looking back, though, we left it to RZA, Divine, and Power to handle those deals for us at the labels; they weren't negotiated in front of the rest of us. And instead of saying we're a family, it feels to me like it was more about RZA putting himself ahead of the rest of us. That was okay (not really, but at least I understand where he's coming from) when we were practically kids in this shit, but now I feel that they're still trying to keep us in the other room. That's harder to swallow as a grown man.

That's why we still kinda fucked up to this day. We can't get it together because at this level of the game, dudes feel like they're being taken advantage of. I still got love for RZA for what he did for me, but it is what it is, and I gotta call it like I see it. As I'm arguing in my lawsuit, it's time for some transparency. And some answers.

If Dirty hadn't died, I think the Wu would be in better standing, and we'd be on a more harmonious wavelength with one another. It still wouldn't be perfect, but it'd be a little better.

Dirty's element—that wild, chaotic energy that helped keep the entire group on the same page—is missing. His element isn't just missing in the Clan, it's missing in today's hip-hop altogether. A raw, wild style of performing. Dudes can't perform the way he could. ODB fans wanted that grit, and Ol' Dirty always gave it to them.

Dirty was always the most paranoid out of all of us; he was on drugs, drinking, and all this crazy shit, but at the end of the day he could pinpoint shit and he saw things we didn't see coming. He was always the one to call people out when he thought they were pullin' shit. Like when RZA bought a mansion in Jersey; it was supposed to be *the* Wu mansion. But it turned out it wasn't no Wu mansion, it was RZA's mansion, and he ran it like it was some kind of church. He wouldn't let anybody bring girls there. No parties, we couldn't get shit popping, we couldn't do none of that fly shit. After a while, we stopped going. He kicked us out and put the keys in it. In other words, it basically was running just like his mansion, but he spun it to seem like it was our mansion to soften the blow that he was in charge.

Dirty used to say this shit all the fucking time. He was the first Clan member to call RZA out; he boycotted shows until he found out who was getting what. "Where's my money at, RZA?" His song "Got Your Money," that song's about fucking RZA.

But Dirty always used to be about, "I want my money. Gimme my money." Dirty was always one step ahead of the rest of us. He was the first motherfucker to call us robots. He basically believed RZA was taking our money. That's why the rest of us can't leave RZA to tell the whole story, Dirty said, because he's going to try and make out like, "No I didn't." If he had his way, he'd try to make out like he was some kind of savior. To which I say get the fuck out of here. I guess we'll find out when the Court gives me the accounting I'm asking for.

If I'm wrong, I will apologize straight to RZA's face. I will man up and stand in front of him and say, "Yo, I didn't know, and I'm sorry for coming at you like I did."

But if I'm right . . . well, it's a good thing I'm not that scrapper in the streets anymore, that I settle my business with lawyers and lawsuits nowadays, instead of with my fists and guns.

After Dirty died, it shifted my brain. He was the wild, crazy motherfucker the fans wanted to see, too. When he died, it took a piece of us away. I know I definitely started seeing things differently.

By the time *8 Diagrams* was released in 2007, more Wu-Tang members were voicing their disapproval of RZA's style.

I kept my thoughts to myself, though. I'd released a half-assed attempt at another solo project called *Mr. Xcitement* (2005) that got all fucked up a year or two prior, including the shutdown of the label, Priority Records, so I was willing to go along with RZA's plans for *8 Diagrams*. When the story broke of how it came out, I think the other members redoubled their efforts to put out more solo projects so each of us could have more creative control.

After four years of work, Rae and Ghost put out *Cuban Linx II* in 2009. Part of the reason *Linx II* was delayed was because we all came together for *8 Diagrams*. That same year, I put out a solo project on Babygrande Records called *Dopium* that drew some critical praise. Ghostface, Cappa, GZA, and Meth all got on tracks for that one.

Then Method Man, Raekwon, and Ghostface put out a project called *Wu-Massacre* in 2010 that had one track produced by RZA. Raekwon took it a step further by releasing *Shaolin vs. Wu-Tang* in 2011, an album with no RZA involvement at all.

The supergroup was splintering apart. When it came time to work on *A Better Tomorrow* in 2013—during the twentieth-anniversary year of the release of *Enter the Wu-Tang (36 Chambers)*—things were still in disarray.

By this time RZA had gone full Hollywood. He was off making pictures, rubbing elbows with movie stars, and pulling down millions; he didn't need this bullshit. Even so, the twentieth anniversary was still an opportunity, so he decided to try to get us all back on the same page by recording *A Better Tomorrow*. Problem was, that better tomorrow never came. Shit wasn't getting better—shit was getting worse.

Before we started recording, RZA went on a world tour of studios and musicians from the Motown days. We heard he took trips to Nashville and Detroit, hunting down that sound so he could chop up the sessions into new beats. I ain't gonna lie, I thought it was a good marketing ploy and was excited to hear what he'd come back with.

During that time, Divine tried to get the rest of us to go to L.A. to record, then to Vegas for a week or two, trying to rekindle the vibe we had when we made those early albums. But this one went the same way as the last three records; a lot of my brothers felt it was too soft. Method Man wanted some hard shit, as did the rest of us. Although I felt like it wasn't that gritty, raw, high-energy sound that we were used to coming with, that made us who we were, I felt I couldn't go against RZA like that . . . most of us couldn't. I think RZA just felt like we're all forty years old now, we can't keep rapping about slanging and banging anymore, we need to be at the BBQ with our families.

I think the thing with RZA is that he's accomplished a lot more. He's been acting, scoring films for Quentin Tarantino, and now he's even directing feature-length movies. He's got Ferraris and millions of dollars. He's in another space altogether, so his music reflects that.

And he had put up his own money—well, I guess it was *our* money, too—to make the album, so ultimately it was his decision as to the direction we were gonna take. Also, some others didn't want to record until the paperwork was redone. It caused us to implode on a small level. We ended up laying down some stuff, but we were never all in one place; it was disjointed, with themes picked out of thin air, so the album never came together as a cohesive unit. We couldn't get it off the way we wanted to get it off.

But it went even deeper than that. First, the music: The beats weren't there, so the foundation was missing. RZA was acting like it was all fine, but the rest of us weren't having it, saying we wanted him to find some new shit. But he wouldn't go and do that, so we were stuck with what he put forward. Then he didn't want to use any outside producers, because he's RZA. And finally, he tried to do a record in two months, which, as I've already said, is practically impossible to do and come up with something great.

And finally, it wasn't just that RZA was, as usual, trying to control every aspect of the production, but I felt like the others just weren't attacking their rhymes like they used to. It seemed like maybe the industry had beaten my brothers all down so that they didn't believe in the power of their rhymes anymore. And when we finally heard the end product, I don't think many of us were happy, but we all decided to roll with it in the end.

With all the rifts and disagreements within the group, when it came to doing what we had to do to ensure the album was a success, we kind of balked. There was just too much internal shit going on. When it came time to shoot a video, some of the guys went MIA. When it came time to do press, cats went missing again. We had mad magazine covers we could have done, but didn't. We did a few shows, though, so that helped a lot in terms of us appearing as a unified front. Even if things were a mess behind the scenes, we still brought the ruckus live. We could have—we *should have* moved at least 150,000 units in the first week. Instead, *ABT* debuted at number 29 on the Billboard chart and moved less than twenty-five thousand copies in its debut week. Womp womp.

As a result, everyone was all over the place and pissed off about how *ABT* had landed, and the ways the business—*our* business— had been run for all these years. Raekwon in particular was very vocal about his disappointment with the album, giving interviews saying he felt it should have been harder, that our team was compromised by how RZA makes music, and all that.

But RZA wasn't hearing any of it. As a leader, sometimes you have to compromise with your soldiers. They're on the battlefield with you, fighting by your side. Everything can't go your way every time, not everybody gonna agree with you every time. You may have put up the money to get the album done, so yeah, you get final say, but you still have to listen and take heed of what your soldiers are saying as they're putting in the work.

And it just keeps happening. In 2017, RZA produced "Don't Stop" with Meth, Rae, and Deck for the *Silicon Valley* soundtrack.

Now, I'm not on that song, and I'm glad I'm not, because it's a wack beat, and I told him so. But RZA didn't want to listen; he thinks everything he does is hot all the time. He's not open to criticism, even when it will make the project better. So he put it out anyway—under the Wu-Tang Clan name—like we'd all decided to put that forth. Other songs on that soundtrack have a million views; DJ Shadow's "Nobody Speak," featuring Run the Jewels, has millions of views. "Don't Stop" has around seventy thousand streams at the time I'm writing this. Shit, I can get seventy thousand streams by my own damn self! So when four original Wu members come together on a song and it only gets seventy thousand streams, that's not cool. That kind of shit hurts our stock, it hurts all of us.

People also been talking about the last album we came together for, *Once Upon a Time in Shaolin,* which exists in only one pressed copy that was put up for sale in 2015.

First of all, to me, what Cilvaringz did with that project was some sucker shit, pure and simple. He went around to each of us individually and paid us money to lay verses down for an independent compilation album, not an official Wu-Tang LP. He collected a nice amount of verses from brothers to piece together a decent record. But he didn't have the motherfucking right to sell it as a Wu-Tang Clan album, as I also argue in my lawsuit. Yet he still tried to do just that—he tried to go out and sell it as an official Wu-Tang Clan record, thought he was gonna make a profit off it. He didn't have the paper to do that; to sell all our masters and all our rights, and neither did RZA. We wouldn't sign off on no sucker shit like that. You know damn well my lawyers, everybody's lawyers would cease-and-desist that shit so goddamn fast his head would turn.

At some point he schemed up this idea to sell it as an art piece, let RZA in on the idea then; at one time, Leonardo DiCaprio was gonna buy it for two million dollars. That didn't happen, so they held an auction, and that pharma guy Martin Shkreli ended up winning with a bid of two million. RZA got in bed with Cilvaringz and sold what was supposed to be a compilation album as an official Wu-Tang album to Shkreli for millions. Of course, I still haven't seen any of that supposed bread either. This is all in my lawsuit, too. And I'm convinced the Court will see it my way, if the case ever has to go that far. 'Cuz like so much else, that shit just ain't right.

# 19

## THE LEGACY

I've been in the game long enough to know people come and go. I've seen the rap world go from Master P to Tupac to Biggie to 50 Cent to the new wave of Lil Wayne and on and on. The real question is how can you stay around forever, how do you remain relevant? Today, with the exception of Nas and Jay-Z, very few rappers from the 1990s are still putting out work. I'll always be grateful for what I've had; even if radio never plays another of my records again, I'm still happy for how long I've been in the game as an artist. And I'll always be thankful that hip-hop saved my life.

But at the same time, I also don't want to be the one that could have been. I don't want to be that dude. Sometimes, even with everything I've done and everywhere I've been, both with the Clan and on my own, I still feel like that's my story. Whether as a solo artist, or whether it's about my time with the Clan, my legacy is inextricably bound up in the group, and although it's still up to me as to how I shape it moving forward, a large part of it has already been written down in hip-hop history. And even today, I feel like I could have been more, I could have been greater.

And one of the questions I'm dealing with going forward is how do I shape the rest of my legacy? Before I'm through with music, I want to put out at least eight solo albums. And I'm trying to make a cornerstone, classic album every time. And making that kind of music takes time. Plus, I'm struggling against my own legacy with Wu-Tang. All the Clan members are. I have to make my own music stand up to the classics like *36 Chambers* and *Wu-Tang Forever.* That's what I'm trying to do every time I step into the studio.

My journey isn't over yet. I'm still climbing the mountain, but I'm not as young as I was back in the day. I also know it's not how many days you have left, it's what you do with the days you have, and that's what I'm focusing on now, doing what I can in my time left on this planet and making the most of every opportunity I get.

The Clan's journey isn't over yet, either. There's a chance the nine remaining members of the Wu-Tang Clan (including Cappadonna) could come together and create a really cool album. There's plenty of egos in the way, of course, and all these years of conflict over money and the business to put behind us. We'd have to start from square one, but this time we're older, more experienced. Maybe that's exactly what we need—a fresh start. And if some of the brothers can put their egos aside and come together like we did back in the day, bring that all-for-one-and-one-for-all mentality like we used to have, there's no limit to what we could create.

Would I be down with all that? Sure, but right now I have to look out for U-God first and foremost. I have to make sure my head is on straight and take care of my own business before I can even begin to think about whether there's any way to truly bring the Clan back together again. And if the project turned out to be anything like *A Better Tomorrow,* forget it. That whole album was just some wack shit from start to finish, and we don't need any more of that.

It's a similar situation with the Clan touring together. Truth be told, I feel like there's been many situations where opportunities have come along that would have been good for Wu-Tang to get back out in the spotlight again, but for one reason or another, they slip through our fingers. A lotta times it's because dudes are worrying about the wrong shit again. They'd rather spend their time complaining about their situation than take steps to rectify it. Because again, I think they're scared of taking it to the next level. It's either that, or somebody's got something over their head that's preventing them from doing anything. I don't know, that's all I can think of, those two options. But in order for us to get back into the spotlight again and take our shit to the next level, we have to put all that worry and fear behind us and just create.

Even today, it's still hard to leave the past behind. See, most people still got this terrible, stereotyped way of looking at us. Even after all our success—gold and platinum records, world tours, and all that—I feel like a lot of motherfuckers still see Wu-Tang as just some fucking derelict thugs that got lucky. Yeah, we grew up grimy. Grew up in Park Hill and Brownsville, slinging crack and running from the cops. When we first came in, we were rough. We were hard as shit then. That's not us now. That's not me today.

Nowadays, I'm still working hard, sometimes as hard as I did back then. I pay my child support, I pay my taxes, I worry about my family, my siblings, my children. They don't understand that I'm done with the streets for good. You may have heard some shit about us back in the day, but you don't hear about any of us running around in the streets nowadays. Other rappers be doing shit like that, not us. I'm just tired of that image of us as wack, derelict dudes.

And it's not just us, either; black people as a whole are dealing with another level of consciousness regarding society today. Too much of the truth that's been hidden from us is coming to light now. Not just in the music industry, but with social and political issues worldwide.

Mainstream America can't front that shit anymore. We're dark skinned, proud, boisterous, and unrelenting in achieving our dreams, with no regard for the outdated ways of thinking this world tries to impose on people of color, particularly black men. Me, RZA, Meth, Raekwon, and all the kids who grew up disadvantaged who are taking the world by creative storm, we're all living proof that we will not be kept down. We will continue to evolve and learn and adapt until our situation improves overall.

We not only evolved, we survived. Everything I did back then I did to survive, but I was always, *always* looking for a way up and out, and I made it. I don't consider myself an ex–drug dealer or an ex-criminal. I consider myself to be an experienced fucking person who went through a lot of hell to come out right and get where I am today. And I'm still going through hell in some aspects of my life. It isn't the hell of my youth, that's for sure, but it's still hell, just a different kind today.

I know there's things in here that some people ain't gonna agree with, but this is how I saw the events that went down. The way I see it today, this story still has to be told. How we were raised. How we were brought up. That doesn't mean it's who we are now. It may have shaped me, but it doesn't define who I am today. Some people can look at me now and recognize that—they can see I'm not the street hustler I was back when I was twenty years old. Other people can't—for whatever reason, they look at me and think they're seeing the same kid who was running the streets back in the day. I still know a bunch of motherfuckers I grew up with that are stuck in the past. They think we're all still back there in Park Hill, and I'm like, "Dawg, you been sittin' there twenty fuckin' years. I'm not even in the hood no more."

And any motherfuckers who claim to represent that gangster

shit nowadays, I guarantee they're faking it. They've never been through that shit for real. They're just caught up in projecting that lifestyle, acting like they've been through some shit when in reality they're just sucka-ass motherfuckers. Acting like they want to go through the shit we went through when we were kids—they have no idea what that was like. Why would you want to go through that fucking hell again or, even worse, brag about it? Makes no sense to me at all.

All the motherfuckers who went through hell growing up and got out of that shit don't want none of it anymore. They're the ones who don't talk about it; they've just left it behind, like it was in another life altogether.

Our journey here was rough, no doubt. We lost our brother Dirty along the way, but the rest of us are still here, still alive, still bringing it. We're not posted up in front of 160 anymore, ducking cops and bullets, scrambling for drug money while dreaming of stardom and getting out of the projects. We've done that. We're not locked up or on parole pissing in cups. We left all that shit behind us years ago. We've achieved fame and success the likes of which most people can only dream about, and in the right circumstances, we'll do it again.

Yeah, we don't always get along, but what family does? But just give us time to come back together, and we'll show everybody that the Wu-Tang Clan *still* ain't nothin' ta fuck wit'!

# ACKNOWLEDGMENTS

I want to thank first and foremost the good Lord for giving me the strength and perseverance to continue on this long journey called life. To my mother, who from the beginning showed me how to turn a negative into a positive from the minute I was born. To my right-hand man and manager, Domingo Neris, aka the Puerto Rican Gandhi, who has taught me the art of good business and being patient, you made me a better person, father, and artist . . . we did it, fat man! To John Helfers for helping me tell my story; it took us over two years, HUNDREDS of HOURS—it was a grind, but we did it! To Jorge, for advising and looking out for Domingo and myself. To my legal team, Ian, Paul, and Jon, for having my back 365 days of the year. To my team at UTA, Marc, Cheryl, Zimmer, Kim, Meredith, and Jamie; and to Pronoy, Greg, and the whole team at Picador and Faber for helping me bring my story to the world. To my family, all of my kids, this is your legacy, too. To my Wu brothers Meth, Rae, Deck, Cappa, Ghost, Just, RZA, MK, and Math, we've come a long way, guys—happy twenty-fifth anniversary! To ODB, the one and only—rest in peace, my brother. In your memory, I'm gonna combine a piece of you into every rhyme I write until the day I die. To all the Wu fans around the world, I started this journey in the slums of Park Hill Projects in Staten Island, New York City, and now the story has been told! I love each and every one of you—I wrote this for all of you . . . SUUUUUUEEEEEY!